INVESTMENT IN HUMAN CAPITAL

THEODORE W. SCHULTZ

Investment in

Human

Capital

The Role of Education
and of Research

Fp

THE FREE PRESS, NEW YORK
COLLIER-MACMILLAN LIMITED, LONDON

Copyright © 1971 by The Free Press
A Division of The Macmillan Company

Printed in the United States of America

All rights reserved. No part of this book may be
reproduced or transmitted in any form or by any means,
electronic or mechanical, including photocopying, recording,
or by any information storage and retrieval system,
without permission in writing from the Publisher.

The Free Press
A Division of The Macmillan Company
866 Third Avenue, New York, New York 10022

Collier-Macmillan Canada Ltd., Toronto, Ontario

Library of Congress Catalog Card Number: 77-122273

printing number
1 2 3 4 5 6 7 8 9 10

Preface

M<small>Y</small> own interest in the contributions of the sciences to production took shape while I was at Iowa State College. I began to see that new biological materials were becoming "substitutes" for land and that the stranglehold that land held on the supply of food was being relaxed. But it became increasingly clear to me that the advances in the sciences could not explain all of the gains in productivity. At the University of Chicago from the late forties on, I began to search for a more complete explanation and I came to see the role of the acquired abilities of human agents as a major source of the unexplained gains in productivity. These acquired abilities were obviously not free. Scarce resources were being allocated to acquire these abilities; and thus, the analytical stage was set for investment in man.

Investment in man meant that the traditional concept of capital had to be extended to make room for human capital. I was perplexed by the omission of human capital in the economic growth models that dominated the economic

literature. At several points in this book I comment on some
of the reasons why economists were shy in coming to
grips with human capital. Although I was aware that there
were several distinguished economists who had looked upon
human beings as capital—Adam Smith, H. von Thünen, and
notably Irving Fisher, I did not know then that others also
had perceived the economic importance of the advances in
knowledge and of the improvements in the "quality" of
the labor force. I have been perhaps unduly critical of the
particular view of Alfred Marshall that it is neither appropriate nor practical to apply the concept of capital to human
beings which he expressed in his objections to Fisher's
approach. Human beings were incontestably capital from
an abstract and mathematical point of view as Marshall
saw the issue, but human capital had no practical meaning
because it was out of touch with the marketplace. But it
has been pointed out by others since I first called attention
to this view of Marshall, that Marshall saw the relevance
of investment in human beings in several parts of his work.
With respect to knowledge also, Marshall anticipated much
of what is now becoming clear in economics; for example,
his dictum that "Knowledge is our most powerful engine
of production."

Frank Knight, so I discovered, in what I now consider
to be one of his classic papers, "Diminishing Returns to
Investment," *Journal of Political Economy*, 1944, perceived clearly and cogently both the improvements in the
"quality" of the labor force and the economic contributions from the advances in the sciences and their effects on
the rate of returns to investment.

Once I saw the pervasive role of human capital in a
modern economy, I also began to see the inadequacies of the
traditional concept of capital. The traditional concept
started down the road of capital homogeneity, a road away

from an all-inclusive concept of capital with its vast hetero-geneity. Human capital is also of many different forms, and it renders many different consumer and producer services. If it were possible analytically to aggregate all of the dif-ferent forms of human capital, it would exceed by a wide margin all nonhuman capital. Although I devote a sub-stantial part of Chapters 3 and 5 to the pervasive attributes of human capital, the discussion is exploratory and far from definitive. The thrust of my studies has been primarily to clarify the investment processes and opportunities that provide the incentive to invest in human capital. In this book, I consider mainly formal education and organized research. The investment approach, however, opens for analysis a wide array of different forms of investment in man, with new vistas that extend far beyond the scope of this set of studies.

There are opportunities to invest in man through on-the-job learning, the search for economic information, migra-tion, and activities that contribute to health; all of these have received considerable attention analytically. A par-ticular class of human capital consisting of "child capital" may hold the key to an economic theory of population. The formation of "child capital" by the household, man and wife, would begin with the bearing of children and pro-ceed through their rearing through childhood. An invest-ment approach to population growth is now breaking new ground.

I have tried to keep the exposition meaningful to readers who would shy away from technical economics. Most of the book pertains to the investment in formal education; my hope is that it is intelligible to those who make such investment decisions, whether they be students, their par-ents, teachers, academic entrepreneurs, or public agencies. Similarly, the treatment of allocating resources to research is oriented toward research workers and research entrepreneurs as much as toward economists.

In parts of this book, I draw upon several of my studies that have appeared in economic journals. I am grateful to the editors of the *American Economic Review*, the *Journal of Political Economy*, the *Journal of Human Resources*, the *American Journal of Agricultural Economics*, and the *Southern Economic Journal* for their permission to do so, and also to the National Bureau of Economic Research.

I acknowledge appreciatively a generous grant from the Ford Foundation for research on human capital and a complementary grant from National Institutes of Mental Health for graduate trainees. I am indebted to Mrs. Phyllis Downes for her careful and painstaking work in seeing the manuscript through several drafts and to Mrs. Virginia K. Thurner, whose editorial skills and scholarly competence have been of great value to me in shaping this book.

THEODORE W. SCHULTZ

December 1, 1969

Contents

List of Tables

INVESTMENT IN HUMAN CAPITAL

1 An Investment Approach in Modernizing an Economy

THE abundance of goods and services, along with more time for leisure, that a modern economy makes possible is a widely known fact. As real income, it has been quantified, and as literature, it has given us the affluent society. But what is not known are the costs of, and returns to, skills and techniques that account for the abundance of a modern economy. They are still shrouded in mystery. In practical affairs, it is obvious that this must be so in view of the ineffective endeavors of many countries bent on modernization. They may, of course, learn by trial and error. In economic theory, also, there is as yet no satisfactory solution of this mystery despite the notable advances in economics. It is not that the problem of economic growth has been absent from the economists' agenda; there has been an intensive search for the "missing" factors of production that might account for the unexplained residual in modern growth. Various attempts have been made in treating

I

"technical change" to find a meaningful economic solution. The search for an explanation of the observed productivity changes using an accounting framework that includes the improvements in the quality of the labor force and in the quality of physical forms of capital is a fruitful approach, although the costs of and returns to the components of quality are not reckoned.

These advances aside, the state of economic knowledge in general continues to be burdened by many obsolete views. There is the view that it is necessary for a country to be well endowed with natural resources if it is to develop a modern economy. But surely this view is no longer tenable. Japan has demonstrated, beyond any doubt, that a rich endowment of natural resources is not necessary in developing a modern economy. Nor is it necessary that a country be large for it to modernize, as is evident from the success of such countries as Denmark and Switzerland, even though they have no coal, iron ore, oil, or even farmland that is naturally highly productive. During recent decades, the predominant view has been that the source of modern abundance is industrialization, namely, steel mills, plants to produce machines, electrification, and an array of complementary light industries. But this view of modernization also has been found wanting, in some countries for lack of a modern agriculture and in others for want of skills to produce industrial products as cheaply as the cost of importing them. Meanwhile, the price of learning from trial and error is high.

As already noted, economists who have been thinking in terms of economic growth have not solved the mystery of modern abundance. That the state of employment really matters in modernizing an economy is not in doubt. That savings and investment are two critical activities is undoubtedly true. That the allocation of investment resources made in accordance with the standard set by the relative rates of return to alternative investment opportunities is surely valid whether such resources are allocated privately or publicly by means of economic planning and governmental decisions. But on the analytical front, economic growth models that treat changes in the labor force by counting the number of workers and that treat changes in the stock of capital by counting physical structures, equipment, and inventories are inadequate analytical tools because they omit critically important sources of modern economic growth. They also fail in explaining the growth of sectors of a modern economy, be the sector agriculture, manufactures, construction, heavy industry, or service. The unsatisfactory state of received economic theory in solving the mystery of modern abundance has turned some economists to an array of explanatory factors that are predominantly cultural, social, and political. Although it would be a serious mistake not to consider the roles that some of these factors play in harmonizing an economy, economic theory can contribute much more than it has to an understanding of the sources of modern abundance.

The tripartite classification of factors of production—land, labor, and capital—that emerged from classical economic thinking still prevails despite its limitations in analyzing modern economic growth. The assumption of diminishing returns of labor and capital applied to land regardless of secular developments has not been abandoned, although it is true that most growth models now leave land aside and concentrate on labor and capital. But labor as a factor of production is generally treated "free of capital," regardless of the secular changes in the skill compositions of the labor force; and capital is restricted, as a rule, to the physical forms and usually treated on the shaky assumption of capital homogeneity. Although the traditional concepts of land, labor, and capital have been subject to strong criticism, notably by Frank Knight, the reformulation or abandonment of them has not been the order of the day. Irving Fisher[1] established the theoretical groundwork for an all-inclusive concept of capital and income more than four decades ago, but it was too abstract and mathematical for traditional analytical taste on no less an authority than that of Alfred Marshall, who wanted economics to be practical and in touch with the marketplace.

An investment approach, I am convinced, is required in thinking about economic growth. In this approach the stock of capital is augmented by investment, and the productive services of the additional capital increase income, which is the essence of economic growth. It is a major step toward a general theory when *all* investment resources are encompassed and allocated in accordance with the meaningful economic standard established by the relative rates of return to alternative investment opportunities. Thus, in theory, this approach is grounded on an all-inclusive concept of investment and an accounting of all additional investments gives a complete and consistent explanation of the marginal changes in the stock of capital, of the marginal changes in the productive services from capital, and of the marginal changes in income and, accordingly, of growth.

In thinking about economic growth, one does not ask the traditional query: What is the area of land, the size of the labor force, and the number of machines and structures? In allocating investment resources, he asks: What is the marginal increase in production from a particular additional investment? The productive services of land can be

1. Irving Fisher, *The Nature of Capital and Income* (New York: The Macmillan Company, 1906).

augmented by investment; investment in man can increase both his satisfactions and the productive services he contributes when he works; and the productive services of machines and structures, also, can be augmented in this manner. In addition and to an increasing extent, there is the investment in organized research to acquire new information, a source of new skills and new materials (techniques), which can alter significantly the investment opportunities in land, man, and machines. In line with this approach, there is no assumption of a rate of technical change but a search to determine the rate of return to organized research; no assumption with regard to population growth to account for the rate of increase in the labor force but a search to determine the rate of return to children (child capital) and to the acquisition of useful skills; no assumption of a fixed supply of natural resources but a search to determine the rate of return to investment in land improvements and in discovering and developing other natural resources; and, similarly, there is the analytical task of determining the rate of return to investment that changes the composition of the reproducible forms of material capital as new and better forms become available from the production activities of organized research.

It is my contention that economic thinking has neglected two classes of investment that are of critical importance under modern circumstances. They are investment in man and in research, both private and public. The central problem of this study is to clarify the nature and scope of these two activities.

From Theory to Classification

Economic theory performs several different functions. We depend on it, as already implied, in organizing an approach to the problem at hand. We also depend on it for a classification of the activities and economic components to be analyzed, for a received set of premises and the analytical core from which hypotheses can be derived, for analytical tools to test empirically the hypotheses that are derived from the theory, and not least, for a concise summary of the state of economic knowledge. It should also be said that advances in economic knowledge are, in general, a joint product of theory and empirical analysis. Although economic theory is indispensable, there are models that have no economic meaning. It is also true that empirical work not guided by theory is, in general, pointless. But such empiricism is no longer the bane of economics.

In classifying with a view to organizing this study, as already noted, I found the classical approach to land, labor, and capital inadequate. Each can be viewed, however, as a form of capital, but the heterogeneity of capital so conceived is inconsistent with the long-standing assumption of capital homogeneity. The concept of a stock that includes all forms of capital is beset with what appear to be insurmountable difficulties when it comes to specifying and measuring the totality of the stock of capital. The services rendered by capital, whatever its form, can be ascertained—as is clear from the progress that has been made in the measurement of income. However, the capitalization of each and every income stream in an attempt to measure the stock of capital is a type of arithmetic that adds little, if anything, to economic knowledge.

But the totality of the existing stock of capital in itself is not an essential component in determining economic growth, because the meaning of economic growth is some rate of increase in the number of income streams in terms of dollars per year. The additions to the existing stock are what matter. In an economy in which the existing "factors of production" are fully employed, additional income streams—that is, economic growth—are some function of the classes and the amount of investment. Thus we want a classification of investment viewed as activities that are subject to private and public decisions.

There is, however, another important part of classical economics that also must be considered and placed aside before turning to the matter of classification. It is the treatment of "the state of the arts." The classical assumption that the state of the arts remains constant must be abandoned in determining the rate of growth of an economy that is being modernized. In no small part, the rate of growth is a consequence of investments that are explicitly made to change the state of the productive arts. Institutions that provide services to the economy are also impounded and held constant under the classical assumption pertaining to the state of the arts. Economic growth, however, is a process that alters the demand for the services of institutions, and a part of the analytical task is to explain the lags in the adjustment of institutions in response to changes in demand from economic growth per se.

Needless to say, there is an increasing awareness that changes in the state of the arts really matter, as is evident in the vast literature on technology. According to much of what is being said on this subject, the values of people and the structure of society are being shapd by technology and technocrats. Most of this literature, however, is naive with respect to the manner in which the economy adjusts and people gain (lose) as workers and as consumers.

Although economists have, in general, been silent on the institutional implications of the advances in technology, they have been concerned about the changes in the techniques of production. The appeal to "technical change" is an attempt to cope with changes in the state of the productive arts. The explanation of productivity change in terms of improvements in the quality of labor and of physical capital, without appealing to technical change, is another approach to this problem. There has been progress, and it is now clear that these improvements in the quality of the "factors of production" are both real and large. Thus the stage is set for determining the classes of investment activities that augment the worthwhile capabilities of the labor force and the state of the productive arts.

Meanwhile, during the past decade, there have been important advances in economic thinking with respect to investment in human capital. This set of investments is classified as follows: schooling and higher education, on-the-job training, migration, health, and economic information. Most of the work thus far has concentrated on the first of this set. It has been extended to the personal distribution of income, international trade, international movement of skilled persons, the allocation of resources in the production of educational services, the effects of discrimination upon motivation in school performance, the treatment of "educated labor" under the production function, and family planning. Earnings foregone, which are, as a rule, a major cost component in the investment in human capital, have been extended to and developed into a theory of the allocation of time.

But there has been less progress in analyzing research as an investment activity. The missing link in the analytical chain that connects research to the economy is in the accounting of the economic value of the contributions of research. It has been difficult to forge this link because of the ambiguity with which the concept of knowledge is burdened. The approach of this study, to which a major chapter is devoted, treats research as a specialized activity requiring special skills and facilities that are used to discover and develop special forms of new information. In accordance with this concept, this class of new information is appropriable and of some economic value. Furthermore, such new information is of two basic parts: 1) that which is transformed into new skills, which, when acquired, are forms of human capital, and 2) that which is transformed into new materials, which when achieved, are new forms of nonhuman capital.

This concept of the discovery and development of such new information leads to the following classification of investment activities: 1) organized research by government agencies, universities, laboratories (also institutes, bureaus, centers, and foundations) that are established "not-for-profit" and by business firms producing for profit; 2) unorganized research by those proceeding on their own, a group that is a vanishing breed; 3) organized endeavors to transform the new information from research into useful techniques and skills; 4) unorganized endeavors in this area that consist mainly of entrepreneurial innovations; 5) organized distribution by government agencies, universities (extension services), foundations, and others operating "not-for-profit" and by business firms that are motivated by profits; and 6) the unorganized (informal) dissemination of new information from research, a classification of many parts and exceedingly hard to identify.

Later on, when we enter the domain of institutions that render economic services, we shall consider the changes in the demand for the services of institutions that are the consequences of the rising economic value of man and attempt to explain some of the observed adjustments in such institutions.

2 The Unsettled Question of Technical Change

F OR purposes of economic analysis, what is meant by "technology"? Why does it change? How is it best dealt with? These are difficult, unsettled questions of major importance in analyzing the sources of economic growth. An all-inclusive concept of technology presumably would comprise the technical attributes of all factors and products. It would, therefore, include the original technical properties of the soil in the Ricardian sense, and thus it would take into account all technical differences among parcels of land. But since they are given by nature, does it mean they are not subject to change? Although nature is not invariant, it is not a significant source of technical change. The technical properties of land are nevertheless an integral part of a technology. An all-inclusive concept of technology presumably also would include the innate abilities of man. These, too, are given by nature, and for time periods relevant in economic analysis, differences in such abilities in any large population are not subject to significant changes. Thus, the idea of technical change pertains to technical attributes other than the original properties of land and the innate abilities of labor. But investment to improve the soil and the acquired abilities of man can alter the technical attributes of land and of man. Hence, by means of investment they, too, are subject to technical change.

Economists, however, have taken a narrow view of technology by restricting it to "capital goods," excluding land and man and concentrating on structures and equipment.[1] While this view includes tools, apparatuses, and instruments, it, as a rule, excludes such biological entities as animals, plants, and other organisms entering as inputs into the process of production. Nor does this view of technology include all of the technical attributes of the output; that is, of consumer goods and services. While all of these entities are subject to technical change, in the sense that ultimately each existing entity can be replaced by another with different technical attributes, the process of technical change consists of an array of marginal changes of the historically acquired capital structure, including that of households.

Although it is obvious that the advance in science and technology has become a major source of economic growth, it is not obvious that the new techniques thus discovered and developed, and which enter into the process of production employed by firms and households, are forms of capital. These techniques are means of production; they require investment; and they are forms of capital. But in laying the foundations of economic theory, econo-

---

1. Edward Ames notes that a telephone system uses 30,000 or more kinds of apparatus, and literally hundreds of kinds of new apparatus are introduced annually. "That's No Paradox: It's a Pin Factory" (Unpublished paper, Department of Economics, Purdue University, 1966).

mists have from the outset abstracted from changes in technology, and they then have introduced technical change as an exogenous process. But as economic growth has become increasingly dependent upon technical change, technology has been crowding capital and labor off the economic stage.

Thus a clarification of the economics of technical change is overdue. But how is technical change to be approached? Much depends on whether we approach it as part of a domain that is outside of economic theory, or as an integral part of that theory. I propose to show that the latter approach is theoretically possible and that it is necessary for any comprehensive analysis of modern economic growth.

The other approach, which is widely used and consists of many variants, is restricted, in general, to treatments of the economic effects of what is assumed to be technical change. In an analysis of the secular process of production and consumption, numerous economic effects may be attributed to technical change. These effects may appear to alter the activities of firms and of households; they may be viewed as labor saving or as capital saving, or they may be neutral in this respect; they may appear to reduce the importance of labor and capital, thus giving rise to an unexplained residual; and then they may appear to be a significant source of gains in productivity, of economic growth, and also of adjustment lags in the tendency toward equilibrium. There is no doubt that studies of these and other apparent economic effects of technical progress have been useful, above all in focusing attention on the increasing importance of technical change. E. D. Domar[2] put it neatly, noting that economists have been recasting the roles of the actors in economic growth by assigning

2. E. D. Domar, "On the Measurement of Technological Change," *The Economic Journal*, 71 (December, 1961), pp. 709-729.

minor parts to labor and capital and the leading role to technology. The adverse consequence of this recasting of roles upon the relevance of much of economic theory has gone unnoticed. It has become patent that in analyses of economic growth, the economic effects of technical change have come to look ever larger and more threatening to the accepted core of economic theory.

Abstracting from Technical Change

The theoretical tradition of economics is to abstract from technical change; one of the basic assumptions of the classical formulation of economic theory is that technology remains constant. For the early economists this was an ingenious simplification, and the resulting theory was, in general, relevant to the problems then under consideration. But now that we must deal with modern economic growth, it has long been obvious that the assumption that technology remains constant is altogether contrary to the facts of modern growth. Yet despite the strong empirical evidence showing that improvements in technology have become a major source of economic growth, technical change is not an integral part of economic theory. It remains apart, exogenous, and this separation is one of the main reasons growth theory is so lacking in relevance in explaining modern economic growth. There is an increasing awareness, however, that an approach that treats technical change as a separate entity outside and beyond the core of theory is quite inadequate. This awareness has come from a realization that this approach is somehow undermining the relevance of capital theory, wage theory, input-output analysis, international trade theory, and that important analytical tool, the production function. Economists have responded by devising particular adaptations for coping with some of the economic effects of technical change. But, as yet, there is no satisfactory general solution, and it is in this sense that the approach to technical change is an unsettled question.

Three Parts of the State of the Arts

In developing the corpus of theory, the early economists took as one of their key assumptions the *state of the arts* remaining constant. The state of the arts included for them not only what has since become known as "technical change" but also institutions and forms of economic organization. In view of the difficulties that subsequently arose in treating changes in each of the three parts of the state of the arts, made especially evident by recent endeavors to deal with them, it was without doubt a master stroke to have begun by abstracting from changes in the state of the arts.

When it comes to relevance, the early economists had a marked advantage over modern economists in abstracting from changes in the state of the arts. In their world, secular changes in institutions occurred with glacial slowness; the stability of economic organizations was not challenged by socialized forms of organization to allocate resources; and, not least of all, technical change could still be viewed as an unusual event requiring only a brief chapter "On Machinery." Economic progress was rooted in the division of labor and in the enlargement of a stock of "homogeneous" capital with some offsetting drag from diminishing returns to land. Despite the limitations of such a concept of capital, their analysis was substantially relevant in accounting for the economic growth of their period. Under present economic circumstances, however, this relevance escapes the modern economist who seeks to determine the sources of economic growth.

Meanwhile, modern economists have clarified two of the three parts of the state of the arts. The major advance has been in treating different forms of economic organization, predominantly with respect to the relevance of price theory. Price theory, originally conceived to determine how resources are allocated and income distributed in a competitive capitalist economy, has now been extended to a planned economy. As Robert M. Solow has noted, modern work has rediscovered the same price theory "in the guise of shadow prices or efficiency prices," and, accordingly, it is now known "that the theory of perfectly-competitive capitalism is in many respects the theory of a planned or socialist economy."[3] The method of treating social institutions, to the extent that they are altered over time and thus change community preferences, has been clarified somewhat. But, in general, this achievement has had less empirical relevance if for no other reason than that such institutional changes continue to occur slowly. That part of the state of the arts pertaining to technical change has remained substantially unclarified.

Interpretations of History and Models

Thus we are back to the search for approaches to analyze changes in technology. Once these changes were excluded from theory, living with them as foreign bodies has not been good for the health of economics. Many leading economists have been looking for a remedy. But in economics as in the history of science, to borrow a phrase

3. Robert M. Solow, *Capital Theory and the Rate of Return* (Amsterdam: North Holland Publishing Company, 1963), p. 15.

from Paul A. Samuelson, the journey between two points is not a straight line. The historical inevitability of technological progress was not the part of Marx's theory that jarred the complacency of economists, although this particular part has become increasingly relevant in modern economic growth. However, recent empirical work, notably that of Moses Abramowitz, Solomon Fabricant, John M. Kendrick, and Simon Kuznets, in which they aim to hold the technical attributes of labor and nonhuman capital constant, has jarred economists because their estimates appeared to leave so much of United States economic growth unexplained. What is apparent from their work is that when labor and nonhuman capital inputs are treated in this way, they are not good proxies of their productive services.

Nor is there a paucity of economic models for dealing with technical change. The least useful is a family of models that introduce technical changes as a *trend variable*.[4] There is not much to be said for them; they do not attempt any meaningful theoretical integration and, as might be expected, produce only naive estimates and projections of technical change.

Solow's early model dealing with technical change and the aggregate production function[5] has the appearance of much more economic sophistication. Nevertheless, it only changes the name to be applied to the economic effects of technical change; it simply transforms it into upward shifts of the aggregate production function, and these shifts are once again trends. Solow's recent model, how-

4. For example, see T. W. Swan, "Economic Growth and Capital Accumulation," *The Economic Record*, 32 (November, 1956), pp. 334-361.

5. Robert M. Solow, "Technical Change and the Aggregate Production Function," *The Review of Economics and Statistics*, 39 (August, 1957), pp. 312-320.

ever, accomplishes more by treating new capital goods as *carriers* of more efficient techniques than those embodied in old capital goods.[6] This way of dealing with technical change achieves a form of theoretical integration by dating the formation of capital goods. In principle, it should also be possible to bring in the improvements in the skills of labor in the same manner.

However, a serious obstacle and a major omission appear when these vintage capital models are applied. At any meaningful level of aggregation, the formation of capital goods, whatever the date, consists partly of goods that are carriers of new techniques and partly of goods that simply augment the stock of capital carrying techniques previously in use. To distinguish empirically between these two parts as they enter into the process of capital formation during any given period seems to be an unsolvable problem. The omission that inevitably arises is the exclusion of many, if not all, of the resources allocated to the discovery and development of new techniques.

Before we turn to another family of models, the work of Edward F. Denison warrants consideration.[7] It has the merit of specifying and then quantifying a number of important sources of economic growth that have been neglected. Denison's concept of labor includes improvements in the skills of the labor force associated with the earnings of labor attributed to education, although in his allocation of such earnings, he uses the arbitrary assump-

6. Robert M. Solow, "Technical Progress, Capital Formation and Economic Growth," *The American Economic Review*, 52 (May, 1962), pp. 76-86.

7. See Edward F. Denison, *The Sources of Economic Growth in the United States and the Alternatives before Us*, Supplementary Paper No. 13 (New York: Committee for Economic Development, 1962).

tion that "three-fifths of the reported income differentials represent the incomes from work *due to* differences in education as distinguished from associated characteristics."[8] But his concept of nonhuman capital as input services does not represent the flow of services contributed by the improvements in such capital.[9]

Meanwhile, recent work on human capital has made it clear that the investment in schooling, on-the-job training, health, job information, and migration enhances the value productivity of man's acquired capabilities, and it has led to the development of measurements of changes in the quality of labor that can be quantified. Moreover, when it comes to dealing with improvements in factor quality, the work on human capital is substantially ahead of that pertaining to nonhuman capital.[10]

Regarding economic models, Zvi Griliches and Dale W. Jorgenson[11] have developed a set of measurements of the increases in the stock of nonhuman capital that are similar in principle to the measurements of the improvements in quality already developed for human capital. This approach is clearly foreshadowed in the earlier work of Griliches in which he had developed models that led him to estimate the improvements in both labor and various nonhuman inputs that have taken place during recent

8. *Ibid.*, p. 69.

9. In Chapter 9, "Factors of Production Concealed under 'Technological Change,'" of my *Transforming Traditional Agriculture* (New Haven, Conn.: Yale University Press, 1964), I previously made this evaluation of Denison's contribution.

10. It is also less complicated empirically because it is much more difficult to identify the economic value of the flow of services from particular new machines and other new forms of nonhuman capital than that from schooling and other new forms of skills.

11. Zvi Griliches and Dale W. Jorgenson, "Sources of Measured Productivity Change: Capital Input," *The American Economic Review*, 56 (May, 1966), pp. 50-61.

decades in United States agriculture.[12] Griliches and Jorgenson fittingly close their paper with the remark, "In explaining economic growth we suggest greater reliance than heretofore on the twin pillars of human and non-human capital, each supporting an important part of the capital structure. Perhaps the day is not far off when economists can remove the intellectual scaffolding of technical change altogether." Since then, Jorgenson and Griliches have generalized the economic theory underlying their approach, and they have applied it empirically to the growth of the United States' domestic private economy, 1945-1965. They propose a social accounting framework, and their "hypothesis is that if real product and real factor input are accurately accounted for, the observed growth in total factor productivity is negligible."[13] Clearly economists have come a long way on the intellectual journey toward dealing with technical change.

Integrating Technical Change into Theory

Building on this advance in economics, two major steps can now be taken that will bring technical changes into the corpus of economic theory. The first, which is indicated by work already under way, is to treat all techniques,

12. Zvi Griliches, "Measuring Inputs in Agriculture: A Critical Survey," *Journal of Farm Economics*, 42 (December, 1960), pp. 1411-1433; "The Sources of Measured Productivity Growth: United States Agriculture, 1940-60," *The Journal of Political Economy*, 71 (August, 1963), pp. 331-346; "Notes on the Measurement of Price and Quality Changes," *Models of Income Determination*, Conference on Research in Income and Wealth, Studies in Income and Wealth, 28 (Princeton, N.J.: Princeton University Press, 1964), pp. 381-404.

13. Dale W. Jorgenson and Zvi Griliches, "The Explanation of Productivity Change," *The Review of Economic Studies*, 34 (July, 1967), pp. 249-283, and especially p. 249.

whether old or new, as forms of capital, thus transforming technology into capital for purposes of economic analysis. The second is to treat much of scientific research, and also a large part of education and other skill-producing activities, as "industries" producing new forms of capital that are more efficient than particular old forms of capital.

The first of these steps is designed to determine the economic value of the entities that contribute to production, whatever their technical attributes; it is not intended to specify and identify each and every technical attribute of such entities, a task far beyond the capacity of economics for the simple reason that it is not within the province of economic analysis. In taking this step, it is imperative not to treat all forms of capital as a single homogeneous capital good, but rather to specify the particular, relevant heterogeneity of capital necessary to advance the determination of its economic value instead of its purely technical properties. In principle this step implies, for purposes of economic analysis, that a technique is no more or less than a unit of capital, that a set of techniques representing a technology is a capital structure, and that a technical change is an alteration of a capital structure. It also implies that the adoption of a new and more efficient technique entails an investment in the formation of that type of capital. It follows that the long-standing endeavor to distinguish between techniques and capital goes by the board, and the pseudo-economic "scaffolding" for dealing with techniques, technical horizons, choice of techniques, and best-practice techniques can be replaced by investment in particular forms of capital, which is an economic scaffold because it is made from the conceptual materials of which the house of economics is built. Moreover, the difficult and vexing distinction between labor-saving and capital-saving technical change becomes straightaway a matter of one form of capital substituting for or complementing another as investment proceeds. The analytical burden then falls on economics proper and on investment analysis in particular.

The second step implies a marked extension of the concept of the industries that produce capital "goods." We want to include all industries that produce capital, whether human or nonhuman. Since the conventionally omitted capital-producing industries entail cost and returns, an efficient allocation requires that these industries be included in any comprehensive analysis of the process of economic growth. I shall have more to say with regard to these industries in later chapters.

Detours and the Right Road

Looking back to where our journey started, we acquire a new perspective on the presumed advantage of abstracting from changes in technology. At the outset there was the question: How else could one deal with capital? Land and labor seemed manageable, but "capital" was ever so elusive analytically. Since the structure of capital is dependent upon the state of technology, what could have been more plausible in reducing the complexity of the capital problem than the assumption that technology remains constant? But the advantage of this assumption is more apparent than real, because the capital heterogeneity problem remains, regardless of the state of technology. It remains because each and every economy, whether it is simple or complex, traditional or modern, or is in or out of equilibrium, and whether its technology is changing or constant, has a particular capital structure which consists of more than one form of capital. Therefore, economists cannot escape the capital heterogeneity problem by holding technology constant.

It can now be seen that technical change is but a part of the general problem of capital heterogeneity, which is the relevant analytical problem. Instead of endeavoring to solve that problem, economists have long sought to bypass it by using the expedient device of a single capital good, and so on down the road of capital homogeneity.

The classical economists put us on the wrong road. John Hicks has taught us that the models implicit in the work of both Adam Smith and David Ricardo assume capital homogeneity.[14] They saw the quantity of land as fixed by nature, although a long controversy ensued on how to deal with the differences in the quality of different parcels of land. Labor presented no such problems for them because they viewed labor as homogeneous in quality, essentially free of any capital components, although Adam Smith's realism is rich with sage remarks referring to acquired skills as forms of capital. Yet without any technical change there was a capital structure consisting of more than one form of capital. Nevertheless, Adam Smith's ". . . pure model is consistently carried through on the assumption that the only form of capital is circulating capital."[15] Except for the explicit introduction of diminishing returns to land, Ricardo follows closely Smith's analysis, and thus "we have the same confinement to circulating capital, and the same capital homogeneity."[16]

Thus, beginning with Adam Smith and Ricardo, economic analysis went astray not because of technical change

14. John Hicks, *Capital and Growth* (Oxford, England: Oxford University Press, 1965), Chapter 4.
15. *Ibid.*, p. 36.
16. *Ibid.*, p. 46.

per se but as a consequence of the failure to recognize the diversity in the forms of reproducible capital goods, whatever the state of technology. To reiterate, the assumption that technology remains constant does not provide a foundation for theory that frees it from capital heterogeneity. It may have been a useful device for preliminary exploration, but it was, as Hicks tells us, "a disaster" for capital theory. "Like other metaphysical entities, it is a boat that is loose from its moorings. It is the big thing that was wrong with classical theory."[17]

A Summary

A preliminary purpose of this chapter has been to clarify particular economic attributes of technical change by showing that what is relevant to the purpose at hand are the attributes of capital. Once this is clear, one can straightaway treat techniques, old and new, as forms of capital, and the stage is set for determining the economic value of capital, whatever its form. Transforming techniques into forms of capital undoubtedly has far-reaching implications for economic theory. For one, it makes ever so explicit the heterogeneity of capital. Also, we see that the economists' traditional practice of abstracting from changes in technology does not free capital from the problem of capital heterogeneity. Although the road is unimproved and poorly marked, I believe we are now on the right road to deal with technical change. This road takes us to the "industries" that produce the new and more efficient forms of capital by means of investment.

17. *Ibid.*, p. 35.

3 Investment in Human Capital[1]

ALTHOUGH it is obvious that people acquire useful skills and knowledge, it is not obvious that these skills and knowledge are a form of capital, that this capital is in substantial part a product of deliberate investment, that it has grown in Western societies at a much faster rate than conventional (nonhuman) capital, and that its growth may well be the most distinctive feature of the economic system. It has been widely observed that increases in national output have been large compared with the increases of land, man-hours, and physical reproducible capital. Investment in human capital is, probably, the major explanation for this difference.

Much of what we call consumption constitutes investment in human capital. Direct expenditures on education,

1. Presidential address delivered at the Seventy-Third Annual Meeting of the American Economic Association, St. Louis, Mo., December 28, 1960. The author is indebted to Milton Friedman for his very helpful suggestions to gain clarity and cogency and to Harry G. Johnson for pointing out a number of ambiguities.

health, and internal migration to take advantage of better job opportunities are clear examples. Earnings foregone by mature students attending school and by workers acquiring on-the-job training are equally clear examples. Yet nowhere do these enter into our national accounts. The use of leisure time to improve skills and knowledge is widespread and it, too, is unrecorded. In these and similar ways, the *quality* of human effort can be greatly improved and its productivity enhanced. I shall contend that such investment in human capital accounts for most of the impressive rise in the real earnings per worker.

I shall comment, first, on the reasons why economists have shied away from the explicit analysis of investment in human capital, and then on the capacity of such investment to explain many a puzzle about economic growth. Mainly, however, I shall concentrate on the scope and substance of human capital and its formation. Finally, I shall consider some social and policy implications.

Shying Away from Investment in Man

Economists have long known that people are an important part of the wealth of nations. Measured by what labor contributes to output, the productive capacity of human beings is now vastly larger than all other forms of wealth taken together. What economists have not stressed is the simple truth that people invest in themselves and that these investments are very large. Although economists are seldom timid in entering on abstract analysis and are often proud of being impractical, they have not been bold in coming to grips with this form of investment. Whenever they come even close, they proceed gingerly as if they were stepping into deep water. No doubt there are reasons for being wary. Deep-seated moral and philosophical issues are ever present. Free men are first and foremost the end to be served by economic endeavor; they are not property nor marketable assets. And not least, it has been all too convenient in marginal productivity analysis to treat labor as if it were a unique bundle of innate abilities that are wholly free of capital.

The mere thought of investment in human beings is offensive to some among us.[2] Our values and beliefs inhibit us from looking upon human beings as capital goods, except in slavery, and this we abhor. We are not unaffected by the long struggle to rid society of indentured service and to evolve political and legal institutions to keep men free from bondage. These are achievements that we prize highly. Hence, to treat human beings as wealth that can be augmented by investment runs counter to deeply held values. It seems to reduce man, once again, to a mere material component, to something akin to property. And for man to look upon himself as a capital good, even if it did not impair his freedom, may seem to debase him. No less a person than J. S. Mill at one time insisted that the people of a country should not be looked upon as wealth because wealth existed only for the sake of people.[3] But, surely, Mill was wrong; there is nothing in the concept of human wealth contrary to his idea that it exists only for the advantage of people. By investing in themselves, people can enlarge the range of choice available to them. It is one way free men can enhance their welfare.

Among the few who have looked upon human beings

2. This paragraph draws on the introduction to my paper, "Investment in Man: An Economist's View," *Social Service Review*, 33 (June, 1959), pp. 109-117.

3. See J. S. Nicholson, "The Living Capital of the United Kingdom," *The Economic Journal*, 1 (March, 1891), p. 95, and J. S. Mill, *Principles of Political Economy*, W. J. Ashley (ed.), (London: Longmans, Green, and Co., 1909), p. 8.

as capital, there are three distinguished names. The philosopher-economist Adam Smith boldly included all of the acquired and useful abilities of all of the inhabitants of a country as part of capital. So did H. von Thünen, who then went on to argue that the concept of capital applied to man did not degrade him nor impair his freedom and dignity but, on the contrary, that the failure to apply the concept was especially pernicious in wars: ". . . for here . . . one will sacrifice in a battle a hundred human beings in the prime of their lives without thought in order to save one gun." The reason is that, ". . . the purchase of a cannon causes an outlay of public funds, whereas human beings are to be had for nothing by means of a mere conscription decree."[4] Also, Irving Fisher presented clearly and cogently an all-inclusive concept of capital.[5] Yet the main stream of thought has held that it is neither appropriate nor practical to apply the concept of capital to human beings. Alfred Marshall,[6] whose great prestige goes far to explain why this view was accepted, held that while human beings are incontestably capital from an abstract and mathematical point of view, it would be out of touch with the marketplace to treat them as capital in practical analyses. Investment in human beings has accordingly seldom been incorporated in the formal core of economics, even though many economists, including Marshall, have seen its relevance at one point or another in what they have written.

The failure to treat human resources explicitly as a form of capital, as a produced means of production, as the prod-

4. Quoted from unpublished translation by B. F. Hoselitz of pp. 140-152 of Vol. II, Pt. 2, of H. von Thünen, *Der isolierte Staat* (3rd ed.; Berlin: Wiegandt, Hempel and Parey, 1875).

5. Irving Fisher, *The Nature of Capital and Income* (New York: The Macmillan Company, 1906).

6. Alfred Marshall, *Principles of Economics* (8th ed.; London: The Macmillan Company, 1930), pp. 787-788.

uct of investment, has fostered the retention of the classical notion of labor as a capacity to do manual work requiring little knowledge and skill, a capacity with which, according to this notion, laborers are endowed about equally. This notion of labor was wrong in the classical period, and it is patently wrong now. Counting individuals who can and want to work and treating such a count as a measure of the quantity of an economic factor is no more meaningful than it would be to count the number of all manner of machines to determine their economic importance either as a stock of capital or as a flow of productive services.

Laborers have become capitalists not from a diffusion of the ownership of corporation stocks, as folklore would have it, but from the acquisition of knowledge and skill that have economic value.[7] This knowledge and skill are in great part the product of investment and, combined with other human investment, predominantly account for the productive superiority of the technically advanced countries. To omit them in studying economic growth is like trying to explain Soviet ideology without Marx.

Economic Growth from Human Capital

Many paradoxes and puzzles about our dynamic, growing economy can be resolved once human investment is taken into account. Let me begin by sketching some that are minor though not trivial.

When farm people take nonfarm jobs they earn substantially less than industrial workers of the same race, age, and sex. Similarly, nonwhite urban males earn much less than white males even after allowance is made for the

7. See Harry G. Johnson, "The Political Economy of Opulence," *Canadian Journal of Economics and Political Science*, 26 (November, 1960), pp. 552-564.

effects of differences in unemployment, age, city size, and region.[8] Because these differentials in earnings correspond closely to corresponding differentials in education, they strongly suggest that the one is a consequence of the other. Negroes who operate farms, whether as tenants or as owners, earn much less than whites on comparable farms.[9] Fortunately, crops and livestock are not vulnerable to the blight of discrimination. The large differences in earnings seem rather to reflect mainly the differences in health and education. Workers in the South, on the average, earn appreciably less than those in the North or West, and they also have less education on the average. Many migratory farm workers earn very little indeed by comparison with other workers. Many of them have virtually no schooling, are in poor health, are unskilled, and have little ability to do useful work. To urge that the differences in the amount of human investment may explain these differences in earnings seems elementary. And yet another example, the curve relating income to age tends to be steeper for skilled than for unskilled persons. Investment in on-the-job training seems a likely explanation.

Economic growth requires much internal migration of workers to adjust to changing job opportunities.[10] Young men and women move more readily than older workers. Surely this makes economic sense when one recognizes that the costs of such migration are a form of human investment. Young people have more years ahead of them than older

8. Morton Zeman, "A Quantitative Analysis of White-Nonwhite Income Differentials in the United States" (Unpublished Ph.D. dissertation in economics, University of Chicago, 1955).

9. Based on unpublished preliminary research by Joseph Willett in his Ph.D. study at the University of Chicago.

10. See Simon Kuznets, "Distribution by Industrial Origin," *Income and Wealth of the United States*, ed. by Simon Kuznets (Cambridge, Eng.: Bowes & Bowes, Ltd., 1952), Sec. IV.

workers during which they can realize on such an investment. Hence it takes less of a wage differential to make it
economically advantageous for them to move, or, to put
it differently, young people can expect a higher return on
their investment in migration than older people. This differential may explain selective migration without requiring
an appeal to sociological differences between young and
old people.

The examples so far given are of investment in human
beings that yield a return over a long period. This is true
equally of investment in education, training, and migration
of young people. Not all investments in human beings
are of this kind; some are more nearly akin to current
inputs, such as expenditures on food and shelter in some
countries where work is mainly the application of brute
human force, calling for energy and stamina, and where
the intake of food is far from enough to do a hard day's
work. On the "hungry" steppes and in the teeming valleys
of Asia, millions of adult males have so meager a diet that
they cannot do a long day of hard work. To call them
underemployed does not seem pertinent. Under such circumstances, it is certainly meaningful to treat food partly
as consumption and partly as a current "producer good,"
as some Indian economists have done.[11] Let us not forget
that Western economists during the early decades of industrialization and even in the time of Marshall and A. C.
Pigou often connected additional food for workers with
increases in labor productivity.

Let me now consider three major, perplexing questions
closely connected with the mystery of economic growth.
First, consider the long-period behavior of the capital-
income ratio. We were taught that a country which

11. See, for instance, P. R. Brahmananda and C. N. Vakil, *Planning for an Expanding Economy* (Bombay: Vora, 1956).

amassed more reproducible capital relative to its land and labor would employ such capital in greater "depth" because of its growing abundance and cheapness. But apparently this is not what happens. On the contrary, the estimates now available show that less of such capital tends to be employed relative to income as economic growth proceeds. Are we to infer that the ratio of capital to income has no relevance in explaining either poverty or opulence? Or that a rise of this ratio is not a prerequisite to economic growth? These questions raise fundamental issues bearing on motives and preferences for holding wealth as well as on the motives for particular investments and the stock of capital thereby accumulated. For my purpose all that needs to be said is that these estimates of capital-income ratios refer to only a part of all capital. They exclude in particular, and most unfortunately, any human capital. Yet human capital has surely been increasing at a rate substantially higher than reproducible (nonhuman) capital. We cannot, therefore, infer from these estimates that the stock of *all* capital has been decreasing relative to income. On the contrary, if we accept the not implausible assumption that the motives and preferences of people, the technical opportunities open to them, and the uncertainty associated with economic growth during particular periods were leading people to maintain roughly a constant ratio between *all* capital and income, the decline in the estimated capital-income ratio[12] is simply a signal that human capital has been increasing relatively not only to conventional capital but also to income.

12. I leave aside here the difficulties inherent in identifying and measuring both the nonhuman capital and the income entering into estimates of this ratio. There are index-number and aggregation problems aplenty, and not all improvements in the quality of this capital have been accounted for.

The bumper crop of estimates that show national income increasing faster than national resources raises a second and not unrelated puzzle. The income of the United States has been increasing at a much higher rate than the combined amount of land, man-hours worked, and the stock of reproducible capital used to produce the income. Moreover, the discrepancy between the two rates has become larger from one business cycle to the next during recent decades.[13] To call this discrepancy a measure of "resource productivity" gives a name to our ignorance but does not dispel it. If we accept these estimates, the connections between national resources and national income have become loose and tenuous over time. Unless this discrepancy can be resolved, received theory of production applied to inputs and outputs as currently measured is a toy and not a tool for studying economic growth.

Two sets of forces probably account for the discrepancy, if we neglect entirely the index number and aggregation problems that bedevil all estimates of such global aggregates as total output and total input. One is returns to scale; the second is the large improvement in the quality of inputs that have occurred, but have been omitted from the input estimates. Our economy has undoubtedly been experiencing increasing returns to scale at some points offset by decreasing returns at others. If we can succeed in identifying and measuring the net gains, they may turn out to have been substantial. The improvements in the quality of inputs that have not been adequately allowed for are no doubt partly in material (nonhuman) capital. My own conception, however, is that both this defect and the omission of economies of scale are minor sources of

13. See Solomon Fabricant, *Basic Facts on Productivity Change*, Occasional Paper No. 63 (New York: National Bureau of Economic Research, 1959), Table 5.

discrepancy between the rates of growth of inputs and outputs compared to the improvements in human capabilities that have been omitted.

A small step takes us from these two puzzles raised by existing estimates to a third mystery, which brings us to the heart of the matter: namely, the essentially unexplained large increase in real earnings of workers. Can this be a windfall? Or a quasi-rent pending the adjustment in the supply of labor? Or, a pure rent reflecting the fixed amount of labor? It seems far more reasonable that it represents a return to the investment that has been made in human beings. The observed growth in productivity per unit of labor is simply a consequence of holding the unit of labor constant over time, although in fact this unit of labor has been increasing as a result of a steadily growing amount of human capital per worker. As I read our record, the human capital component has become very large as a consequence of human investment.

Another aspect of the same basic question, which admits of the same resolution, is the rapid postwar recovery of countries that had suffered severe destruction of plant and equipment during the war. The toll from bombing was all too visible in the factories laid flat, the railroad yards, bridges, and harbors wrecked, and the cities devastated. Structures, equipment, and inventories were all heaps of rubble. Not so visible, yet large, was the toll from the wartime depletion of the physical plant that escaped destruction by bombs. Economists were called upon to assess the implication of these wartime losses for recovery. In retrospect, it is clear that they overestimated the prospective retarding effects of these losses. Having had a small hand in this effort, I have had a special reason for looking back and wondering why the judgments that we formed soon after the war proved to be so far from the mark. The explanation that now is clear is that we gave altogether too much weight to nonhuman capital in making these assessments. We fell into this error, I am convinced, because we did not have a concept of *all* capital and, therefore, failed to take account of human capital and the important part that it plays in production in a modern economy.

Let me close this section with a comment on poor countries, for which there are all too few useful estimates. I have been impressed by repeatedly expressed judgments, especially by those who have a responsibility in making capital available to poor countries, about the low rate at which these countries can absorb additional capital. New capital from outside can be put to good use, it is said, only when it is added "slowly and gradually." But this experience is at variance with the widely held impression that countries are poor fundamentally because they are starved for capital and that additional capital is truly the key to their more rapid economic growth. The reconciliation is again, I believe, to be found in emphasis on particular forms of capital. The new capital available to these countries from outside as a rule goes into the formation of structures, equipment, and sometimes also into inventories. But it is generally not available for additional investment in man. Consequently, human capabilities do not stay abreast of physical capital, and they do become limiting factors in economic growth. It should come as no surprise, therefore, that the absorption rate of capital to augment only particular nonhuman resources is necessarily low. The B. Horvat[14] formulation of the optimum rate of investment, which treats knowledge and skill as a critical investment variable in determining the rate of economic growth, is both relevant and important.

14. B. Horvat, "The Optimum Rate of Investment," *The Economic Journal,* 68 (December, 1958), pp. 747-767.

Scope and Substance of Human Investments

What are human investments? Can they be distinguished from consumption? Is it at all feasible to identify and measure them? What do they contribute to income? Granted that they seem amorphous compared to brick and mortar, and hard to get at compared to the investment accounts of corporations, but they assuredly are not a fragment; they are rather like the contents of Pandora's box, full of difficulties and hope.

Human resources obviously have both quantitative and qualitative dimensions. The number of people, the proportion entering upon useful work, and hours worked are essentially quantitative characteristics. To make my task tolerably manageable, I shall neglect these and consider only such quality components as skill, knowledge, and similar attributes that affect particular human capabilities to do productive work. Insofar as expenditures to enhance such capabilities also increase the value productivity of human effort (labor), they will yield a positive rate of return.[15]

How can we estimate the magnitude of human investment? The practice followed in connection with physical capital goods is to estimate the magnitude of capital formation by expenditures made to produce the capital goods. This practice would suffice also for the formation of human capital. However, for human capital there is an additional problem that is less pressing for physical capital goods: how to distinguish between expenditures for current consumption and those for capital formation. This distinction bristles with both conceptual and practical difficulties.

15. Even so, our *observed* return can be either negative, zero, or positive because our observations are drawn from a world where there is uncertainty and imperfect knowledge and where there are windfall gains and losses and mistakes aplenty.

We can think of three classes of expenditures: for current consumption, for a durable consumer component, and for a durable producer component. Both of these durable capabilities represent investments; one becomes human capital that renders consumer services, and the other is a form of human capital that enhances the producer-capability of the person.

The task of identifying each component is formidable. While any capability produced by human investment becomes a part of the human agent and hence cannot be sold, it is nevertheless "in touch with the marketplace" by affecting the wages and salaries the human agent can earn. The resulting increase in earnings is the yield on the investment.[16]

Despite the difficulty of exact measurement at this stage of our understanding of human investment, many insights can be gained by examining some of the more important activities that improve human capabilities. I shall concentrate on five major categories: 1) health facilities and services, broadly conceived to include all expenditures that affect the life expectancy, strength and stamina, and the vigor and vitality of a people; 2) on-the-job training, including old-style apprenticeships organized by firms; 3) formally organized education at the elementary, secondary, and higher levels; 4) study programs for adults that are not organized by firms, including extension programs notably in agriculture; and 5) migration of individuals and families to adjust to changing job opportunities. Except for education, little that is germane is known of these activities.

16. In principle, the value of the investment can be determined by discounting the additional future earnings it yields, just as the value of a physical capital good can be determined by discounting its income stream.

I shall refrain from commenting on study programs for adults, although in agriculture the extension services play an important role in transmitting new information and in developing new skills of farmers.[17] Nor shall I elaborate further on internal migration related to economic growth.

Health activities have both quantity and quality implications. Some economists are engaged in determining the effects of improvements in health[18]—that is, health measures that enhance the quality of human resources, as, for example, additional food and better shelter, especially in underdeveloped countries.

The change in the role of food as people become richer sheds light on one of the conceptual problems already referred to. I have pointed out that extra food in some poor countries has the attribute of a "producer good." This attribute of food, however, diminishes as the consumption of food rises, and there comes a point at which any further increase in food becomes pure consumption.[19] The same may be true for clothing, housing, and perhaps medical services.

My comment about on-the-job training will consist of a conjecture on the amount of such training, a note on the decline of apprenticeship, and then a useful economic theorem on who bears the costs of such training. The ex-

17. See T. W. Schultz, "Agriculture and the Application of Knowledge," *A Look to the Future* (Battle Creek, Mich.: W. K. Kellogg Foundation, 1956), pp. 54-78.

18. Health economics is in its infancy. Selma J. Mushkin's survey, "Toward a Definition of Health Economics," *Public Health Reports*, 73, U.S. Dept. of Health, Education, and Welfare (September, 1958), pp. 785-793, is very useful with its pertinent economic insights.

19. For instance, the income elasticity of the demand for food continues to be positive even after the point is reached where additional food no longer has the attribute of a "producer good."

pansion of education has not eliminated it. It seems likely that some of the training formerly undertaken by firms has been discontinued and other training programs have been instituted to adjust both to the rise in the education of workers and to changes in the demands for new skills. The amount invested annually in such training can only be a guess. Harold F. Clark places it near to equal to the amount spent on formal education.[20] Elsewhere, too, it is thought to be important. For example, some observers have been impressed by the amount of such training under way in plants in the Soviet Union.[21] Meanwhile, apprenticeship has all but disappeared, partly because it is now inefficient and partly because schools now perform many of its functions. Its disappearance has been hastened no doubt by the difficulty of enforcing apprenticeship agreements. Legally they have come to smack of indentured service. The underlying economic factors and behavior are clear enough. The apprentice is prepared to serve during the initial period when his productivity is less than the cost of his keep and of his training. Later, however, unless he is legally restrained, he will seek other employment when his productivity begins to exceed the cost of keep and training, which is the period during which a master would expect to recoup on his earlier outlay.

20. Based on comments he made in the summer of 1959; see also Harold F. Clark, "Potentialities of Educational Establishments outside the Conventional Structure of Higher Education," *Financing Higher Education: 1960-70*, ed. by D. M. Keezer (New York: McGraw-Hill Book Company, 1959), pp. 257-273. Since this paper was written, the pioneering study by Jacob Mincer has appeared. See his "On-the-Job Training: Costs, Returns, and Some Implications," *The Journal of Political Economy* (Supplement), 70 (October, 1962), pp. 50-79.

21. Based on observations made by a team of United States economists of which I was a member; see "Inside the Soviet Economy," *Saturday Review*, January 21, 1961, pp. 37-39.

In analyzing on-the-job training, Gary S. Becker[22] distinguishes between *general* and *specific* skills and observes that most if not all on-the-job training produces general skills. With respect to such general skills, he advances the theorem that in competitive markets employees pay all the costs of this training and none of these costs are ultimately borne by the firm. Becker points out several implications. The notion that expenditures on training by a firm generate external economies for other firms is not consistent with this theorem. The theorem also indicates one force favoring the transfer from on-the-job training to attending school. Since on-the-job training reduces the net earnings of workers at the beginning and raises them later on, this theorem also provides an explanation for the "steeper slope of the curve relating income to age" for skilled than unskilled workers, referred to earlier.[23] What all this adds up to is that the stage is set to undertake meaningful economic studies of on-the-job training.

Happily we reach firmer ground in regard to education. Investment in education has risen at a rapid rate and by itself may well account for a substantial part of the otherwise unexplained rise in earnings. I shall do no more than summarize some preliminary results about the total costs of education (including income foregone by students), the apparent relation of these costs to consumer income and to alternative investments, the rise of the stock of education in the labor force, returns to education, and the contribution

22. In his study undertaken for the National Bureau of Economic Research, a part of his *Human Capital* (New York: National Bureau of Economic Research, 1964).

23. Becker also has noted still another implication arising out of the fact that the income and capital investment aspects of on-the-job training are tied together, which gives rise to "permanent" and "transitory" income effects that may have substantial explanatory value.

that the increase in the stock of education may have made to earnings and to national income.

It is not difficult to estimate the conventional costs of education consisting of the costs of the services of teachers, librarians, and administrators, maintaining and operating the educational plant, and interest on the capital embodied in the educational plant. It is far more difficult to estimate another component of total cost, the income foregone by students. Yet this component should be included, and it is far from negligible. In the United States, for example, well over half of the costs of higher education consists of income foregone by students. As early as 1900, this income foregone accounted for about one-fourth of the total costs of elementary, secondary, and higher education. By 1956, it represented over two-fifths of all costs. The rising significance of foregone income has been a major factor in the marked upward trend in the total real costs of education, which, measured in current prices, increased from $400 million in 1900 to $28.7 billion in 1956.[24] The percentage rise in education costs was about three and a half times as large as in consumer income, which would imply a high income elasticity of the demand for education, if education were regarded as pure consumption.[25] Educational costs also rose about three and a half times as rapidly as did the gross formation of physical capital in dollars. If we were to treat education as pure investment, this result would suggest that the returns to education were relatively more attractive than those to nonhuman capital.[26]

24. See Chapter 6 of this volume, Tables 6.3 through 6.7.
25. Had other things stayed constant this suggests an income elasticity of 3.5. Among the things that did change, the prices of educational services rose relative to other consumer prices, perhaps offset in part by improvements in the quality of educational services.
26. This of course assumes, among other things, that the relation-

Much schooling is acquired by persons who are not treated as income earners in most economic analysis, particularly, of course, women. To analyze the effect of growth in schooling on earnings, it is therefore necessary to distinguish between the stock of education in the population and the amount in the labor force. Years of school completed is far from satisfactory as a measure because of the marked increases that have taken place in the number of days enrolled students attend school and because much more of the education of workers consists of high school and higher education than formerly. My preliminary estimates suggest that the stock of education in the labor force rose about eight and a half times between 1900 and 1956, whereas the stock of reproducible capital rose four and a half times, both in 1956 prices. These estimates are, of course, subject to many qualifications.[27] Nevertheless, both the magnitude and the rate of increase of this form of human capital have been such that they could be an important key to the riddle of economic growth.[28]

---

ship between gross and net have not changed or have changed in the same proportion. Estimates are from my essay, "Education and Economic Growth," *Social Forces Influencing American Education*, Sixtieth Yearbook of the National Society for the Study of Education, ed. by Nelson B. Henry (Chicago: University of Chicago Press, 1961), Part II, pp. 46-86.

27. Drawn from *ibid.*, Sec. 4, they are tentative and incomplete. They are incomplete in that they do not take into account fully the increases in the average life of this form of human capital arising out of the fact that relatively more of this education is held by younger people in the labor force than was true in earlier years; and they are incomplete because no adjustment has been made for the improvements in education over time, increasing the quality of a year of school in ways other than those related to changes in the proportions represented by elementary, high school, and higher education.

28. In value terms this stock of education was only 22 percent as large as the stock of reproducible capital in 1900, whereas in 1956 it already had become 42 percent as large.

The exciting work under way is on the return to education. In spite of the flood of high school and college graduates, the return has not become trivial. Even the lower limits of the estimates show that the return to such education has been in the neighborhood of the return to non-human capital. This is what most of these estimates show when they treat as costs all of the public and private expenditures on education and also the income foregone while attending school, and when they treat all of these costs as investment, allocating none to consumption.[29] But surely a part of these costs are consumption in the sense that education creates a form of consumer capital[30] that has the attribute of improving the taste and the quality of consumption of students throughout the rest of their lives. If one were to allocate a substantial fraction of the total costs of this education to consumption, say one-half, this would, of course, double the observed rate of return to what would then become the investment component in education that enhances the productivity of man.

Fortunately, the problem of allocating the costs of education in the labor force between consumption and investment does not arise to plague us when we turn to the contribution that education makes to earnings and to

29. An interesting speculation is whether the consumption component in education will ultimately dominate, in the sense that the investment component in education will diminish as these expenditures increase and a point will be reached where additional expenditures for education will be pure consumption (a zero return on however small a part one might treat as an investment). This may come to pass, as it has in the case of food and shelter, but that eventuality appears very remote presently in view of the prevailing investment value of education and the new demands for knowledge and skill inherent in the nature of our technical and economic progress.

30. The returns on this consumer capital will not appear in the wages and salaries that people earn.

national income because a change in allocation only alters the rate of return, not the total return. I noted at the outset that the unexplained increases in United States national income have been especially large in recent decades. How much of this unexplained increase in income represents a return to education in the labor force? I shall return to this question later.

A Note on Policy

One proceeds at his own peril in discussing social implications and policy. The conventional hedge is to camouflage one's values and to wear the mantle of academic innocence. Let me proceed unprotected!

1. Our tax laws everywhere discriminate against human capital. Although the stock of such capital has become large and even though it is obvious that human capital, like other forms of reproducible capital, depreciates, becomes obsolete, and entails maintenance, our tax laws are all but blind to these matters.

2. Human capital deteriorates when it is idle because unemployment impairs the skills that workers have acquired. Losses in earnings can be cushioned by appropriate payments, but these do not keep idleness from taking its toll from human capital.

3. There are many hindrances to the free choice of professions. Racial discrimination and religious discrimination are still widespread. Professional associations also hinder entry, for example, into medicine. Such purposeful interference keeps the investment in this form of human capital substantially below its optimum.[31]

31. See Milton Friedman and Simon Kuznets, *Income from Independent Professional Practice* (New York: National Bureau of Economic Research, 1945).

4. It is indeed elementary to stress the greater imperfections of the capital market in providing funds for investment in human beings than for investment in physical goods. Much could be done to reduce these imperfections by reforms in tax and banking laws and by changes in banking practices. Long-term private and public loans to students are warranted.

5. Internal migration, notably the movement of farm people into industry, made necessary by the dynamics of our economic progress requires substantial investments. In general, families in which the husbands and wives are already in their late thirties cannot afford to make these investments because the remaining payoff period for them is too short. Yet society would gain if more of them would pull stakes and move because, in addition to the increase in productivity currently, the children of these families would be better located for employment when they were ready to enter the labor market. The case for making some of these investments on public account is by no means weak. Our farm programs have failed miserably these many years in not coming to grips with the costs and returns from off-farm migration.

6. The low earnings of particular people have long been a matter of public concern. Policy all too frequently concentrates only on the effects, ignoring the causes. No small part of the low earnings of many Negroes, Puerto Ricans, Mexican nationals, indigenous migratory farm workers, poor farm people, and some of our older workers, reflects the failure to have invested in their health and education. Past mistakes are, of course, bygones, but for the sake of the next generation we can ill afford to continue making the same mistakes over again.

7. Is there a substantial underinvestment in human beings

other than in these depressed groups?[32] This is an important question for economists. The evidence at hand is fragmentary. Nor will the answer be easily won. There undoubtedly have been overinvestments in some skills, for example, too many locomotive firemen and engineers, too many people trained to be farmers, and too many agricultural economists! Our schools are not free of loafers, and some students lack the necessary talents. Nevertheless, underinvestment in knowledge and skill relative to the amounts invested in nonhuman capital would appear to be the rule and not the exception for a number of reasons. The strong and increasing demands for this knowledge and skill in laborers are of fairly recent origin and it takes time to respond to them. In responding to these demands, we are heavily dependent upon cultural and political processes, and these are slow and the lags are long compared to the behavior of markets serving the formation of nonhuman capital. Where the capital market does serve human investments, it is subject to more imperfections than in financing physical capital. I have already stressed the fact that our tax laws discriminate in favor of nonhuman capital. Then, too, many individuals face serious uncertainty in assessing their innate talents when it comes to investing in themselves, especially through higher education. Nor is it easy either for public decisions or private behavior to untangle and properly assess the consumer and producer components. The fact that the rate of return to investment in high school and to higher education has been as large as or larger than the rate of return to conventional forms of capital—when all of the costs of such education, including

32. See Gary S. Becker, "Underinvestment in College Education?," *The American Economic Review*, 50 (May, 1960), pp. 346-354.

income foregone by students, are allocated to the investment component—creates a strong presumption that there has been underinvestment since, surely, much education is cultural and in that sense is consumption. It is no wonder, in view of these circumstances, that there should be substantial underinvestment in human beings, even though we take pride, and properly so, in the support that we have given to education and to other activities that contribute to such investments.

8. Should the returns from public investment in human capital accrue to the individuals in whom it is made?[33] The policy issues implicit in this question run deep and they are full of perplexities pertaining both to resource allocation and to welfare. Physical capital that is formed by public investment is not transferred as a rule to particular individuals as a gift. It would greatly simplify the allocative process if public investment in human capital were placed on the same footing. What then is the logical basis for treating public investment in human capital differently? Presumably it turns on ideas about welfare. A strong welfare goal of our community is to reduce the unequal distribution of personal income among individuals and families. Our community has relied heavily on progressive income and inheritance taxation. Given public revenue from these sources, it may well be true that public investment entering into schooling, elementary and secondary, is an effective and efficient set of expenditures for attaining this goal.

9. My last policy comment is on assistance to low-

33. I am indebted to Milton Friedman for bringing this issue to the fore in his comments on an early draft of this paper. See Preface to Friedman and Kuznets, *op. cit.*, and also Jacob Mincer's pioneering paper, "Investment in Human Capital and Personal Income Distribution," *The Journal of Political Economy*, 66 (August, 1958), pp. 281-302.

income countries to help them achieve economic growth. Here, even more than in domestic affairs, investment in human beings is likely to be underrated and neglected. It is inherent in the intellectual climate in which leaders and spokesmen of many of these countries find themselves. Our export of growth doctrines has contributed. These typically assign the stellar role to the formation of nonhuman capital and take as an obvious fact the superabundance of human resources. Steel mills are the real symbol of industrialization. It is assumed that the early industrialization of England did not depend on investments in the labor force. New funds and agencies are being authorized to transfer capital for physical goods to these countries. This one-sided effort is under way in spite of the fact that the knowledge and skills required to take on and use efficiently the superior techniques of production are usually in very short supply in these countries. Some growth, of course, results from the increase in more conventional capital even though the labor that is available is lacking both in skill and knowledge. But the rate of growth will be seriously limited. It simply is not possible to have the fruits of a modern agriculture and the abundance of modern industry without making large investments in human beings.

Truly, the most distinctive feature of our economic system is the growth in human capital. Without it there would be only hard, manual work and poverty, except for those who have income from property. In William Faulkner's *Intruder in the Dust*, there is an early morning scene of a poor, solitary cultivator at work in a field. Let me paraphrase that line: "The man without skills and knowledge leaning terrifically against nothing."

4 Human Capital Analysis: Criticism and Response

THE concept of capital as it is used in this study consists of entities that have the economic property of rendering future services of some value. This concept is not to be confused with capital defined as a fungible entity. In classifying capital that renders future services, it is helpful to begin with a dichotomy, namely, human capital and nonhuman capital. Neither of these two classes of capital is homogeneous; on the contrary, each, as a matter of fact, consists of many different forms of capital and each is therefore exceedingly heterogeneous. Nevertheless, the distinction between human and nonhuman capital is real and analytically fundamental.

The distinctive mark of human capital is that it is a part of man. It is *human* because it is embodied in man, and it is *capital* because it is a source of future satisfactions, or of future earnings, or of both. Where men are free agents, human capital is not a negotiable asset in the sense that it can be sold. It can, of course, be acquired not as an asset that is purchased in a market but by means of investing in oneself. It follows that no person can separate himself from the human capital he possesses. He must always accompany his human capital whether it serves him in production or consumption. From these basic attributes of human capital, there arise many subtle differences between human and nonhuman capital in explaining the economic behavior pertaining to the formation and utilization of these two classes of capital.

A consideration of some of the differences as well as of some of the similarities between human and nonhuman capital is the purpose of the two responses to particular criticisms of the concept of human capital. The first is a response to the critique presented by Professor Harry G. Shaffer.[1] The second pertains to the valuation problem presented by Professor Jack Wiseman.[2]

On Professor Shaffer's Critique

Professor Shaffer states at the outset, "I shall grant unequivocally that theoretical models, incontestable from an abstract or mathematical point of view, can be built on the basis of the application of the capital concept to man."[3] He then contends, however, "that it is generally inadvisable to treat man as human capital."[4] In his critique, he presents several reasons for his contention.

He discusses briefly some minor difficulties that arise in practice in distinguishing between consumption and investment expenditures and then examines with care, and in my

1. Harry G. Shaffer, "Investment in Human Capital: Comment," *The American Economic Review*, 51 (December, 1961), pp. 1026-1035.
2. Jack Wiseman, "Cost-Benefit Analysis in Education," *The Southern Economic Journal*, 32 (July, 1965), Part 2, pp. 1-12.
3. Harry G. Shaffer, *op. cit.*, p. 1026.
4. *Ibid.*

judgment correctly, some major difficulties in identifying and measuring the earnings (return) that are associated with a particular investment in man. Shaffer does not object to the concepts of investment in man and human capital; on the contrary, he explicitly accepts the underlying theory. Also, he is careful to disassociate himself from those who believe that it is morally wrong to apply the concepts of investment and capital to people. However, if any new knowledge were attainable by the use of these concepts, despite the empirical difficulties, Shaffer appears to believe that such knowledge would be grossly misused—by implication, more so than other economic knowledge—in making policy decisions. This view of the relation between economic analysis and policy seems unreal and irrelevant.

Shaffer's first point is addressed to the question: When are educational expenditures for consumption and when are they for production? This question deserves careful investigation because so much depends upon the correctness of the answer. To follow the conventional procedure of treating all such costs as serving only consumption will not do. But to allocate all of these costs to investment in future earnings is fully as extreme and unwarranted. Although the economic logic for allocating the costs of education is clear and compelling, no one has as yet developed a wholly satisfactory empirical procedure for identifying and measuring the particular resources that enter into each of these components. Faced with this difficulty, any allocation that one makes, based on such clues as seem relevant, must in all honesty be labeled "arbitrary." There is little intellectual comfort in the fact that a similar brand of arbitrariness characterizes other areas of analysis, for example, in the way expenditures for electricity and for automobiles used by farmers are divided and distributed between household and farm expenses, or the way a part of the costs of some private residences used for offices, libraries, or studies are treated as business expenses.

In discussing the central question of allocating resources between consumption and production capabilities, Shaffer emphasizes two facts; namely, that most students attend public schools and that up to a certain age, school attendance is compulsory. But neither of these facts is relevant to a logical basis for distinguishing between consumption and production capabilities. If education were altogether free, a person would presumably consume it until he were satiated and "invest" in it until it would no longer increase his future earnings. If a part of the educational expenditures were borne on public account, the direct private costs of education would of course be less than the total costs of education, and to the extent that such education increased the future earnings of the student, his private rate of return to what he spent on education would be higher than the rate of return to total educational expenditures entering into this part of his education. Thus private incentives to consume and to invest in education are affected by public educational expenditures, but that there are such public expenditures has no bearing on the question of whether education is consumption or production capabilities. The fact that some schooling is compulsory is also irrelevant to the question at hand. To argue that it applies is analogous to saying that a city ordinance that requires private owners of houses to install plumbing and sewage disposal facilities is a factor in determining whether such facilities are a consumer or producer durable. Clearly, the compulsory city ordinance does not provide a logical basis for distinguishing between these two types of durables.

Although Shaffer is clear in seeing the positive effects of education upon the future earnings of students, he believes that the economic motivations of students and parents to invest in education are weak or even nonexistent. They are, in Shaffer's view, strongly motivated as current consumers of education but only weakly or not motivated at all as investors in education. Such a dichotomy with respect to economic motivations is far from convincing. It is undoubtedly true, as Shaffer points out, that some education is wholly for current consumption, and obviously in that case there would be no investment opportunity, hence no bases for an investment motivation. But are there no economic motivations in the case of students who attend our medical schools, schools for dentists, lawyers, and engineers to invest in each of these particular skills with an eye to increases in future earnings? I am sure that the prospects of larger future earnings play a strong motivating role in these situations. Let me observe again, however, that private incentives either to consume currently or to invest in education are affected by the amount and the nature of public expenditures for education. It is, of course, true that any attempt to explain total behavior with regard to the allocation of all public and private resources entering into education takes one beyond the scope of the conventional private economic calculus of people. In studying the responses of private individuals to whatever investment opportunities education affords, it should be borne in mind 1) that where the capital market does serve human investment, it is subject to more imperfections than in financing physical capital; 2) that most investment in people, notably in the case of education, is in a long-period capacity, for it has a relatively long life and it is thus subject to the additional uncertainties this implies; 3) that many individuals face serious uncertainty in assessing their innate talents when it comes to investing in themselves; and 4) that our laws discriminate against human investments. These factors affect the observed responses, and their adverse effects may be confused with the real economic response, other things equal, to a given rate of return that is then thought to be weak or nonexistent.

Let me do no more than restate the effects of education upon consumption and earnings. The consumption component of education is either for current consumption, satisfying consumer well-being in the present, like food, or for future consumption, like houses. Education can also improve the capabilities of people and thus enhance their future earnings. The investment formed by education is, therefore, of two parts: a future consumption component and a future earnings component.

In "Education and Economic Growth,"[5] in examining education for consumption, I emphasized the current consumption component. It is now clear to me that most education that satisfies consumer preferences is for future consumption and that this component has substantial durability and it is, therefore, to the extent that it serves consumption, mainly an *enduring* consumer component, even more so than other consumer durables. As an enduring consumer component, it is the source of future utilities (and thus this component also contributes to future real income), which in no way enters into *measured* national income. This component, accordingly, is like investment in a house, automobile, or refrigerator. Thus we have the following: 1) education for current consumption; 2) education for long-period future consumption, making it an investment in an enduring consumer component, which is

5. In *Social Forces Influencing American Education,* Sixtieth Yearbook of the National Society for the Study of Education, ed. by Nelson B. Henry (Chicago: University of Chicago Press, 1961), Part II, pp. 46-86.

undoubtedly of considerable importance; and 3) education for skills and knowledge useful in economic endeavor and, thus, an investment in future earnings.

Shaffer's second point, which presents a number of the real difficulties that arise when one attempts to identify and measure the increase in earnings that are associated with education, is well founded. Differences in innate abilities, race, employment, mortality, and family connections all enter and must be faced. It should not distract from the merits of his presentation to observe that these several difficulties are very much in the forefront in the work of the economists engaged in studying this set of problems. Gary S. Becker's study[6] is a landmark on this score as well as on other relevant theoretical and empirical issues, and a major one by Edward F. Denison[7] is both bold and original in bringing aggregate analysis to bear on the *sources* of economic growth in the United States. He finds education to be one of the major sources of economic growth after adjusting for differences in innate abilities and associated characteristics that affect earnings independently of education. Shaffer introduces a concept that he calls "maintenance costs," which in terms of the studies available to him has been neglected. But Burton A. Weisbrod[8] in his paper "The Valuation of Human Capital" builds on "the proposition that the value of a person to others is measured by any excess of his contribution to production over what he consumes from production—this difference being the amount by which everyone else benefits from his produc-

6. Gary S. Becker, *Human Capital* (New York: National Bureau of Economic Research, 1964).

7. Edward F. Denison, *The Sources of Economic Growth in the United States and the Alternatives before Us,* Supplementary Paper No. 13 (New York: Committee for Economic Development, 1962).

8. Burton A. Weisbrod, "The Valuation of Human Capital," *The Journal of Political Economy,* 69 (October, 1961), pp. 425-436.

tivity." Weisbrod then proceeds to estimate the relevant consumption, or if you please, "maintenance costs" thus conceived, and subtracts such costs from gross earnings to obtain net earnings.

I am reluctant to tread upon the boulders Shaffer has collected in his comments on policy. I suspect, however, from what he says about them that they are conglomerates of compressed sand and at best weak materials for his conclusions. To have started off by lecturing "liberals" on their rationalization of federal aid to education is not conducive to a calm and reasoned discussion of the policy implications of expenditures for education. If the argument were that the knowledge now available about the increases in earnings from education is still too fragmentary to be used in making policy decisions, it would deserve careful consideration. If the argument were that knowledge about the effects of education upon future earnings will be misused by people and therefore any efforts to acquire such knowledge should be very much discouraged, this conclusion from such an argument would be patently false.

The principal source of Shaffer's confusion in discussing policy arises from his belief that, if it were to become known that particular forms of education pay in terms of increases in future earnings, policy decisions that took this fact into account would necessarily no longer take into account any of the other important contributions of education. People, including those who make policy decisions, are simply not that monolithic in their evaluation of education. Shaffer's implied apprehension that society will proceed to deny advanced education to women merely because most of them do not enter the labor market is a pure illusion. If Shaffer only means that knowledge about economic returns accruing from investment in human capital, in terms of future earnings, *should not* be the exclusive basis for public policy decisions in making expenditures for education, I am in full agreement. My view on this issue can be stated very simply: It is altogether proper that people should prize highly the cultural contributions of education and they will continue to do exactly that; but it is very shortsighted of us not to see its contributions to earnings. Education has become a major source of economic growth in winning the abundance that is to be had by developing a modern agriculture and industry. It simply would not be possible to have this abundance if people were predominantly illiterate and unskilled. Education, therefore, in addition to having high cultural values, is presently also an investment in people to the extent that it improves their capabilities and thereby increases the future earnings of people.

Shaffer says that there are specific studies that "clearly show . . . the income differential correlated with additional education is considerably higher for whites than for Negroes"[9] and suggests the inference that less rather than more should therefore be spent on education for Negroes, provided this were the sole criterion. The specific studies in this case are based on national averages, making no adjustments for the effects of city size, different rates of unemployment, regions, and the quality of education. Nor is any account taken of the differences in the cost of education, including income foregone by the students, which is fully half of the total cost of college education. These factors account for a part of the difference in earnings between white and Negro workers.[10] The poor quality of schooling that Negroes have acquired and still do, with few

9. Harry G. Shaffer, *op. cit.*, p. 1031.
10. Morton Zeman, "A Quantitative Analysis of White-Nonwhite Income Differentials in the United States" (Unpublished doctoral dissertation in economics, University of Chicago, 1955).

exceptions, is also an important factor.[11] But more important still, as Welch has shown, is the blight of discrimination against Negroes.[12]

On Professor Wiseman's Critique of the Valuation of Education

The valuation problem to which Professor Wiseman has addressed himself is obviously fundamental. The propositions on which his approach rests are traditional propositions of economics and the formal inferences that he derives from them are integral parts of the theoretical corpus of economics. The empirical counterparts of these formal inferences raise exceedingly difficult problems, which are at many points beyond solution given the state of our knowledge. Professor Wiseman also reminds us of our enduring professional obligation to Frank Knight, who has consistently and cogently stressed that economics cannot be made to rest on "any balance-sheet view of life," that want-satisfaction is not the final criterion of value "because we do not in fact regard our wants as final," and that man "in a real sense creates values."[13]

It is undoubtedly true that many parts of the empirical edifice of economics are imperfect, marked by flaws resultant from unresolved problems inherent in valuation. I know of no economic estimates that will pass close inspection by this test. As a rule, the more aggregative the estimates the greater the difficulty on this score. The impli-

11. Finis Welch, "The Determinants of the Return to Schooling in Rural Farm Areas, 1959" (Unpublished doctoral dissertation in economics, University of Chicago, 1966).

12. Finis Welch, "Labor Market Discrimination: An Interpretation of Income Differences in the Rural South," *The Journal of Political Economy*, 75 (June, 1967), pp. 225-240.

13. Quoted by Jack Wiseman, *op. cit.*, p. 5.

cations are clear when we consider how aggregative analysis has flourished. One view is to look on these empirical imperfections as unavoidable and forget about them. But this view is all too convenient, hard as it is to show precisely what can be done to reduce such flaws in our estimates of the costs and benefits of schooling. We should not only be on our guard in recognizing the limitations of these estimates but also develop alternative approaches to check our confidence in these matters.

A difficulty in Wiseman's treatment of the valuation problem is that he does not provide us with any standard to determine the importance of the issues he raises. This is not to say that these issues are not relevant. For example, the schooling a person has acquired may increase his future earnings; it obviously cannot be sold as a stock of capital in the manner that material capital, a machine, can be sold. But how important is this distinction? The same question arises with respect to changes in patterns of preferences over time, and again with regard to compulsory schooling. To clarify what I mean, let me elaborate somewhat on each of these.

To have Wiseman sip and enjoy the taste of Mrs. Joan Robinson's vintage of capital comes as a surprise. Her assertion which he cites with approval[14]—namely, that acquired skills that increase future personal earnings have no financial meanings—is obviously invalid when put to an empirical test. For instance, the capital market when it provides personal loans distinguishes markedly between doctors, lawyers, and engineers with good jobs on the one hand and unskilled farm workers and coal miners with jobs on the other.

The rise in personal earnings is an important part of the explanation of the increase in life insurance, as Michael

14. *Ibid.*, p. 3.

Lynch[15] has shown. Clearly, also, the amount of financial payment that is legally awarded in cases of accidental injury or death is increasingly tailored to the earnings of the victim of the accident.

Wiseman is on firm ground in his belief that education "changes attitudes, expectations and preference patterns." One hopes it transforms Beatlemaniacs into Bach lovers. But since this is nonreversible (one hopes), Wiseman worries about the implicit valuation problem and its implications. He worries too much. Had he taken this attribute of education and applied it to the advance in knowledge with regard to nutrition, he also might worry. No doubt as people learn about nutrition, their preferences are changed somewhat. Such changes, I feel sure, are concealed in our estimates of the income elasticity of demand for food. Frank Knight would be reluctant to take these estimates seriously because of such blemished logic. Wiseman is no doubt correct in pointing out these blemishes. But when it comes to the uses to which these estimates are put, this class of flaws is of minor marginal importance.

The effect of compulsory schooling is another case in which the relevance of the fine logic is small to the point of being indiscernible because of institutional considerations. Toward the end of the paper, Wiseman correctly, in my judgment, stresses the importance of institutional arrangements and changes in them. But in his comments on compulsory schooling, he seems unaware that at least in the United States, as George J. Stigler has noted,[16] laws specifying the number of years or the age for compulsory

15. Michael Lynch, "The Expected Utility Hypothesis and the Demand for Insurance" (Unpublished doctoral dissertation in economics, University of Chicago, 1967).

16. George J. Stigler, *Employment and Compensation in Education,* Occasional Paper No. 33 (New York: National Bureau of Economic Research, 1950), p. 8 and Appendix B.

schooling came after the fact: school attendance for the most part preceded the law.

I applaud the logic distinguishing between the valuation that parents and children place on education. It also is applicable to the valuation of clothing, housing, and food. But nowhere do economists go back of consumer behavior of the family in devising concepts to organize and measure the revealed preferences of consumers. Thus the distinction in the valuations between parents and children is concealed. No doubt there is, as a consequence, a loss in logical rigor and in potential economic knowledge. But is it more important in elementary schooling than in food? I doubt it.

Wiseman's point that estimates of foregone earnings are not to be trusted when it comes to making global changes in educational opportunities is certainly valid. Nor for that matter are any other estimates of the components that determine the supply of and the demand for education satisfactory for this purpose. There are many strong reasons, in addition to the two on which Wiseman commented, why global changes in educational opportunities go beyond the range of usefulness of such estimates. But why concentrate on global changes since the behavior of people, be it private or public, is not of that character?

I fully share Wiseman's view that it is untenable to place the decisions with respect to educational policy wholly in the hands of the educated. But I see no basis for believing that this is a viable issue in our society.

Wiseman closes his paper with an appeal for studies that are market-oriented. Studies thus oriented provide a basis for economic analysis. There is much more to be won by going this route than Wiseman sees. For example, the difference in the quality of schooling and the costs and returns to these quality components await economic analysis. I am convinced a real contribution can be made by economists in undertaking such studies.

The list of complementary studies to distinguish between types of education, to integrate analytically economic and social goals, and to determine the extent of market discrimination with respect to jobs, with which Wiseman concludes his paper, is of major importance.

5 Search for Empirical Implications[1]

THE approach here begins with the proposition that people enhance their capabilities as producers and as consumers by investing in themselves. It implies that not all of the economic capabilities of a people are given at birth, or at age fourteen when some of them enter upon work, or at some later age when some complete their schooling; but that many of these capabilities are developed through activities that have the attributes of an investment. These investments in people turn out not to be trivial; on the contrary, they are of a magnitude to alter radically the usual measures of the amount of savings and capital formation. They also alter the structure of wages and salaries and the amount of earnings relative to income from property.

These alterations are clues to long-standing puzzles about economic growth, structure of relative earnings, and the

1. I am indebted to Larry A. Sjaastad and George J. Stigler for helpful comments.

62

distribution of personal income. Inasmuch as these alterations are a consequence of investment in human capital, I wish to propose the following hypotheses in pursuing these matters: 1) in economic growth, on the assumption that the fundamental motives and preferences that determine the ratio of *all* capital to income remain essentially constant, the hypothesis here advanced is that the inclusion of human capital will show that the ratio of *all* capital to income is not declining. Reproducible physical capital—structures, equipment, and inventories—a particular class of capital, has been declining relative to income. Meanwhile, however, the stock of human capital has been rising relative to income. If the ratio of *all* capital to income remains essentially constant, then the unexplained economic growth that has been so puzzling originates mainly out of the rise in the stock of human capital. 2) A second assumption is that the economic capabilities of man are predominantly a *produced means of production* and that, except for some pure rent (in earnings) for differences in inherited abilities, most of the differences in earnings are a consequence of differences in the amounts that have been invested in people. Here, then, the hypothesis is that the structure of wages and salaries is primarily determined by investment in schooling, health, on-the-job training, searching for information about job opportunities, and by investment in migration. 3) With respect to the distribution of personal income, based on the assumption that the rise in the investment in human capital relative to that invested in nonhuman capital increases earnings relative to property income and to the extent that the more equal distribution of investments in man equalizes earnings among human agents, the hypothesis here proposed is that these changes in the investment in human capital are a major factor reducing the inequality in the distribution of personal income.

Gary S. Becker[2] gives us an overview of the pervasiveness of human capital and reveals many vistas awaiting to be explored. As is well known, the precise analytical tools that are required when one enters upon basic research are, as a rule, among the unknown in the game of research. Becker started his study with the aim of estimating the return to college and high school education in the United States. He soon discovered, however, that the investment activities associated with education were akin to other investments in people and that all of these activities had a number of attributes in common for which received theory, tailored to investments in structures and equipment, required reformulation. I shall return to Becker's contribution below; before doing so, however, there are a number of general implications of investment in man that deserve a brief comment.

I restrict myself mainly to the role that investment in man plays as a source of economic growth, and thus I do not examine the two other basic matters. It is now generally agreed that the conventional measures of inputs are inadequate for studying growth. Without an assessment of the claims that the increases in the amount of capital represented by structures, producer equipment, and even of inventories are underestimated because improvements in such resources are not reckoned, there can be no doubt whatsoever that the concept of a labor force, or of man-hours worked, fails to take into account the improvements in the capabilities of man. It is as if we had a map of resources excluding a mighty river and its tributaries. This particular river is fed by schooling, learning on the job, advances in health, and the growing stock of information

2. Gary S. Becker, "Investment in Human Capital: A Theoretical Analysis," *The Journal of Political Economy* (Supplement), 70 (October, 1962), pp. 9-49.

about the economy. Each of these is an investment activity that develops human capital. Migration is also treated in this way because analytically a misplaced resource is equivalent to a less productive resource properly located.

But does this not give too much weight to the growth in the *quality* of human resources? Let me illustrate in a rough way the possible implications of the quality component. Suppose there were an economy with the land and the physical reproducible capital, including the available techniques of production that we now possess in the United States, but which attempted to function under the following restraints: there would be no person available who had any on-the-job experience; none who had any schooling; no one who had any information about the economy except of his locality; each individual would be bound to his locality; and the average life span of people would be only 40 years. Surely, production would fall catastrophically. It is certain that there would be both low output and extraordinary rigidity of economic organization until the capabilities of the people were raised markedly by investing in them. Let me now suppose a set of human resources with as many but no more capabilities per man than existed as of 1929 in the United States. The adverse effects on production would undoubtedly be large. To continue these speculations, suppose that by some miracle India or some other low-income country acquired overnight, as it were, a set of natural resources, equipment, and structures, including techniques of production comparable per person to ours. What could they do with them, given the existing skills and knowledge of the people? Surely the imbalance between the stock of human and non-human capital would be tremendous. Last, in this vein, let me suggest an imbalance between these two forms of capital that would be the converse, namely, a country long on human capital relative to her stock of reproducible nonhuman capital. The circumstances that characterized a number of countries, notably West Germany and Japan, immediately following World War II may have been an imbalance of this type; and consistent with this characterization, the rate of return to subsequent investment in nonhuman capital appears to have been exceedingly high.

There is excitement in the recent search for a conception of economic growth that would explain past growth and indicate future growth. The frequently observed divergency between increases in national product and increases in resources left much to be explained. The puzzle confronting economists has been that the rate of growth in the output that was being observed has been much larger than the rate of increase in the principal resources that were being measured.[3] It is now clear that this puzzle is largely of our own making because we have been using estimates of capital and labor that had been refined and narrowed in ways that excluded many of the improvements made in the quality of these resources. Thus by no stretch of the imagination is it possible to explain the growth in the real national income of the United States, say between 1929 and some recent date, using only these "refined" estimates of stock of physical capital and of man-hours worked. Meanwhile, economists have come upon numerous signs pointing to improvements in the quality of human resources as one of the major sources of economic growth. To explore what lies back of these signs, a theory of investment that includes people is essential.

Simon Kuznets long ago directed attention to large gains in the income of workers, which he attributed to "shifts

3. I elaborated on this puzzle in "Investment in Man: An Economist's View," *Social Service Review*, 33 (June, 1959), pp. 114-115, and in Chapter 3 of this study.

from industries with lower to industries with higher income per gainfully occupied."[4] These interindustry shifts in the labor force, according to Kuznets, have accounted for about four-tenths of the total rise in income per worker.[5] Are these gains a windfall? Or are they a quasi-rent caused by a persistent lag in the adjustment in the supply of labor? It seems far more reasonable that they represent a return to an investment in skills and knowledge and in information about job opportunities and in migration. The treatment by George J. Stigler[6] of the search for information about jobs in terms of the costs of acquiring such information and the return it fetches and a comparable treatment of migration by Larry A. Sjaastad[7] present new hypotheses based on investment in human capital for analyzing a part of these interindustry shifts. The new skills are here also treated as an investment in man.

Kuznets, as already observed, attributed four-tenths of the large increases in real earnings per worker to interindustry shifts. Thus six-tenths of these increases were left "unexplained." Here, again, these gains in real earnings may not be windfalls or quasi-rents to labor. As before, they are probably predominantly a return to investment in skills and in related capabilities. Learning on the job and in schools has undoubtedly been an important source.

4. Simon Kuznets, *National Income: A Summary of Findings* (New York: National Bureau of Economic Research, 1946), pp. 42-49.

5. *Ibid.*, p. 48; and his "Long-Term Changes in the National Income of the United States of America since 1870," *Income and Wealth of the United States*, ed. by Simon Kuznets (Cambridge, Eng.: Bowes & Bowes, Ltd., 1952), p. 126.

6. George J. Stigler, "Information in the Labor Market," *The Journal of Political Economy* (Supplement), 70 (October, 1962), pp. 94-105.

7. Larry A. Sjaastad, "The Costs and Returns on Human Migration," *The Journal of Political Economy* (Supplement), 70 (October, 1962), pp. 80-93.

Jacob Mincer[8] treats "training on the job" as an investment that employees make in themselves. He presents estimates of the amounts invested in such training by males in the United States labor force, which came to $5.7 billion during 1939 and to $12.5 billion in 1958, both in 1954 dollars.[9]

Mincer's estimates are annual gross investments. Since they are made by workers when they are relatively young, they have a long productive life. Accordingly, the accumulative effects, or, if you wish, the annual net investment, must be large indeed. When we turn to schooling, estimates can be obtained more directly than for training on the job, although earnings foregone become important after elementary schooling. My estimate of the total costs of elementary, high school, and college and university education, including earnings foregone by students, comes to $28.7 billion for 1956.[10] The stock of "educational capital" in the United States labor force rose from $180 billion to $535 billion between 1930 and 1957, in 1956 dollars.[11] Edward F. Denison[12] has developed an approach to the *sources* of economic growth in which the contri-

8. Jacob Mincer, "On-the-Job Training: Costs, Returns, and Some Implications," *The Journal of Political Economy* (Supplement), 70 (October, 1962), pp. 50-79.

9. For males, Mincer's hypothesis and estimating technique place the total costs of the learning acquired on the job at four-fifths of the total costs of learning acquired in schools during 1939; whereas about two decades later, during 1958, the total cost of on-the-job learning was only two-thirds that of learning in schools, *ibid.*, Table 2.

10. See Chapter 6 of this study, Table 6.7.

11. See my "Education and Economic Growth," *Social Forces Influencing American Education*, Sixtieth Yearbook of the National Society for the Study of Education, ed. by Nelson B. Henry (Chicago: University of Chicago Press, 1961), Part II, pp. 46-86.

12. Edward F. Denison, "Education, Economic Growth, and

bution of labor is adjusted for particular improvements in the quality of labor. His technique of estimating the increases in national product associated with these quality components is not based on first ascertaining the investment made by means of schooling, on-the-job training, and the like and then attempting to gauge the return to these investments. His approach goes directly to particular quality components and relates them to the increases in earnings. This is not the occasion to pursue the analytical challenge implicit in Denison's "comprehensive" set of *sources*. Suffice it to say that his estimates attribute to education about one-fifth of the economic growth of the United States between 1929 and 1957.[13] The historical comparisons shown in his Table 1 lend support to the following inferences: 1) The contribution of education to growth between 1909 and 1929 was a little more than one-half of that between 1929 and 1957; 2) the projected further growth from this source from 1960 to 1980 is a little less than that from 1929 to 1957; 3) for the longer run, it is impossible to maintain the *rate of increase* in the amount of schooling achieved during recent decades; 4) whereas physical capital contributed almost twice that of education between 1909 and 1929, the contribution of education to economic growth between 1929 and 1957 exceeded that of physical capital.[14]

Gaps in Information," *The Journal of Political Economy* (Supplement), 70 (October, 1962), pp. 124-128.

13. His Table 1, *ibid.*, p. 125, indicating the sources of the growth in real national product, allocates 23 percent of the growth rate in 1929-1957 to education. This is a gross figure. Since there are among his "sources" some that have had a negative effect, his positive percentage points total 109, and the 23 percentage points attributed to education represent, therefore, about 21 percent of the positive sources of economic growth.

14. Denison has not adjusted physical capital for improvements in

In theory, investment is obviously a means and the amount of investment a critical magnitude in economic growth. But in studies made of economic growth, the amounts invested appear to be a weak factor. A practical difficulty in determining the effects of investment upon growth arises out of the narrowness of the concept of investment on which the available estimates are based. A concept restricted to structures, producer equipment, and inventories is all too narrow for studying either the growth that is being measured (national income) or, what is more important, all gains in well-being from economic progress that would also include the satisfactions that people derive from more leisure, from the growing stock of consumer durables, and from the satisfactions that come to people from better health and more education—all of which are omitted in estimates of national income.

Kuznets sees the matter clearly at one point in his monumental 1961 study when he observes that for "the study of economic growth over long periods and among widely different societies—the concept of capital and capital formation should be broadened to include investment in health, education, and training of the population itself, that is, investment in human beings. From this point of view the concept of capital formation followed here is too narrow."[15] Only the most diligent reader, however, will see and keep this limitation in mind in drawing inferences

---

quality except to the extent they require larger use of resources. Among his sources of growth, almost one-third is allocated to the "increase in output per unit of input," including one-fifth allocated to the "advance of knowledge," *ibid*. Much of this contribution is made effective through improvements in capital goods.

15. Simon Kuznets, assisted by Elizabeth Jenks, *Capital in the American Economy: Its Formation and Financing*, a National Bureau of Economic Research study (Princeton, N.J.: Princeton University Press, 1961), p. 390.

Table 5.1—Estimates of Different Stocks of Capital and Annual Rates of Increase in the United States between 1929 and 1957

| | CAPITAL STOCKS (billions, in 1956 dollars) | | ANNUAL RATE OF GROWTH (percent) | RATE APPLIED TO 1957 (billions, in 1956 dollars) |
| | 1929 | 1957 | | 2 x 3 |
CLASS	1	2	3	4
Reproducible tangible wealth[1]	$727	$1,270	2.01	$25.5
Educational capital in population[2]	317	848	3.57	30.3
Educational capital in labor force[3]	173	535	4.09	21.9
On-the-job training of males in labor force[4]	(136) for 1939	347	5.36	18.6
Total lines 3 and 4				40.5

1. Raymond W. Goldsmith, *The National Wealth of the United States in the Postwar Period* (Princeton, N.J.: Princeton University Press, 1962), Statistical Appendix, Table A-2, adjusted to 1956 dollars and quoted with permission of Goldsmith.

2. T. W. Schultz, "Education and Economic Growth," *Social Forces Influencing American Education,* Sixtieth Yearbook of the National Society for the Study of Education, ed. by Nelson B. Henry (Chicago: University of Chicago Press, 1961), Part II, Table 14, p. 73, with 1930 estimates reduced by 3.57 and 4.1 percent, respectively, to give estimates for 1929.

3. *Ibid.*

4. Rough guesses based on Table 2, p. 57, in Jacob Mincer, "On-the-Job Training: Costs, Returns, and Some Implications," *The Journal of Political Economy* (Supplement), 70 (October, 1962). An estimate for 1958 was adjusted downward by 5.36 percent to obtain the 1957 figure, and both 1939 and 1957 are on a 1956 dollar basis; the 1954 dollar estimates were increased by 4.6 percent.

from Kuznets' estimates and findings. It is the slowing down in the pace at which his "capital" is formed that will be seen. But this fact will not be related to the quickening pace in the formation of human capital, nor to the even tempo of capital, as an aggregate. Thus a concept of capital that is restricted to structures, producer equipment, and inventories (the omission of expenditures on research is also serious) may unwittingly direct attention to issues that are not central or critical in understanding economic growth over long periods. The concern about the distinct downward trend in the ratio of this type of investment (net "capital" formation) to national income is one of these issues. Another is the importance that is attributed to the decline in the ratio of this class of capital to national income. There are no compelling reasons why the stock of any particular class of capital should not fall (or rise) relative to national income over time. Producer goods— structures, equipment, and inventories—are such a class. It is a fact that investment in this class has been declining relative to the investment in human capabilities acquired by learning on the job and in schools and in other ways.

The estimates presented in Table 5.1 show that when the different average annual rates of increase for the period between 1929 and 1957 are applied to the respective stocks, the incremental increase of "reproducible tangible wealth" is $25.5 billion and that of the sum of the two classes of human capital is $40.5 billion.

But the average annual rates of increase shown in Table 5.1 for the period of 1929 to 1957 are low because of the severe depression of the thirties. The sub-periods associated with 1929 and 1957 show substantially higher average annual rates of increase, as is shown in Table 5.2.

The estimates appearing in Table 5.2 support two important inferences: 1) the sum of the amounts of "physical capital" and of human capital that is formed is *large* relative to the net national product and 2) the sum of these two classes of capital formed was equal to about 26 percent of the net national product, both for 1929 and 1957.

No doubt the growth in investment in man has improved markedly the quality of work entering into economic endeavor, and these improvements in quality have been a major source of economic growth. But what explains the

Table 5.2—Estimates of Different Stocks of Capital and Annual Rates of Increase for 1929 and 1957 Relative to Net National Product in the United States[1]

CLASS	CAPITAL STOCKS (billions, in 1956 dollars)		ANNUAL RATE OF GROWTH (percent)		INCREASE IN STOCK (billions, in 1956 dollars) year following	
	1929	1957	1929	1957	1929 3 x 1	1957 4 x 2
	1	2	3	4	5	6
1. Reproducible tangible wealth	$727	$1,270	4.22 (1922-29)	3.93 (1950-57)	$30.7	$49.9
2. Educational capital in population	317	848	3.75 (1920-30)	3.74 (1950-57)	11.9	31.7
3. Educational capital in labor force	173	535	3.54 (1920-30)	5.90 (1950-57)	6.1	31.6
4. On-the-job training of males in labor force	66 (136 for 1939)	347	7.50 (1939-49)	3.10 (1949-58)	5.0	10.8
5. Total of lines, 1, 3, and 4					41.8	92.3

	NET NATIONAL PRODUCT (billions, in 1956 dollars)	
	7	8
6. Net national product	$ 159	$ 359

	PERCENT INCREASE	
7. Increase in stock relative to net national product	26.3	25.7

1. For sources, see Table 5.1.

correspondingly high rate of increase in the demand for these acquired abilities? Nowhere have we come to grips with this question. Is this demand for skills and knowledge in labor specific to our economy? Or is it also to be observed in low-income countries? It is hard to believe that the demand for these quality components in labor increased rapidly during the early industrialization in western Europe. Labor was then abundant and "cheap"; it was mainly illiterate and unskilled; and it did mostly manual work that required much brute force. Improvements in skills and knowledge and health of workers generally appear not to have been prerequisites to the impressive economic growth of that period.[16]

Despite a flood of workers schooled beyond the elementary grades entering the labor market, the earning differentials in favor of workers with such schooling imply that the *rate* of return to the costs of the additional schooling has not been beaten down. It appears to have risen since 1939. Meanwhile, between 1940 and 1958 the proportion of workers who had completed one to four years of high school rose from 38 to 52 percent, and the proportion of those with some college (completed one to more than four years) rose from about 13 to 19 percent of the United States labor force.[17] If the rate of return had fallen sharply as a consequence of this flood, it might be argued that the demand for these capabilities had not shifted so much to the right.[18] But this seems not to have happened.

16. See my "Investment in Human Capital in Poor Countries," *Foreign Trade and Human Capital*, ed. by Paul D. Zook (Dallas, Tex.: Southern Methodist University Press, 1962), pp. 3-15.

17. Percent distribution by years of school completed for the labor force 18 to 64 years old, *Statistical Abstract of the United States, 1960*, Table 139. Inasmuch as the length of the school year has been increasing, these estimates understate to this extent the rise in real schooling. There is some upward bias in the reports on which these estimates are based. Whether it has changed over time is not evident.

18. Larry A. Sjaastad, in a comment on this, points out that since these are internal rates of return they can be deceptive. For example, the increase in the working life may have held them up. Also, if costs of schooling were to fall relative to earnings, the rates again would be deceptive. The knowledge acquired in school and on the job, like techniques of production, is being improved, and the increase in the supply of educated people quite possibly creates its own demand.

Therefore, the same hard question: What factors account for the high rate of growth in the demand for these capabilities of schooling beyond the eighth grade?

Not all investment in human capital is for future earnings alone. Some of it is for future well-being in forms that are not captured in the earnings stream of the individual in whom the investments are made. Benefits that do not show up in earnings are hard to identify and measure. They are important, nevertheless, and deserve careful thought and investigation. They are least likely in connection with training on the job and in searching for information about jobs. There are some associated with migration. They are, however, more likely to be important in health and education, as is clear in Selma J. Mushkin's[19] treatment of health and especially so in Burton A. Weisbrod's[20] examination of the benefits of education.

Among the different classes of future contributions from investment in people, it is useful to distinguish between those that accrue to the individual or his family and those that are captured by other individuals or families. Those that accrue to the individual are of two parts: a future earnings component and a future consumption component. In education, this consumption component has substantial durability, even more than (physical) consumer durables. This enduring consumer component attributed to education is the source of future satisfactions that in no way enter into *measured* earnings or into *measured* national income.

Weisbrod examines a large set of benefits from education

19. Selma J. Mushkin, "Health as an Investment," *The Journal of Political Economy* (Supplement), 70 (October, 1962), pp. 129-157.
20. Burton A. Weisbrod, "Education and Investment in Human Capital," *The Journal of Political Economy* (Supplement), 70 (October, 1962), pp. 106-123.

other than the future productivity returns that are revealed
in estimates of earnings as these have been treated. One of
these benefits is "the value of the 'option' to obtain still
further education and the rewards accompanying it." The
value of this option is real for many students who are discovering their talents through education. Whether this
particular benefit is to be counted among the returns, say,
to the high school education for these students who at
that point discover they have the talent to reach for a
college education, or to the subsequent college education
will depend upon the aim of the analysis. It is important,
of course, that this particular return not be counted twice.
Several nonmarket returns associated with education that
come to the individual who has acquired the schooling
are also examined. These are then the benefits that do not
accrue to those who have received the schooling. Other
families capture some benefits as neighbors and as tax-
payers, both seen in relation to the place in which the
person with the schooling resides. Then, too, there are
employment-related benefits that go to co-workers and to
employers. It is Weisbrod's belief that these several benefits
of education "are reasonably identifiable." There then
remains a residual category of benefits, which are widely
diffused in society.

Returning to Becker's theoretical analysis of investment
in human capital, it has become a rich source of hypotheses
to be tested. These hypotheses reach into old issues that
have long perplexed investigators and into new exciting
ones. Becker derives the "general relations between earnings, rates of return, and the amount invested" and shows
"how the latter two can be indirectly inferred from earnings." Thus at the level of formal economic analysis human
investment offers a unified explanation of a wide range of
empirical phenomena.

The three basic matters mentioned at the outset—economic growth, structure of wages and salaries, and the distribution of personal income—are being clarified. The findings thus far support the hypotheses advanced at the beginning of this presentation of analytical scaffolds and their empirical implications.

6 Cost of Capital Formation by Education[1]

ALTHOUGH education is in some measure a consumption activity rendering satisfactions to the person at the time he obtains an education, it is predominantly an investment activity undertaken for the purpose of acquiring capabilities that render future satisfactions or that enhance future earnings of the person as a productive agent. Thus a part of it is a consumer good akin to conventional consumer durables, and another part of it is a producer good. I propose, therefore, to treat education as an investment and to treat its consequences as a form of capital. Since education becomes a part of the person receiving it, I shall refer to it as *human capital*. Since it becomes an integral part of a person, it cannot be bought or sold or treated as property under our institutions. Nevertheless, it is a

1. This study was started while I was a Fellow at the Center for Advanced Study in the Behavioral Sciences. In it I have been assisted by Marto Ballesteros and Jacob Meerman. I have benefited from the criticisms of Gary S. Becker, Zvi Griliches, and Albert Rees.

form of capital if it renders a service of value. The principal hypothesis underlying this treatment of education is that some important increases in national income are a consequence of additions to this form of capital. Although it will be far from easy to put this hypothesis to the test, there are many indications that some, and perhaps a substantial part, of the unexplained increases in national income in the United States are attributable to the formation of this kind of capital.[2]

I shall use the term "education" to include both schooling and higher education. I shall concentrate on the resource costs of organized formal education in the United States. It will become apparent that a large stream of resources is allocated to education. My principal task is to present a set of estimates of the value of the resources that have been entering into education. These resources consist chiefly of two components—the earnings that students forego while attending school and the resources to provide schools. My estimates begin with 1900, cover the next five decennial years, and close with 1956. The annual factor costs are first given in current prices. A major section is devoted to the earnings that students forego while they attend school, both because of their importance and because these foregone earnings have heretofore been neglected. More than half the total resources that enter

2. By "unexplained" I mean here the increases in measured national income that exceed the increases in measured resources, treated as inputs. For approximately the same period covered by this study, Solomon Fabricant, in *Basic Facts on Productivity Changes*, Occasional Paper No. 63 (New York: National Bureau of Economic Research, 1959), Table 5, presents estimates that show the output of the United States private domestic economy as having increased at an average annual rate of 3.5 percent between 1889 and 1957, whereas total inputs increased at an annual rate of only 1.7 percent. Between 1919 and 1957, these annual rates of increase were 3.1 and 1 percent, respectively.

into high school, college, and university education consists of the time and effort of students. The section on costs of the educational services that the schools provide introduces estimates of the value of services of school property used for education, along with current expenditures for salaries, wages, and materials.

Capital formation by means of education is neither small nor a neat constant in relation to the formation of non-human capital. It is not small even if a substantial part of the total cost of education were strictly for consumption. What our estimates show is that the stream of resources entering into elementary education has increased less than that entering into either high school or higher education. But, even so, it has been increasing at a higher rate than has the gross formation of physical capital. In 1900 the total cost of elementary education was equal to about 5 percent of gross physical capital formation compared to 9 percent in 1956. Comparable figures for high school and higher education combined are 4 percent in 1900 and almost 25 percent in 1956.

Two more introductory comments seem necessary, one on the neglect of the study of human capital and the other on the moral issue of treating education as an investment in man. A serious fault in the way capital is treated in economic analysis has been the omission of human capital.[3] Had economists followed the conception of capital laid down by Irving Fisher,[4] instead of that by Alfred Marshall,[5]

3. See my "Investment in Man: An Economist's View," *Social Service Review*, 33 (June, 1959), pp. 109-117.

4. Irving Fisher, *The Nature of Capital and Income* (New York: The Macmillan Company, 1906).

5. Alfred Marshall, *Principles of Economics* (8th ed.; London: The Macmillan Company, 1930). In discussing definitions of capital, Marshall commented on Fisher's concept as follows: "The writ-

this omission, so it seems to me, would not have occurred.

It is held by many to be degrading to man and morally wrong to look upon his education as a way of creating capital. To those who hold this view, the very idea of human capital is repugnant; for them education is basically cultural and not economic in its purpose, because education serves to develop individuals to become competent and responsible citizens by giving men and women an opportunity to acquire an understanding of the values they hold and an appreciation of what they mean to life. My reply to those who believe thus is that an analysis that treats education as one of the activities that may add to the stock of human capital in no way denies the validity of their position; my approach is not designed to show that these cultural purposes should not be, or are not being, served by education. What is implied is that, in addition to achieving these cultural goals, some kinds of education may improve the capabilities of a people as they work and manage their affairs and that these improvements may increase the national income. These cultural and economic effects may thus be joint consequences of education. My treatment of education will in no way detract from, nor disparage, the cultural contributions of education. It takes these contributions for granted and proceeds to the task of determining whether there are also some producer benefits from education that may appropriately be treated as capital that can be identified and estimated.

---

ings of Professor Fisher contain a masterly argument, rich in fertile suggestion, in favour of a comprehensive use of the term. Regarded from the abstract and mathematical point of view, his position is incontestable. But he seems to take too little account of the necessity for keeping realistic discussions in touch with the language of the market-place . . . ," Appendix E.

Ideally, we should like to have estimates of the formation of human capital, both gross and net, and of the size of the stock. We should also like to know how much, if any, of the increase in national income is attributable to increases in the stock of human capital and what the "rate of return" to investment in education has been. There will then be the question, How do parents and students and public authorities respond to these investment opportunities?[6] Here, I take only one small step toward answering these questions.

Let me now present the sources of the estimates that follow, making explicit the underlying assumptions and commenting on the data so that the reader may have a basis for determining the limitations of these estimates. The more important economic implications that emerge from this study will be left until later.

Earnings That Students Forego

It will be convenient to draw an arbitrary line between elementary and secondary schools and to assume that no earnings are foregone by children who attend elementary schools.[7] Beyond the eighth grade, however, these earnings become important. The time and effort of students may usefully be approached as follows: 1) Students study,

6. Surely some individuals and families make decisions to invest in some kinds of education, either in themselves or in their children, with an eye to the earnings that they expect to see forthcoming from such expenditures on education. It should be possible to analyze these decisions and their consequences as one does other private decisions that give rise to physical capital formation throughout the economy.

7. This assumption is plausible enough in the case of our society at the present time. But no longer ago than 1900, many of these children were of considerable economic value as workers, and some parents were keeping them from school for that reason.

which is work, and this work, among other things, helps create human capital. Students are not enjoying leisure when they study, nor are they engaged wholly in consumption; they are here viewed as "self-employed" producers of capital. 2) Assume, then, that if they were not in school, they would be employed producing (other) products and services of value to the economy, for which they would be "paid"; there is, then, an opportunity cost in going to school. 3) The average earnings per week of those young men and women of comparable age who are not attending school or the earnings of students while they are not in school are a measure of the (alternative) value productivity of the students' time and effort. 4) The cost of living of students and nonstudents may be put aside because it goes on whether young people go to school or enter the labor market and is about the same except for minor items, such as books, extra clothes, and some travel in getting to and from school.

Estimates of the earnings that students have foregone were made in the following manner: High school students were treated separately from college and university students; the year 1949 was taken as a base year in determining the "earnings" per week of young people, both males and females, for each of four age groups; students' foregone earnings were calculated on the assumption that, on the average, students forego 40 weeks of such earnings, and then expressed in earning-equivalent weeks of workers in manufacturing in the United States. The results appear in Table 6.1; they indicate that high school students forego the equivalent of about 11 weeks and college or university students about 25 weeks of such earnings. These 1949 earnings ratios were applied to particular years between 1900 and 1956; an adjustment was then made for unemployment, as set forth in Table 6.2.

Table 6.1—Estimates of Earnings Foregone by High School and College or University Students in 1949

Age	Median Income[1]	Weeks Worked[2]	Income per Week[3]	Annual Earnings Foregone in Attending School[4]	In Weeks Equivalent to Average Earnings of Workers in Manufacturing[5]
	1	2	3	4	5
14-17:					
Male	$ 311	24	$13.00	$ 520	
Female	301	20	15.00	600	
18-19:					
Male	721	32	22.50	900	
Female	618	29	21.30	852	
20-24:					
Male	1,669	40	41.70	1,669	
Female	1,276	36	35.40	1,416	
25-29:					
Male	2,500	44	57.70	2,308	
Female	1,334	33	40.40	1,616	
Per Student:					
High School				583[6]	11 weeks
College or University				1,369[7]	25 weeks

1. *United States Census of Population, 1950, Special Report on Education, 1953,* Table 13, except for figures for age group 20-24, which are from Herman P. Miller, *Income of the American People* (New York: John Wiley & Sons, 1955), Table 29. Virtually all the income in these age groups would appear to be from "earnings," according to Miller's Table 34.

2. *United States Census of Population, 1950, Special Report on Employment and Personal Characteristics, 1953,* Table 14. Of the persons who did work in 1949, the Census shows the percent who worked 1-13, 14-26, 27-39, 40-49, and 50-52 weeks, and, on the assumption that these classes averaged out to 7, 20, 33, 45, and 51 weeks, respectively, these were used as weights.

3. Col. *1* divided by col. *2.*

4. Assumes that students forego, on the average, 40 weeks of earnings: col. *3* multiplied by 40.

5. *Economic Report of the President, January, 1957,* Table E-25. The average gross weekly earnings for all manufacturing was $54.92. Col. *4* is thus divided by 54.92.

6. Of students enrolled in high school approximately half were males and half were females; 92.7 percent were allocated to the age group 14-17, and 7.3 percent to ages 18-19. In making this allocation, it was assumed that those

below the age of 14 offset those above the age of 19 *(Statistical Abstract of the United States, 1956,* Table 126).

7. College or university students were distributed as follows:

Ages	Males (percent)	Females (percent)
14-17	3.5	5.0
18-19	18.2	16.0
20-24	30.6	11.5
25-29	14.7	0.5
	67.0	33.0

These percentages were used as weights in calculating the estimate of $1,369 (based on *Statistical Abstract of the United States, 1956,* Table 126).

Table 6.2—Annual Earnings Foregone by Students, Adjusted and Not Adjusted for Unemployment, 1900-1956, in Current Prices

Annual Earnings Foregone per Student While Attending

Year	Average Weekly Earnings, All Manufacturing[1]	HIGH SCHOOL		COLLEGE OR UNIVERSITY	
		Unadjusted[2]	Adjusted for Unemployment[3]	Unadjusted[4]	Adjusted for Unemployment[5]
	1	2	3	4	5
1900	$ 8.37	$ 92	$ 84	$ 209	$ 192
1910	10.74	118	113	269	259
1920	26.12	287	275	653	626
1930	23.25	256	224	581	509
1940	25.20	277	236	630	537
1950	59.33	653	626	1,483	1,422
1956	80.13	881	855	2,003	1,943

1. *Economic Report of the President, January, 1957,* Table E-25, and U.S. Dept. of Labor; and *Historical Statistics of the United States, 1789-1945,* a supplement to *Statistical Abstract of the United States, 1949,* Ser. D, pp. 134-144.

2. For high school students, col. *1* multiplied by 11; based on Table 6.1.

3. The percent unemployed is based on Clarence D. Long, *The Labor Force under Changing Income and Employment,* a National Bureau of Economic Research study (Princeton: Princeton University Press, 1958), Appendix C, Table C-1 and for 1956, Table C-2. Unemployed adult male equivalents in percent of the labor force were as follows: 1900, 8.2; 1910, 3.9; 1920, 4.2; 1930, 12.4; 1940, 14.7; 1950, 4.1; and 1956, 3.0.

4. For college and university students, col. *1* multiplied by 25; based on Table 6.1.

5. See Note 3.

Two sorts of limitations need to be borne in mind in interpreting and in using these estimates. The first pertains to the 11-*week* and 25-*week* estimates for the base year 1949; the other is inherent in applying the 1949 relationships to other years.

Many of the young people who did work in 1949 were employed for only a few weeks during the year. It seems plausible that their earnings per week would be below those of workers of equivalent abilities who worked most or all of the year. To this extent, our estimates are too low.[8] Also, it could be that students rate somewhat higher per person in the particular abilities for which earnings are received than do those not in school who are earning income. To the extent that there are such differences, other things being equal, our estimates of earnings foregone are again too low. On the other hand, some students have held jobs while they were attending school; the earnings they have received from such jobs should have been subtracted from our estimates. (Chapter 7 presents some evidence on students working for pay.) Then, too, young people are burdened with more unemployment relative to the number employed than is the labor force as a whole.[9] Thus, of the

8. Of males aged 14 to 17 who worked in 1959, 44 percent worked only about 7 weeks (an average) and 19 percent worked about 20 weeks (average). Similarly, in the case of females aged 14 to 17 who worked, 53 percent worked only about 7 weeks and 21 percent about 20 weeks (averages). For ages 18 to 19, these figures are lower—that is, for males, 24 percent worked only 7 weeks and 19 percent about 20 weeks; and for females aged 18 to 19, the two figures are 29 and 23 percent, respectively. For ages 20 to 24, they are 10 and 12 percent for males and 17 and 15 percent for females.

9. *The Economic Report of the President, January, 1960*, Table D-18, gives some figures that appear relevant. They show total unemployed equal to 5.2 percent of the total employed, whereas for the 14- to 19-year age group, it was 11.8 percent.

four factors just mentioned, two pull in one direction and two in the other.

There is also the question: What would the earnings of school-age workers have been if all of them had entered the labor market? But it is not relevant because our problem is not one that entails a large shift in the number of human agents. The elasticity of the demand, either in the short or the long run, for such workers over so wide a range is not at issue. Instead, we want to know what earnings a typical student has been foregoing at the margin. Even so, our estimates of earnings foregone are substantially reduced by the effects of the large shift of students into summer employment;[10] the earning figures that we are using, drawing on the 1950 census, are heavily weighted by this summer employment. As pointed out above, many who did work for pay worked only a couple of months or so.[11]

The other difficulties stem from applying the 1949

10. In 1955, for example, 1.2 million individuals aged 14 to 19 entered the labor force between May and July, in contrast to about 0.4 million in the ages 20 to 24.

11. One can know something about the relation of the number of individuals in these age groups who are gainfully employed to the number enrolled in school. As one might expect, in the youngest of the three age groups, the number gainfully employed (April, 1950) was a little more than one-third the number enrolled in school (October, 1950), whereas for the age group 20 to 24 there were fully seven times as many in the gainfully employed group as there were enrolled in school. The figures for 1950 are as follows:

Ages	Enrolled in School (October) (millions)	Gainfully Employed or in Labor Force (April) (millions)
16-17	3.06	1.12
18-19	1.19	2.39
20-24	0.96	7.09
Total	5.21	10.60

"structural" relationships to other periods. The only adjustment that has been introduced is that for movements in unemployment. It is not easy to isolate the changes resulting from legislation. George J. Stigler[12] suggests that "on the whole compulsory school attendance laws have followed more than led the increase in enrollments of children over 14." Child labor laws may have done likewise. In any case, these laws may be viewed as a comprehensive private and public effort to invest in education, the child labor laws having the effect of eliminating some job opportunities.[13]

There is a presumption in favor of the view that high school students in 1949 were attending school more weeks per year than did high school students in earlier years. Such evidence as I have been able to uncover, however, suggests that for 1900, 1910, and 1920 most high school students, including those who were attending secondary preparatory schools, were being instructed so that they could win entrance into a college or university and that these students were attending school about as many weeks per year as high school students in more recent years. Between the early twenties and the mid-forties there may have been a small dip in this variable as a consequence of

12. George J. Stigler, *Employment and Compensation in Education*, Occasional Paper No. 33 (New York: National Bureau of Economic Research, 1950), p. 8 and Appendix B.

13. In commenting on child labor laws, Albert Rees has called my attention to the *Census of Manufactures* of 1890, which shows that 121,000 children (males under sixteen and females under fifteen) were employed and that their annual earnings were 31 percent of those of all manufacturing wage earners. This is a substantially higher ratio than that implied for this age group in tables 6.1 and 6.2. Thus, using 11 weeks' earnings foregone for 1900 may understate the investment in high school education at the beginning of this period. Also, see Chapter 7.

the large increases in high school enrollment and the fact that high school instruction was no longer devoted primarily to the preparation of students for college.[14]

The weekly earnings of workers who possess the capabilities of students and who are of that age group may have changed substantially since 1900 relative to the earnings of those employed in manufacturing. But it is not possible even to guess whether their earnings have become more or less favorable relative to the earnings of workers in manufacturing. The age groups that appear in Table 6.1 represent young people who had had more years of schooling than did the same age groups in 1900. But this would also be true of workers in manufacturing. The fact that the wage ratio between skilled and unskilled workers has narrowed may imply that our estimates of earnings foregone by high school students during the earlier years are somewhat too high, or more plausible, that the esti-

14. Unfortunately for our purposes, data for the United States do not separate elementary and high school attendance. The data are mainly for the 5- to 17-year age group with two sets of figures: (1) the average number of days that schools were in session, and (2) the average number of days attended by each enrolled pupil 5 to 17 years of age. These are: 1900, 144 and 99 days, respectively; 1910, 156 and 113 days; 1920, 163 and 121 days; 1930, 173 and 143 days; 1940, 175 and 152 days; 1950, 178 and 158 days; and 1956, 178 and 159 days. Thus there has been a 60 percent increase in the average number of days that each enrolled student attended schools. This rise, however, has been dominated by changes that have occurred in the attendance of elementary students. In the early years, high school students were heavily concentrated in states that had already established long school sessions and good attendance records. For example, the average number of days attended by high school students in a sample of such states was 170 days in 1920; a 1925-1926 set of 31 states shows 151 days, and another set of states for 1937-1938 shows 168 days, rising to 178 days in 1945-1946 and 176 days in 1959-1960.

mates for college and university students are on the low side for those years.[15] It would be exceedingly difficult, however, to isolate the effects of these changes.

Costs of Services Provided by Schools

Ideally, we want a measure of the annual flow of the productive services employed for education. This flow consists of the services of teachers, librarians, and school administrators, of the annual factor costs of maintaining and operating the school plant, and of depreciation and interest. It should not include expenditures to operate particular auxiliary enterprises, such as providing room and board for students, operating "organized" athletics or other noneducational activities. School expenditures for scholarships, fellowships, and other financial aids to students should also be excluded, because they are here treated as transfer payments; the real costs involved in student time are already fully covered by the opportunity cost estimates.

Tables 6.3 and 6.4 give these costs of schools for elementary, secondary, and higher education.

Total Costs of Education

The estimates of the costs of elementary education were complete as set forth in col. (11) of Table 6.3, inasmuch as no earnings were foregone in accordance with our assumption.

15. Paul G. Keat, "Changes in Occupational Wage Structure, 1900-1956" (Unpublished Ph.D. dissertation in economics, University of Chicago, 1959), p. 77, estimates the wage ratio of skilled to unskilled workers to have been 205 in 1900 and 149 in 1949.

Table 6.3—Annual Resource Costs of Educational Services Rendered by Elementary and Secondary Schools in the United States, 1900-1956, in Current Prices

(millions of dollars except Col. 4 in billions)

PUBLIC SCHOOLS

Year	Gross Expenditures[1]	Capital Outlay[2]	Net Expenditures[3]	Value of Property[4]	Implicit Interest and Depreciation[5]	Total Public[6]
	1	2	3	4	5	6
1900	$ 215	$ 35	$ 180	$ .55	$ 44	$ 224
1910	426	70	356	1.1	88	444
1920	1,036	154	882	2.4	192	1,074
1930	2,317	371	1,946	6.2	496	2,442
1940	2,344	258	2,086	7.6	608	2,694
1950	5,838	1,014	4,824	11.4	912	5,736
1956	10,955	2,387	8,568	23.9	1,912	10,480

	PRIVATE SCHOOLS		PUBLIC AND PRIVATE SCHOOLS		
Year	Gross Expenditures[7]	Total Private[8]	Total[9]	Secondary[10]	Elementary[11]
	7	8	9	10	11
1900	$ 27	$ 28	$ 252	$ 19	$ 233
1910	54	56	500	50	450
1920	104	108	1,182	215	967
1930	233	246	2,688	741	1,947
1940	227	261	2,955	1,145	1,810
1950	783	769	6,505	2,286	4,219
1956	1,468	1,404	11,884	4,031	7,853

1. Lines 1-6 from *Statistical Abstract of the United States, 1955,* Table 145; line 7 from *Biennial Survey of Education in the United States, 1954-56.*

2. Lines 1-6 from *Biennial Survey of Education in the United States, 1948-50,* Chapter 2, Table 1; line 7 from *Biennial Survey of Education in the United States, 1954-56.*

3. Obtained by subtracting col. *2* from col. *1.*

4. See note 2.

5. Obtained by taking 8 percent of col. *4.* The distribution of physical assets is placed at 20 percent land, 72 percent buildings, and 8 percent equipment, following Robert Rude's study, "Assets of Private Nonprofit Institutions in the United States, 1890-1948" (unpublished study, National Bureau of Economic Research, 1954), Table II-2a. With no depreciation or obsolescence on land, 3 percent on buildings (more obsolescence than for colleges and universities

(Table 6.3 cont'd. next page)

Table 6.3 (cont'd.)

because of changing local and community populations to which high schools must adjust) and 10 percent on equipment, and with an implicit interest rate of 5.1 percent, we have an 8 percent rate per $100 of assets per year.

6. Obtained by adding cols. *3* and *5*.

7. From same sources as col. *1*, except that line 1 is based on the same ratio as line 2 between cols. *1* and *7*; line 3 is based on the same ratio as line 4; and line 7 is based on the same ratio as line 6.

8. Obtained by taking the percentage that col. *7* is of col. *1* and multiplying by col. *6*. The gross expenditures of private schools ranged from 9.7 to 13.4 percent of that of public schools. This procedure assumes that capital outlays, value of physical property, and imputed interest and depreciation bear the same relationship to gross expenditures for private as for public schools.

9. Total of cols. *6* and *8*.

10. Obtained by allocating the total of col. *9* between elementary and secondary schools on the basis that it costs 88 percent more per student in secondary than in elementary schools. Expenditures for high schools determined by using George J. Stigler's estimates appearing in *Employment and Compensation in Education,* Occasional Paper No. 33 (New York: National Bureau of Economic Research, 1950), Tables 7 and 12. Enrollment in elementary schools is given as 33, and in secondary schools as 21 per teacher (using the average for the last five years in Stigler's table); average salary of elementary school teachers in 1938 was $1,876, and for secondary school teachers, $2,249. This is as 100 to 120. Accordingly, per student, we have: $\frac{120 \div 21}{100 \div 22} \times 100 =$ an index of 188 for teacher salary per student in secondary schools compared to 100 for that in elementary schools. A slightly lower ratio appears in the *Biennial Survey of Education in the United States, 1939-40,* Chap. 1, Table 42, n. 1, in which secondary school costs per student are placed 74 percent higher than those in elementary schools. There are, however, no estimates in the *1939-40 Survey* that permit one to determine expenditures per student for elementary and secondary schools.

11. *Ibid.*

Table 6.4—Annual Resource Costs of Educational Services Rendered by Colleges and Universities in the United States, 1900-1956, in Current Prices

(millions of dollars)

Year	Gross Expenditures[1]	Auxiliary Enterprises[2]	Capital Outlay[3]	Net Expenditures[4]
	1	2	3	4
1900	$ 46	$ 9	$ 17	$ 20
1910	92	18	30	44
1920	216	43	48	125
1930	632	126	125	381
1940	758	152	84	522
1950	2,662	539	417	1,706
1956	4,210	736	686	2,788

Table 6.4 (Cont'd.)

	Value of Physical Property[5]	Implicit Interest and Depreciation[6]	Total[7]
	5	6	7
1900	$ 254	$ 20	$ 40
1910	461	37	81
1920	741	59	184
1930	1,925	154	535
1940	2,754	220	742
1950	5,273	422	2,128
1956	8,902	712	3,500

1. Lines 1-6 from *Statistical Abstract of the United States, 1955*, Table 145; and line 7 from *Biennial Survey of Education in the United States, 1954-56*. These expenditures by public and private institutions were as follows:

	Public	Private
	(in millions of dollars)	
1920	$ 116	$ 100
1930	289	343
1940	391	367
1950	1,429	1,233
1956	2,375	1,835

2. Lines 5-7, same source as col. *1*. For the two sets of institutions these were as follows:

	Public	Private
	(in millions of dollars)	
1940	$ 59	$ 93
1950	255	284
1956	364	372

Lines 1-4 were obtained by letting these auxiliary enterprises equal one-fifth of gross expenditures.

3. Lines 4-7 from *Biennial Survey of Education in the United States, 1954-56*, Chapter iv, Sec. II; lines 1-3 obtained by taking 6.5 percent of col. *5*, lines 1-3.

4. Obtained by subtracting the sums of cols. *2* and *3* from col. *1*.

5. From *Biennial Survey of Education in the United States, 1948-50*, Chapter iv, Sec. II, Table I, and *Biennial Survey, 1954-56*. These estimates check closely with those of Robert Rude, "Assets of Private Nonprofit Institutions in the United States, 1890-1948" (Unpublished study, National Bureau of Economic Research, 1954).

6. Obtained by taking 8 percent of col. *5*; assumptions are no depreciation and obsolescence on land, 2 percent on buildings and improvements, and 10 percent on equipment. Following Rude's study, Table II-2a, these physical assets were distributed 15 percent to land, 70 percent to buildings and improvements, and 15 percent to equipment. Assuming an interest rate of 5.1 percent, we have per $100 of assets:

Interest on all assets	$5.10
Depreciation and obsolescence	
On buildings and improvements	1.40
On equipment	1.50
Total	$8.00

7. Sum of cols. *4* and *6*.

Table 6.5 summarizes the principal components entering into the costs of high school education. A comparison of cols. (3) and (6) shows at once the importance of the earnings that students forego relative to total costs of this education. That such foregone earnings should have been a higher proportion of total costs of high school education during the earlier years (and a higher proportion of total costs of high school than of college and university education in all years) comes as a surprise. Earnings foregone while attending high school were well over half the total costs in each of the years; they were 73 percent in 1900 and 60 percent in 1956; the two low years were 1930 and 1940, when they fell to 57 and 58 percent of total costs. During 1950 and 1956, they were 62 and 60 percent, respectively. Other and more general economic implications

Table 6.5—Earnings Foregone and Other Resource Costs Represented by High School Education in the United States, 1900-1956, in Current Prices

Year	Number of Students[1] (millions)	Earnings Foregone per Student[2]	Total Earnings Foregone[3]	School Costs[4]	Additional Expenditures[5]	Total[6]
				(millions of dollars)		
	1	2	3	4	5	6
1900	.7	$ 84	$ 59	$ 19	$ 3	$ 81
1910	1.1	113	124	50	6	180
1920	2.5	275	688	215	34	937
1930	4.8	224	1,075	741	54	1,870
1940	7.1	236	1,676	1,145	84	2,905
1950	6.4	626	4,006	2,286	200	6,492
1956	7.7	855	6,584	4,031	329	10,944

1. *Statistical Abstract of the United States, 1955,* Table 145, and *Biennial Survey of Education in the United States, 1954-56,* Chapter 2, Table 44.
2. From Table 6.2, col. *3.*
3. Col. *1* multiplied by col. *2.*
4. From Table 6.3, col. *10.*
5. Expenditures for books, supplies, extra clothes, and travel to and from school estimated at 5 percent of total earnings foregone; hence, 5 percent of col. *3.*
6. Cols. *3 + 4 + 5.*

of these changes in resource costs of high school education will be considered later.

Table 6.6 provides similar estimates for college and university education. Here, too, earnings foregone by students are exceedingly important [see cols. (3) and (6)]. In 1900 and 1910 these earnings were about half of all costs, rising to 63 percent in 1920 and then falling to 49 percent in 1930 and 1940. With inflation and full employment, they then rose to 60 and 59 percent in 1950 and 1956.

Table 6.6—Earnings Foregone and Other Resource Costs Represented by College and University Education in the United States, 1900-1956, in Current Prices

Year	Number of Students[1] (thousands)	Earnings Foregone per Student[2]	Total Earnings Foregone[3]	School Costs[4]	Additional Expenditures[5]	Total[6]
				(millions of dollars)		
	1	2	3	4	5	6
1900	238	$ 192	$ 46	$ 40	$ 4	$ 90
1910	355	259	92	81	9	182
1920	598	626	374	184	37	595
1930	1,101	509	560	535	56	1,151
1940	1,494	537	802	742	80	1,624
1950	2,659	1,422	3,781	2,128	378	6,287
1956	2,996	1,943	5,821	3,500	582	9,903

1. *Statistical Abstract of the United States, 1955,* Table 145, and the *Biennial Survey of Education in the United States, 1954-56,* Chap. 1, Tables 4 and 45.
2. From Table 6.2, col. **5.**
3. Col. **1** multiplied by col. **2.**
4. From Table 6.4, col. **7.**
5. Expenditures for book, supplies, extra clothes, and travel to and from school estimated at 10 percent of earnings foregone; thus 10 percent of col. **3.**
6. Cols. **3 + 4 + 5.**

Some Implications

When costs of all levels of education are aggregated, the proportion of total costs attributable to earnings foregone has clearly risen over time. This is due to the much greater

importance of secondary and higher education in more
recent years, a change that outweighs the decline in the
foregone-earnings proportion of high school education
alone. For all levels of education together, earnings foregone were 26 percent of total costs in 1900 and 43 percent in 1956. Probably the actual 1900 figure should be
somewhat higher than this because of foregone earnings
of children in the higher grades of elementary school (ignored here). (See Chapter 7.)

Between 1900 and 1956, the total resources committed
to education in the United States rose about *three and
one-half times* relative to consumer income in dollars and
the gross formation of physical capital in dollars. Accordingly, if we look upon all the resources going into education as "consumption" based on consumer behavior, our
estimates would not be inconsistent with the hypothesis
that the demand for education has had a high income
elasticity.[16]

If, however, we treat the resources entering into education as "investments" based on the behavior of people
seeking investment opportunities, our estimates then are
not inconsistent with the hypothesis that the rates of return
to education were relatively attractive; that is, they were
enough higher than the rate of return to investments in
physical capital to have "induced" the implied higher
rate of growth of this form of human capital.[17]

16. A 1 percent increase in real income was associated with a 3.5
percent increase in resources spent on education, implying an income elasticity of 3.5, had other things stayed constant. Among
other changes, the price of educational services rose relative to
other consumer prices, offset perhaps in considerable part by improvements in the "quality" of educational services.

17. Of course, other relevant factors may not have remained
constant. For example, it seems plausible to believe that the grip
of capital rationing is much less severe presently than it was during
the earlier years covered by this study.

Again, it should be stressed that the underlying private and public motives that induced the people of the United States to increase so much the share of their resources going into education may have been cultural in ways that can hardly be thought of as "consumption," or they may have been policy determined for purposes that seem remote from "investment." Even if this were true, it would not preclude the possibility that the rates of return to the resources allocated to education were large simply as a favorable by-product of whatever purposes motivated the large increases in resources entering into education. If so, the task becomes merely one of ascertaining these rates of return. If, however, consumer and investment behavior did play a substantial role in these private and public decisions, to this extent economic theory will also be useful in explaining these two sets of behavior.

Not only have the streams of resources entering into elementary, high school, and higher education increased markedly, but they have changed relative to one another. I shall briefly summarize four of these changes.

1. Though elementary education has increased at a slower rate than has either of the other two education levels, it has come close to doubling its position relative to gross physical capital formation; it rose from 5 to 9 percent of the latter between 1900 and 1956.[18]

The total costs of elementary education have been strongly affected by changes in enrollment and attendance.

18. References to estimates of gross nonhuman or gross physical capital formation are based on Simon Kuznets, *Annual Estimates 1869-1953* (New York: National Bureau of Economic Research, 1958), Table T-8, technical tables in supplement to summary volume on "Capital Formation and Financing" (mimeographed), used with his permission. An estimate for 1956, roughly comparable with that of Kuznets' series, is the $67.4 billion appearing in *The Economic Report of the President, January, 1960*, Table D-1, raised

Increases in the average number of days that enrolled students have attended school played almost as large a part as did the increase in enrollment; the first of these rose 60 and the second 73 percent between 1900 and 1956. However, it should be noted that this factor of attendance has nearly spent itself: average daily attendance is now within about 10 percent of its apparent maximum. Enrollment, on the other hand, will turn upward in response to the growth in population. Meanwhile, the salaries of elementary school teachers were declining relative to wages generally.[19] Altogether, however, it seems plausible that investment in elementary education will not continue to rise at the rate that it did during the period covered by our estimates.

As previously noted, some earnings were undoubtedly foregone by elementary pupils, especially by children attending the upper grades. We have data that suggest that these earnings were appreciable during the early part of this period. (See Chapter 7.) Farm families, particularly, at that time still placed a considerable value on the work that their children could do for them; moreover, fully a third of the population had farm residences in 1900 and 1910. Surely, a poor country endeavoring to establish a comprehensive program of elementary education must reckon the cost entailed in the earnings that older children will have to forego. (See Chapter 7.)

---

by 26.4 percent (the percent by which Kuznets' estimate for 1950 exceeds the U.S. Dept. of Commerce estimate of that year). Thus we have the total costs of elementary education increasing from $230 million to $7,850 million and gross physical capital costs increasing from $4,300 million to $85,200 million.

19. Keat, *op. cit.*, Table 7, p. 25, presents estimates showing that these teachers in 1903 received 58 percent more earnings than did the average full-time employee in manufacturing during the year, compared to only 19 percent more in 1956. Comparable figures for high school teachers are 188 and 36 percent; and for professors, 261 and 73 percent.

2. The annual national cost of high school education has risen markedly, so much so that in 1956 it was equal in amount to nearly 13 percent of gross physical capital formation compared to somewhat less than 2 percent in 1900.[20]

Enrollment in high school advanced from 0.7 to 7.7 million between 1900 and 1956. It had already reached 7.1 million in 1940. The effect of the upsurge in population that began in the early forties had started to make itself felt by 1956, the proportion of young people embarking upon a high school education being very large—indeed, it was approaching its maximum. The increases in this ratio were striking; for example, in 1900 only about 11 percent of the 14- to 17-year age group was enrolled in secondary schools; by 1956 about 75 percent were.[21]

Let me emphasize once more that earnings foregone have made up well over half the total costs of high school education. In 1956 they were three-fifths of total costs, which is somewhat less than at the beginning of this period. From this experience one may infer that poor countries, even when they are no less poor than were the people of the United States in 1900, will find that most of the real costs of secondary education are a consequence of the earnings that students forego while attending school.

3. The trend of total cost of higher education has been similar to that for high school. It rose at a slightly lower rate than did total high school cost in the early part of the period, and at a higher rate later.

20. Beginning with 1940, the total costs of high school education exceeded those of elementary education; by 1956 they were almost 40 percent higher. In 1900 it was the other way around, with elementary education costs nearly three times as large as those of high school, measured in resources used (see cols. (2) and (3) of Table 6.7).

21. However, of this 14- to 17-year age group, 88 percent was enrolled either in elementary school, high school, or college.

Table 6.7—Total Costs of Elementary, High School, and College and University Education in the United States, 1900-1956, in Current Prices

Year	Elementary[1]	High School[2]	College and University[3]	Total[4]
		(millions of dollars)		
	1	2	3	4
1900	$ 230	$ 80	$ 90	$ 400
1910	450	180	180	810
1920	970	940	600	2,510
1930	1,950	1,870	1,150	4,970
1940	1,810	2,900	1,620	6,330
1950	4,220	6,490	6,290	17,000
1956	7,850	10,950	9,900	28,700

1. From Table 6.3, col. *11*. Figures have been rounded throughout.
2. From Table 6.5, col. *6*.
3. From Table 6.6, col. *6*.
4. Cols. *1* + *2* + *3*.

Enrollment in higher education increased from 328,000 in 1900 to 2,996,000 in 1956. Of the 18- to 21-year age group, 4 percent were in residence and enrolled as undergraduates in higher education in 1900; by 1956, 32 percent of this age group were thus enrolled. The upper limit is not as near at hand as it is for elementary and high school education; there are many indications that it will continue to increase rapidly for some time to come.

Earnings foregone by students attending colleges and universities were also about three-fifths of total costs in 1956.

4. Altogether, total costs of education have increased much more rapidly than have the total costs of the resources entering into physical capital. Between 1900 and 1956, the total costs of the three levels of education covered by this study have risen from 9 to 34 percent of the total entering into the formation of physical capital.

Several more steps must be taken, however, before we

can gauge the increases in the stock of capital developed by education and its contribution to economic growth. These steps will entail allocating the costs of education between consumption and investment, determining the size of the stock of human capital formed by education, and ascertaining the rate of return to this education.

7 Changing Patterns of Earnings Foregone

THERE are some empirical clues to the changing patterns of earnings foregone by students in the United States. I shall consider those that have become sufficiently clear to warrant some revision of the estimates in the preceding chapter and some estimates for more recent years. I shall begin with the earnings foregone pertaining to children attending elementary schools, and then those of students in high school and college. I shall close with a comment on what appears to be taking place in this respect during graduate work.

As opportunity costs, the concept of earnings foregone is cogent and precise; for our purpose it is the value of the time that students allocate to schooling (education). The empirical task of estimating earnings foregone is, however, beset with some difficulties. The fact that earnings foregone as of any given date differ widely for different levels of schooling is well known. They also differ by regions and sectors, by race and sex, by type of college, and for different levels of personal incomes. It is difficult to take account of all of these differences in any national estimate for any given date. But what is not well known are the patterns of change in the earnings foregone over time. The value of the time of children to their parents for work in the home and on the farm is relatively high, and thus the decline of the agricultural sector has an effect. So does the rise of married women participating in the labor force. The extension of minimum wage laws reduces the job opportunities for teen-aged children. In general, under conditions of modern economic growth and of rising family income, the value of the time that children work for their parents declines, whereas the labor market value of the time of high school and college students rises. While the job opportunities for youth fluctuate widely as unemployment varies over time, the participation rate of enrolled students in the labor force increases as a larger proportion of students of any age group attend high school or college, presumably because more of them come from low income homes and for this reason desire to work part time for pay while attending school. In the case of graduate students, it appears that an increasing number of them perform duties for the university and are committed to attend the university for which they are paid.

It is generally accepted that parents in countries where people are poor are constrained from sending their children even to elementary school. They cannot afford to make the investment in this schooling because the value of children's time for work even at these tender ages is substantial to such parents. But there has been all too little analysis of why the time of such children is of considerable value in production and in household activities and why it declines for parents who are not so poor. To see the reasons for the change in the value of the time of children, consider the differences in the work of children of

a poor rural family in India and of a moderately high income family in a suburban community in the United States.
The household production activities in the case of the Indian family are labor intensive. Consumer goods are few
in number, and they are dear relative to labor. There are
in India virtually none of the consumer durables that play
such an important role in the household of the suburban
family in the United States. There are no refrigerators,
gas stoves, vacuum cleaners, or a score of other consumer
durables; nor are there precooked foods, frozen foods, cake
mixes, meats available in convenient packages, milk in con-
tainers, and cereals ready to serve. The United States household is relatively goods-intensive, whereas the Indian
household is very much labor-intensive. Children are capable of rendering many minor services of some value in
the Indian household, while it is hard to keep children occupied at anything of interest to them in the United States
household. Then, too, on an Indian farm, at the peak season
of work, children as young as ten are drawn into the labor
force, girls somewhat younger than boys. Even during
the off-season, there are all manner of little farm jobs that
children can do that have some value. In contrast, the urban
family in the United States is hard put to find useful work
for children outside the home.[1] In addition, when the
mother of the United States household enters the labor

1. For an excellent comparison of children in a *kibbutz* in Israel
and children in middle-class homes in the United States, see Bruno
Bettelheim, "Alienation and Autonomy," *Changing Perspectives on
Man*, ed. by Ben Rothblatt (Chicago: University of Chicago Press,
1968). But this comparison does not exhaust the differences in
economic possibilities between the poor rural family in India and
the moderately high income family in a suburban U.S. community,
as Barry Chiswick has noted. The productivity of schooling in
India may be lower than in the U.S. The household work in
India may be better on-the-job training than it is in the U.S. household, given the difference in later job (work) opportunities.

force either part time or full time, it is, in part, because the children are in school that she has the time for such work; then, even for the first years of school it is not empty to say that the school, among other things, is a place where the children are in safe hands while the mother is at work.

During Elementary Schooling

In my estimates, I assumed for reasons of empirical convenience that by 1900 in the United States the value of children's time had approached zero because of the level of economic development that had been attained, and therefore, there were no earnings foregone entering into the cost of elementary schooling. Although I called attention to some evidence that implied that a considerable number of children were in the labor force, the earnings data available to me at the time did not permit me to make any firm estimates.

Earnings foregone in 1900 for all students—college, high school, and elementary—according to Albert Fishlow[2] were $214 million, whereas my estimate, with none for children attending elementary schools, is $105 million. Fishlow states, "What creates this magnification beyond Schultz's $105 million total is the inclusion in these calculations not only of high school and college students but also of elementary pupils ten years of age and older. Historically, the observed participation in the labor force of such children testifies to a positive, even if perhaps increasingly

2. Albert Fishlow, "Levels of Nineteenth Century American Investment in Education," *Journal of Economic History*, 26 (December, 1966), pp. 418-436. Fishlow's statement (p. 427) that "Not until 1900 did scholastic endeavors impinge upon the agricultural work years," is not plausible, and as Lewis C. Solmon has shown, is not supported by his estimates cited in the text below.

small, marginal product. Specifically, in the United States over the period 1870-1900 children ten to fifteen represented six percent of the total labor force. Logically, the imposition of compulsory elementary education does not alter the present social cost associated with such a deployment of resources." There is little room for doubt that these earnings foregone were still real and important as of 1900 and probably for one or two decades later. Lewis C. Solmon's study covering 1880 and 1890 provides additional evidence on these earnings foregone.[3]

Solmon's earnings foregone and direct costs for elementary schooling, United States, 1880 and 1890, are as follows:[4]

Earnings Foregone	1880	1890
	(millions)	
Rural	$ 54	$ 68
Urban	78	142
Total	132	210
Direct Cost		
Rural and urban	92	151

These estimates have two characteristics that support the inference that earnings foregone during elementary school were not negligible at the turn of the century: 1) they were not decreasing appreciably relative to total cost from 1880 to 1890, representing almost three-fifths of total cost in both of these two census years and 2) in absolute terms, according to Solmon, they came to $132 and $210 million, respectively (Fishlow's estimate for 1880 is $72 million).[5]

3. Lewis C. Solmon, "Capital Formation by Expenditures on Formal Education, 1880 and 1890" (Unpublished Ph.D. dissertation in economics, University of Chicago, 1968).
4. *Ibid.*, Table 7, p. 49.
5. Fishlow, *op. cit.*, Table 2, p. 423.

The omission of the value of the time of farm children at farm work by Fishlow results in an underestimation. Solmon provides us with estimates for this component. But neither Fishlow nor Solmon has attempted to estimate the value of the time of children to their parents from work that the children could have done in connection with the activities of the household at that time had they not attended elementary schools.

High School and College

The estimates of earnings foregone while attending high school and college are still far from ideal. To see why this is so, it is necessary to specify once again what is meant by these opportunity costs and what is actually quantified in view of the limitations of the data. Opportunity costs are the earnings that a student foregoes *at the time* he is attending school or college. It is not what he earned during the preceding year even if he worked full time because he is a year older than he was then and thus he is more mature and more experienced as a result of what he learned on the job. It is not the earnings of another youth of the same age with one year less education who is working full time because the youth who is not enrolled in school is probably, on the average, somewhat less capable than the youth who continues his formal education. Even if the high school graduates who do not enroll in college the following year were identical in their capabilities with those who do go on to college, their *reported* earnings would be less than their *actual* earnings because their actual earnings are the sum of the reported earnings and the amount by which these reported earnings are reduced to compensate the employers for the cost of the *general* on-the-job training that they provide.[6]

Ideally we require 1) the full earnings opportunity of the student, 2) the earnings he realizes while he is attending school, and 3) by subtracting (2) from (1) we obtain the actual earnings foregone. The concept of the full earnings opportunity is the amount the "student" would earn if he were participating in the labor force instead of attending school during the year. It follows, of course, that if the student, while he is attending school, devotes all of his time to his schooling and if, the value of leisure aside, he participates in no work while he is on vacation during the off-period when he is not attending school, his actual earnings foregone would be equal to his full earnings opportunity. Under these conditions, therefore, none of the student's time would be devoted to production or to household activities in his home or to work for others for pay.

In general, however, the actual earnings foregone are substantially less than the full earnings opportunities as defined above. The value of leisure aside, they are less by the amount the student earns during vacation and also by the amount of the value of whatever work he performs in and about his home. They are reduced further by the amount he earns during the period he is attending school. The issue of how to treat scholarships and fellowships is unsettled. If the student performs no duties for such an award and if he is not committed by it to a particular school, it has the attributes of an income transfer. As such, it would not reduce his actual earnings foregone. In the case of high school and undergraduate college students,

6. See Jacob Mincer, "On-the-Job Training: Costs, Returns, and Some Implications," *The Journal of Political Economy* (Supplement), 70 (October, 1962), pp. 50-79.

these awards appear, in general, to have the attributes of income transfer. But as I shall show later, the stipends that graduate students receive are, in substance, payments for the services of graduate students.

In his classic study, *Human Capital*, Gary S. Becker treats with much care the empirical problem of determining earnings foregone. His estimates for college students are lower than mine; for 1940, his estimate is about one-tenth lower, and for 1950 it is about one-third lower than mine. Becker's assumption is ". . . that college students earn about one-quarter of the amount earned by high school graduates of the same age. . . ."[7] The assumption is supported by two independent sources of information.[8]

In evaluating Becker's estimates, it is necessary to distinguish between the implications of his assumption and the implications of developments that presumably are not encompassed in the assumption. The assumption would appear to underestimate the full earnings opportunities of college students. Among the developments during recent decades, there is the increase in the employment of college students while they are attending college. The thrust of this development has probably been strong enough to make not only my estimates of earnings foregone but also Becker's too high for the more recent dates.

Regarding the assumption, leave aside whatever real difference there may be in the capabilities between the high school graduates who enter college and those who do not, and consider only the difference between the reported and actual earnings. High school graduates who are not enrolled in college are investing in themselves through on-the-job training, and the amount thus invested reduces their

7. Gary S. Becker, *Human Capital* (New York: National Bureau of Economic Research, 1964), Appendix A, p. 171.
8. *Ibid.*, Table A-10, p. 170.

reported earnings at the time they acquire the training. Meanwhile, the high school graduate who is attending college is investing a much larger amount in himself. For males in the United States in 1949, Jacob Mincer's estimates of these two components are as follows:[9]

After High School

AGE	On-the-Job Training of Those not in College (Cost)	Attending College (Cost)	Difference 3 — 2 (Cost)
1	2	3	4
18	$ 860	$ 1,881	$1,021
19	801	2,268	1,467
20	672	2,778	2,106
21	585	3,304	2,719
4-year total	$2,918	$10,231	$7,313

These estimates for 1949 measure the accumulated difference, and they show that after four years the high school graduate who entered the labor force had invested about $2,900 in himself compared to about $10,200 that the high school graduate who entered and attended college invested in himself. The $7,300 difference, if it were to earn a 10 percent rate of return, suggests a difference of $730 in earnings from these sources in favor of the college student.

But for reasons that are presumably not encompassed by the assumption, Becker's estimates are a better approximation than mine for the period after 1940. Even so, they are probably too high, mainly because, as indicated earlier, college students are working increasingly more for pay while attending college, aside from what they earn during the vacation period. The participation rate in the labor force of students who are enrolled in school, ages 18 to 24, has risen markedly since World War II. The search for

9. Jacob Mincer, *op. cit.*, Table A 6, p. 77.

Table 7.1—Employment Status of Enrolled College Students, Ages 18-24, October, 1966[1]

College Attendance	Enrolled In College (in thousands)	EMPLOYED COLLEGE STUDENTS			
		Total (in thousands)	Percent of Those Enrolled	Percent[2] of 3 Employed Full Time	Percent of 3 Employed Part Time
1	2	3	4	5	6
Males					
full-time college	2,633	846	32	25	75
part-time "	337	312	93	91	8
Females					
full-time college	1,647	429	26	8	92
part-time "	277	233	84	80	20
Both Sexes					
full-time college	4,280	1,275	30	19	81
part-time "	614	545	89	86	14
Total	4,894	1,820	37	39	61

1. From a table prepared for me by Sophia C. Travis, Chief of the Division of Labor Force Studies, U.S. Dept. of Labor, which I obtained from her in correspondence February 7, 1968.

2. The 17,000 males and 6,000 females employed in agriculture are distributed between full-time and part-time employment in the same proportion as those engaged in nonagricultural work. It should be noted that the numbers working in agriculture are exceedingly small.

work ". . . on the part of college youth has caused the labor force rate for 18- to 24-year old students to rise (from 23 to 40 percent) between 1947 and 1959."[10] Seven years later the report for 1966 opens with the statement that "The number of young people who work while going to school has increased sharply in recent years."[11] Supporting data for this statement are then presented in the report.

When we look back, it is becoming increasingly clear

10. *The Employment of Students*, Special Labor Force Report No. 6, U.S. Dept. of Labor, October, 1959, republished in *Monthly Labor Review*, July, 1960, p. 3, also Table 3.

11. From *Employment of School Age Youth*, Special Labor Force Report No. 87, U.S. Dept. of Labor, October, 1966.

that since World War II there has been a tendency toward more employment on the part of students while
they are attending high school and college. With respect
to college students, the increases in enrollment have been
large, and the inference is that relatively more of them
are seeking jobs than formerly and that they have been
finding job opportunities. As of October, 1966, the number of students enrolled in colleges in the United States
had reached 4.9 million. Slightly more than 1.8 million of
them were employed, and about two-fifths of them were
employed full time, and three-fifths on a part-time basis,
as shown in Table 7.1.

There also were 829,000 enrolled students 18 to 24
years old who were still attending elementary or high
school. Of these, 42 percent were employed, most of them
(63 percent) part time and the rest (37 percent) full
time.[12] The secular changes in school enrollment and labor
force participation as reported by Robert M. Fearn are
shown in Table 7.2. In interpreting his estimates, which
begin with 1947, it should be borne in mind that between
1940 and 1947 the labor force participation rate of 14- to
19-year-old enrolled students and nonstudents increased
from 38 to 51 percent for males and from 20 to 32 percent
for females.[13] Between 1947 and 1965, the labor force participation rate of school-enrolled males 18 to 19 years old
increased from 23 to 29 percent and that of females from
13 to 20 percent.[14]

12. From data supplied by Sophia C. Travis; see note 1, Table 7.1.

13. Robert M. Fearn, "Labor Force and School Participation of
Teenagers" (Unpublished Ph.D. dissertation in economics, University of Chicago, 1968), Table 1.

14. Ibid., Table 1. These estimates are all for October of the year
shown.

Table 7.2—School Enrolled and Labor Force Participation Rates of 14- to 19-Year-Old Youth, United States, 1947-1965[1]

	Males			Females		
	School Enrolled Rate	LABOR FORCE PARTICIPATION RATE		School Enrolled Rate	LABOR FORCE PARTICIPATION RATE	
Year		Enrolled Students	Non-students		Enrolled Students	Non-students
	1	2	3	4	5	6
1947	64	23	92	58	13	59
1950	69	31	93	63	19	58
1956	77	30	87	68	20	57
1960	79	28	88	71	18	57
1965	82	29	88	75	20	59

1. From Robert M. Fearn, "Labor Force and School Participation of Teenagers" (Unpublished Ph.D. dissertation in economics, University of Chicago, 1968).

Giora Hanoch's estimates for males, from a one-in-a-thousand sample drawn from the United States 1960 Census, are the sources for the following two sets of estimates. I shall comment below on the qualifications that must be borne in mind in using these estimates:

I. *Low Set of Estimates*[15]

	EARNINGS		EARNINGS FOREGONE
	Not Enrolled in School	Enrolled in School	1 — 2
	1	2	3
Whites			
Ages 14-18	$ 696	$ 200	$ 496
" 19-24	2,659	1,404	1,255
Nonwhites			
Ages 14-18	352	101	251
" 19-24	1,591	628	963

	Per Student
Earnings Foregone	
High school (weighted by enrollment)	$ 513
College " " "	1,191

15. Giora Hanoch, "Personal Earnings and Investment in Schooling" (Unpublished Ph.D. dissertation in economics, University of

II. *High Set of Estimates*[16]

	EARNINGS		EARNINGS FOREGONE
	Not Enrolled in School	Enrolled in School	1 — 2
	1	*2*	*3*
High School (with 9-11 years of school completed)			
White, North	$1,306	$ 390	$ 916
White, South	1,151	372	779
Nonwhite, North	757	229	528
Nonwhite, South	757	89	668
College (with 13-15 years of school completed)			
White, North	3,651	1,518	2,133
White, South	3,247	990	2,257
Nonwhite, North	2,148	1,226	922
Nonwhite, South	1,516	148	1,368

	Per Student
Earnings Foregone	
High School (weighted by enrollment)	$ 820
College " " "	2,105

For purposes of comparison, I have calculated the high school and college earnings foregone for 1960 using the same assumptions underlying my estimates from 1900 to 1956. In 1960, average weekly wage for all manufacturing was $89.72, and the rate of unemployment was 5.5 percent. The earnings foregone per high school student by this method is $933 and per college student, $2,120 for 1960. Although the high estimates derived from Hanoch's data are much the same as mine, in view of the marked secular increase in the proportion of enrolled students who are also in the labor force and working either part time or full time for pay, the actual earnings fore-

---

Chicago, 1965). The above estimates are from a special tabulation, which does not appear in the dissertation; it was made available by Hanoch to Lewis C. Solmon, July 1, 1966. Solmon calculated the estimates that appear in the first four lines.

16. *Ibid.*; col. (1) is from Table 4, p. 55, of his doctoral dissertation; and col. (2) is from Table 5, p. 66.

gone are closer to Hanoch's lower estimates, in my judgment, than to the upper set.

But it must be borne in mind that there is an ambiguity in the estimates that I have derived from Hanoch's data. It arises out of the limitations of the 1960 Census data. The earnings are for 1959, whereas the status of the person with regard to whether or not he is enrolled in school is for 1960. Thus, in the case of students enrolled in school in 1960, it is not possible to distinguish between those who were also attending school in 1959 and those who were not in school in 1959 and who therefore presumably were working for pay all or most of the time during 1959. It is possible, for this reason, that earnings data of those enrolled in school in 1960 are too high and to this extent the earnings foregone shown in both sets are underestimated.

Graduate Students

The puzzle about the economic behavior of graduate students is that in spite of the apparent low private rate of return on the investment in graduate instruction and research, the growth rate of graduate degrees is high. Hanoch's estimate for 1960 places the rate of return at 7 percent;[17] yet, the number of earned degrees continues to increase; between 1959 and 1965 earned master's degrees (or equivalent) rose 60 percent and doctor's degrees (or equivalent) 75 percent.[18] The key to this puzzle is in the earnings foregone; they are not what they seem to be.

Graduate students have been enjoying a highly favorable labor market for their services. It is not fully revealed

17. *Ibid.*, p. 86, Table 7, for white male students.
18. U.S. Dept. of Health, Education and Welfare, *Trends*, 1965 edition, Table S-49.

in most of the estimates. The value of time of graduate students is underestimated somewhat; their earnings while in graduate schools are very much underestimated; and as a result, their actual earnings foregone are overestimated appreciably.

The best comprehensive estimates of the full earnings opportunities of graduate students are those obtained by Hanoch from a one-in-a-thousand sample of the 1960 United States Census. The expected earnings of males, out of school in 1959, who had completed 16 years of schooling and who were 27 years old are as follows:[19]

White—North:	$5,602
White—South:	4,965
Nonwhite—North:	3,249
Nonwhite—South:	2,169

There are several reasons, however, why the full earnings opportunities of graduate students are higher than this. The college graduate who enters the labor market is investing less in himself per year in terms of on-the-job training than the graduate student is investing in himself. The rental to superior abilities is probably higher in graduate instruction and research than it is for college graduates who have entered the labor force. It is also plausible that the annual average of the full earnings opportunities of graduate students covering all of the years allocated to graduate work is higher than it would be when it is linked to age 27.[20] For these several reasons, it is highly probable that the value of the full earnings opportunities of white males who were graduate students in the United

19. Hanoch, *op. cit.*, Table 4, pp. 55-56.
20. The median age at which the doctoral degree was obtained during the late fifties ranged from 29 in the physical sciences to 35 in the humanities.

States in 1959, including not only first-year students but all years, was at least $6,000 per year.[21]

The puzzle with which we began is not a consequence of overestimating the full earnings opportunities of graduate students; if anything, they are underestimated somewhat. But the *actual* earnings foregone are much less than the full earnings opportunities because of the large amounts that graduate students earn during their graduate work. The critical question is, Are stipends earnings? Although I treat scholarships and fellowships that undergraduate students receive as income transfers, stipends in graduate work have the attributes of earned income. Two-fifths of all stipends, according to a federal survey,[22] require the performance of specific duties; the list of duties covers teaching, research, constructing examinations, grading papers, resident counseling, administration, clerical tasks, professional services, and others. There is, however, a more general obligation; namely, the student is required to undertake graduate work at the university that pays or arranges for his stipend. These stipends have, therefore, the attributes of payments for work. Thus the student earns his stipend because the university competes for his services, and it pays him the competitive (among universities) market price. On this matter, I find the approach by Frank P. Stafford appropriate for this task.[23] According to his estimates, which are derived from the *1963 Survey of Graduate Student Finances* by the National

21. Frank P. Stafford, "Graduate Student Income and Consumption" (Unpublished doctoral dissertation in Graduate School of Business, University of Chicago, 1968), p. 68; estimate for 1963 is $6,600.

22. U.S. Dept. of Health, Education and Welfare, *The Academic and Financial Status of Graduate Students, Spring, 1965*, 1967, p. 33, Table 20.

23. Stafford, *op. cit.*, Chap. 4.

Opinion Research Center, the following income data are for full-time graduate students:[24]

Income per Student From:	Amount[25]	Distribution (percent)
Stipends	$2,520	51
Employment	900	18
Spouse's employment	995	20
Gifts from parents	220	4
Other	335	7
Total	4,970	100

The earnings of graduate students come to $3,420 per student (stipends, $2,520, and employment other than stipend, $900). Stafford's estimate of the full earnings opportunities of these graduate students in 1963 before taxes is $6,600.[26] Accordingly, the *actual* earnings foregone for this sample of students is $3,180 per student.

What then are the rate-of-return implications of this approach in determining the earnings of graduate students during the time they are doing their graduate work? When stipends are treated as earnings, they are sufficient to double the 7 percent private rate of return as estimated by Hanoch.[27] Meanwhile, Yoram Weiss has proceeded too far in the opposite direction, for he treats the gross income of graduate students, regardless of source, as earnings. According to Weiss, ". . . the average student spends 5-7 years in graduate school. During his schooling period, he

24. *Ibid.*, Chap. 4, Table 19.
25. *Ibid.* Stafford's data are for income after taxes. The tax per student according to Stafford is $170. I have distributed and added this tax to employment, spouse's income, and other; accordingly, my estimates are before taxes.
26. *Ibid.*, p. 88.
27. Hanoch, *op. cit.*, p. 64. But his qualification is very much to the point. It is that "In graduate school, however, earnings from all sources may well exceed the direct private costs, because a large proportion of students receive fellowships and scholarships."

works in part-time jobs, and receives an annual income of $5,000."[28] Weiss' estimate of the average private rate of return is 17 percent; but it is too high because a part of the income of graduate students is from sources other than for services that they render. About 30 percent of this income is from such sources (spouses' earnings, gifts from parents, and "other"); it is easy to adjust for this.[29] The adjustment places the private rate of return between 14 and 15 percent. Thus the puzzle with which we began is solved.

28. Yoram Weiss, "Allocation of Time and Occupational Choice" (Unpublished doctoral dissertation in economics, Stanford University, 1968), p. 83. Earlier (p. 76) the earned gross income of the average graduate student in 1966 is given as $5,230.

29. *Ibid.*; Table 3.3, p. 74 makes this calculation easy.

8 Measurement of Changes in the Capital Stock of Education

THE natural endowment, the reproducible structures, equipment, and inventories and the human agents, also reproducible, are all stock concepts. Each of these resources as of a given date is a stock. By means of investment, the quantity and quality of these resources can be altered over time. There is, however, the very difficult problem of measurement. Education has various measurable dimensions. School years completed are measurable. But a school year is far from constant over time; in the United States the school year increased 60 percent between 1900 and 1957 in daily school attendance per pupil. The number of constant school years can be estimated; this measurement, however, does not take account of the difference between a year of elementary schooling and that in high school or college. In 1956 prices, a year of college cost 12 times as much as a year of elementary schooling. The real costs entering into education are, therefore, an approximate economic measure of the stock of education and of changes in it over time. The magnitude of the investment to change the stock is equal to the real costs of making the change. Furthermore, there is the secular change in the distribution of educated persons between those in the labor force and those who are not. In countries that are relatively advanced in modernizing their economy, an increasing part of the stock of education in the population is in the labor force.

Estimates of the stock of education may seem remote and academic to those who are concerned about expenditures for classrooms and for teachers' salaries. There are, however, issues that can be clarified by knowledge about the stock of education. What are our scientific and engineering resources? At what rates are they increasing? We are constantly devising measures of inventories, equipment, structures, natural resources, and other forms of capital, because such measures are necessary in gauging changes in them. Similarly, there is a growing awareness that measures are also required of changes in the stock of human capabilities.[1]

Widely held views of the differences in the levels of skills between countries rest as a rule on crude guesses of the respective stocks of education. In the United States the number of people with a high school or a college education has been rising relative to the size of the labor force. A similar change in education also has been taking place in other countries. Yet the differences among them in the rates are impressive. Countries in Western Europe have lagged in this respect compared to the United States, whereas Japan and, more recently, the Soviet Union, both starting from lower levels, have been moving ahead at a

---

1. There is already a substantial body of literature treating human resources, talents and skills, and the demand for and the supply of scientific and other personnel.

higher rate than the United States. Moreover, it is altogether possible for the stock of education in the labor force to decline, as it may have some years ago in East Germany, mainly as a consequence of the large out-migration of doctors, teachers, lawyers, and skilled technicians. The unique pattern of in-migration of Israel is also instructive. There came to Israel a large number of highly educated people and the supply of high skills exceeded the demand for some of these skills. A later wave of in-migration was at the other extreme in terms of skills.

International comparisons aside, the economist turns to human capital to see if changes in the stock of such capital may account for the otherwise large unexplained increases in output. As things stand, combined increases in non-human capital and man-hours account for only a small fraction of the increases in national income.

But as is well known, the connections between additions to the stock of capital and the corresponding additions in the value of output in a particular year are very intricate.[2] Resources that differ only with respect to durability may represent stocks that differ in value, although the value of the services each renders in a given year is the same. Consider two engineers who are equally capable and who do the same amount of engineering work during a particular year. Their respective contributions as engineers during that year are equal, although each may be very different when viewed as a stock of engineering resources because one of them may be a young engineer, just starting his career and with a long productive life ahead of him; the other may be an old man, doing his last year of work before he retires. The age of engineers is, therefore, im-

2. Trygve Haavelmo, *A Study in the Theory of Investment* (Chicago: University of Chicago Press, 1960), pp. 12-17.

portant in gauging the value of the stock of engineering resources.

Education is more durable than most forms of nonhuman reproducible capital. A high school education may serve the person over the rest of his life, and of this period, 40 years or more are likely to be in productive work. Most nonhuman capital has a shorter productive life than this. Education can be augmented because it is durable, and the fact that it has a relatively long life means that a given gross investment adds more to the stock than the same gross investment typically adds to the stock of nonhuman capital.

In the United States, young people entering the labor force have, on the average, more education than older workers. When the young people who enter the labor force have more education than the old people who retire, the value of the stock of education in the labor force will rise even if there is no change in the number of workers. In the United States, the younger workers in 1900 had only little more schooling than older workers, but a large difference between them has developed, much to the advantage of those in the younger age groups. The stock of education, accordingly, becomes more valuable in two ways: 1) The level of education of the population rises, and 2) a larger share of the total education is carried by the younger persons than formerly.

Three Measures of the Stock of Education

The following alternative measures are at this stage only clues to what we are seeking. First, we examine the concept of *years of school completed* as a unit of measurement. National statistics based on this concept are readily available, and they are widely used. Next we present *constant school years completed* based on 1940, when the average school attendance per student was 152 days. A third measure will then be presented using the *real cost of a year of school.*

1 *Years of School Completed* This is a convenient unit of measurement. But it is like counting the acres of farmland without taking any account of the differences in land: an acre of low productive semidesert land and an acre of highly productive irrigated land are simply added together. Likewise, we can aggregate the education of a population by counting the number of years of school completed as one might count acres, houses, or tractors.

**Table 8.1—Years of School Completed by the Population
14 Years and Older and by the Labor Force in the United States,
1900-1957**

| | | POPULATION | | | LABOR FORCE | |
Year	Population (millions)	Years of School Completed per Person	Total Years of School Completed (millions)	Labor Force (millions)	Years of School Completed per Person	Total Years of School Completed (millions)
			2 x 3			5 x 6
1	2	3	4	5	6	7
1900	51.2	7.64	391	28.1	7.70	216
1910	64.3	7.86	505	35.8	7.91	283
1920	74.5	8.05	600	41.4	8.12	336
1930	89.0	8.32	741	48.7	8.41	410
1940	101.1	8.85	895	52.8	9.02	476
1950	112.4	9.95	1,118	60.1	10.10	607
1957	117.1	10.70	1,253	70.8	10.96	776
1957 (1900 = 100)	229	140	320	252	142	359

Table 8.1 presents the results of such a count for education. It shows that the years of school completed per person rose about two-fifths from an index of 100 in 1900 to 140 in 1957 (see col. (3)); the increase is virtually the

same for the labor force as shown in col. (6). It follows, of course, that the total number of years of school completed rose relative both to the population and to the labor force. If each year of school completed were the same in amount and value, the inference would be that the stock of education in the labor force, measured in this way, increased from an index of 100 to 359 between 1900 and 1957 (see col. (7)).

2 *Constant School Years Completed* As a standard, a year of school completed is a whit too elastic, for it is now 60 percent longer than it was six decades ago. The average attendance of enrolled pupils, ages 5 to 15, was only 99 days in 1900, whereas it had leveled off at 159 days in 1957. Moreover, the labor force of 1900 consisted mostly of workers who had been in school when the attendance was even less than 99 days; most of those who were then 35 to 45 years of age were presumably in school in 1870 when the average daily attendance was only 78 days (this leaves aside the schooling of immigrants).

I have adopted a procedure developed by Clarence D. Long[3] to transform changes in school attendance into 1940 constant school years equal to 152 days of school attendance per year. This simple adjustment for changes in school attendance alters the picture markedly. As shown in Table 8.2, the rise in constant school years completed is much larger than it is for the unit of measurement used in constructing Table 8.1. For the labor force, for example, whereas years of school completed rose about two-fifths per person, measurement in terms of constant school

3. Set forth in his study, *The Labor Force under Changing Income and Employment* (Princeton, N.J.: Princeton University Press, 1958). See especially Appendix F. Professor Long has very kindly made available to me his basic worksheets, which provide the adjustment factors on which my estimates of "constant school years" are based. I am very much indebted to him.

years rose from an index of 100 to 252 between 1900 and 1957. Even more telling is the fact that the total number of constant school years completed in the labor force rose from an index of 100 to 638 between 1900 and 1957.

Table 8.2—Constant School Years Completed by the Population 14 Years and Older and by the Labor Force in the United States, 1900-1957

| | | POPULATION | | | LABOR FORCE | |
	Population (millions)	Constant 1940 School Years Completed per Person	Total Constant School Years Completed (millions) 2 x 3	Labor Force (millions)	Constant 1940 School Years Completed per Person	Total Constant School Years Completed (millions) 5 x 6
Year						
1	2	3	4	5	6	7
1900	51.2	4.13	212	28.1	4.14	116
1910	64.3	4.65	299	35.8	4.65	167
1920	74.5	5.21	388	41.4	5.25	217
1930	89.0	6.01	535	48.7	6.01	293
1940	101.1	7.07	715	52.8	7.24	382
1950	112.4	8.46	951	60.1	8.65	520
1957	117.1	10.02	1,173	70.8	10.45	740
1957 (1900 = 100)	229	243	553	252	252	638

3 *Costs of Education as a Measure* The two concepts presented above treat a year of elementary school the same as a year of either high school or college, although they differ greatly in value. A year of high school costs five times as much as a year of elementary school, and a year of college almost twelve times as much. I shall use the following 1956 price tags of a year of schooling:[4]

4. These estimates are based on 1956 costs. The reader should bear in mind that these estimates of costs include *earnings foregone* by mature students and that this component in the real costs of education is large both for high school and for college and university education.

Elementary: $ 280
High school: $1,420
College: $3,300

Table 8.3 shows that in 1957 members of the labor force had on the average 7.52 years of elementary, 2.44 of high school, and 0.64 of college and university education. Using 1956 prices, an average year of school of this composition costs $723. Two estimates were made for 1900, and these may be viewed as a lower and an upper limit of schooling and costs. In the lower estimate, high school and college education are allocated within the labor force roughly as they were distributed in the population for comparable age groups; in the higher estimate, all of this education was allocated to the labor force. Table 8.4 gives the years of

Table 8.3—Costs of Education per Member of the Labor Force in 1957[1]

	Constant School Years per Member	Costs per Year in 1956 Prices	Costs per Member of Labor Force	Distribution of Col. 3 (percent)
			1 x 2	
	1	2	3	4
Elementary	7.52	$ 280	$2,106	28
High school	2.44	1,420	3,458	45
College and university	0.64	3,300	2,099	27
Total	10.6		7,663	100

(Average cost per school year = $723)

1. Based on Table 138 of the *Statistical Abstract of the United States, 1959*, which gives the percentage distribution by years of school completed for the labor force 18 to 64 years old, 1957. The elementary subtotal is (4 × 5.6) + (7 × 26.2) + (8 × 68.3) ÷ 100 = 7.522; the high school subtotal is (2.5 × 19.8) + (4 × 48.5) ÷ 100 = 2.435; and the college subtotal is (2 × 8.8) + (5 × 9.2) ÷ 100 = 0.636. Col. 3 is based on these numbers, whereas those that appear in col. 1 have been rounded. The average cost per school year is obtained by dividing $7,663 by 10.6, which equals $723. It should be noted that the years of school completed of 10.6 is slightly larger than the 10.45 constant school years completed shown in Table 8.2 for the labor force because of small differences in data and in the procedures that were employed.

school per member of the labor force for both estimates and then the costs for the upper limit based on col. (1b). Using 1956 prices, the cost of an average year of school of these two compositions comes to $540 for the upper and to $423 for the lower of these two estimates.

Table 8.4—Costs of Education per Member of the Labor Force in 1900[1]

	Constant School Years per Member		Costs per Year in 1956 Prices	Cost per Member of Labor Force (upper limit)	Distributic of Col. 3 (percent)
	(lower)	(upper)			
				1b x 2	
	1a	1b	2	3	4
Elementary	3.75	3.437	$ 280	$ 962	43
High school	0.31	0.556	1,420	790	35
College and university	0.08	0.147	3,300	485	22
Total	4.14	4.14		2,237	100

(Average cost per school year, upper limit: $2,237 ÷ 4.14 = $540

1. These estimates are from a study of high school enrollment and graduates and also of college enrollment and graduates from 1900 back to 1850. High school enrollment represented about 0.636 of 1 percent and graduates, 0.351 of 1 percent of the population; for college, the two comparable estimates were 0.270 and 0.135 of 1 percent. Distributing all of these among the labor force of 1900, we have for elementary school, (83.5 × 2.53) + (16.5 × 8) ÷ 100 = 3.43; high school, (2 × 5.16) + (4 × 11.33) ÷ 100 = 0.556; and college, (2 × 2.46) + (4 × 2.46) ÷ 100 = 0.147. The average cost per year of school is obtained by dividing $2,237 by 4.14 which gives $540 per year of school. Using col. 1a, the average cost per year of school becomes $423 instead of $540, both in 1956 prices.

The results of these preliminary steps in using costs to measure the stock of education are shown in Table 8.5. It should be observed that in Table 8.5, I have used the upper estimate of costs for 1900. Education in the labor force, thus measured, rose from an index of 100 to 849 between 1900 and 1957. Had we used the lower costs figure for 1900, that is, $423 instead of $540, the stock of education in the labor force would have risen virtually 11 times be-

tween 1900 and 1957. The stock of nonhuman reproducible
wealth by Raymond W. Goldsmith's estimates rose only
four and one-half times as shown in col. (5) of Table 8.5.

**Table 8.5—Changes in the Stock of Education Measured by Costs
and the Stock of Reproducible Nonhuman Wealth
in the United States, 1900-1957[1]**

Year	Cost of Constant School Years Weighted by Composition (in 1956 prices in dollars)	Cost of Educational Stock, Population 14 Years and Older (billions)	Cost of Educational Stock, Labor Force 14 Years and Older (billions)	Stock of Reproducible Nonhuman Wealth (billions)	Percent Col. 4 Is of Col. 5
1	2	3	4	5	6
1900	$540	$114	$ 63	$ 282	22
1910	563	168	94	403	23
1920	586	227	127	526	24
1930	614	328	180	735	24
1940	650	465	248	756	33
1950	690	656	359	969	37
1957	723	848	535	1,270	42
1957 *(1900=100)* 134	744	849	450	191	

1. The procedure for deriving the estimates in col. **2** for 1900 is shown in
Table 8.4, and that for 1957 in Table 8.3. A similar procedure was used for
1940. Estimates for the other years were obtained by extrapolation. Col. **3** is
obtained by multiplying col. **4** of Table 8.2 by col. **2** of Table 8.5, and col. **4**
is obtained by multiplying col. **7** of Table 8.2 by col. **2** of Table 8.5. Cols. **3**
and **4** are based on 1956 prices; col. **5** is from Raymond W. Goldsmith, who
kindly made available to me his estimates of United States (national) reproducible wealth in 1947-49 prices, which I then adjusted to 1956 prices.

The following seven points summarize the implications
of these estimates.

1. The increase in stock of education in the U.S. labor
force between 1900 and 1957 differs markedly depending
on how education is measured.

Measure	Increase between 1900 and 1957 (1900 = 100)
Years of school completed	359
Constant school years completed	638
Costs of schooling	
(a) Upper limit costs in 1900	849
(b) Lower limit costs in 1900	1092

By comparison the stock of reproducible nonhuman wealth increased four and a half times in the same period.

2. Years of school completed understates greatly the increases in the "stock" of education over time if for no other reason than that the average daily attendance of enrolled pupils rose 60 percent between 1900 and 1957.

3. Constant school years completed also understates the increase in the "stock" of education because it does not distinguish between elementary, high school, and college and university years of school. Each year, regardless of the level, is given the same weight. From a cost and investment point of view a year of elementary school is much less than a year of high school or college, and the latter two have been increasing much more rapidly, as the following estimates show.

Level of Schooling	Constant School Years Completed per Member of the Labor Force		Increase (1900 = 100)
	1900 (upper estimate)	1957	
Elementary	3.437	7.52	219
High school	.556	2.44	439
College and university	.147	.64	435
Total	4.14	10.60	256

4. Our next measure based on costs of schooling is also an incomplete estimate of the stock of education. It does not distinguish between the younger and older workers in the labor force in measuring their education; for example, a year of high school is given the same weight whether the worker is 25 or 60 years of age. There is also the implicit assumption that a year of school of a given level (elementary or high school or college) whether acquired recently or many years ago is comparable once an adjustment has been made for differences in school attendance. Nor is there any allowance for obsolescence of education. Surely some instruction is better now than it was several decades ago, and some education is subject to obsolescence.

5. Constant school years completed per member of the labor force has risen more for those in the younger than in the older age groups, as the following estimates make clear.

Age Group	NUMBER OF YEARS OF SCHOOL COMPLETED 1900	1957	Increase (1900 = 100)
14-19	4.2	11.0	262
20-24	4.6	12.8	278
25-44	4.2	12.2	290
45-64	3.8	7.8	205
65 and over	3.3	5.6	170

6. Despite the larger increase in education of workers in the younger relative to those in the older age groups, the average productive life of the entire stock of this education may not have changed appreciably. A crude estimate indicates, assuming a productive life up to the sixty-eighth year and the same rate of prior deaths and disabilities for each age group, that the average productive life of all of the education in the labor force was slightly more than thirty years in 1900 and about the same in 1957. The reason for this result seems to be that young people now enter the labor force at a somewhat older age than they did in former years, mainly because they continue their schooling for more years.

7. If the above inference pertaining to the average productive life of education of the labor force proves to be approximately correct, our estimate that the stock of education in the labor force has increased eight and one-half times compared to the increase in the stock of reproducible nonhuman wealth of four and one-half times, between 1900 and 1957, takes on added significance.[5]

5. See T. W. Schultz, "Education and Economic Growth," *Social Forces Influencing American Education*, Sixtieth Yearbook of the National Society for the Study of Education, ed. by Nelson B. Henry (Chicago: University of Chicago Press, 1961), Part II, pp. 78-82.

9 The Rate of Return in Allocating Resources to Education[1]

 HE advance that has been made in determining the economic value of education, since I last considered this problem,[2] is impressive. The advantages in thinking in terms of the rate of return, provided allowance is made for the lack of efficiency prices in the capital market serving private investment in education and for omissions of particular forms of capital when planning for economic development, deserve comment. I then want to evaluate the new crop of estimates of earnings from education and of the costs of education before concentrating on the limits of the rate of return as a guide in allocating investment resources to education.

The formation of capital by education is obviously rele-

---

1. Here I benefited much from dialogues with Yoram Ben-Porath and Zvi Griliches, from Harry G. Johnson's critical and clarifying pen, from incisive comments by Robert M. Solow, Dale W. Jorgenson, Edward F. Denison, Mary Jean Bowman, and Jacob Mincer, and from a correction and suggestions by Samuel Bowles, Martin Carnoy, W. Lee Hansen, and Finis Welch.
2. T. W. Schultz, *The Economic Value of Education* (New York: Columbia University Press, 1963).

vant in planning for economic development when the objective is that of achieving an efficient allocation of investment resources in accordance with the priorities set by the relative rates of return to alternative investment opportunities. But economists are still far from clear on the connections between the rate of return and capital theory and growth theory and technical change. It is now fairly evident that these connections are unclear because of the partial (incomplete) specification of capital and because of the confusion about the distinction between capital and technical change. Conventional concepts and measures of capital include only a part of all capital. There are, of course, no compelling reasons why the stock of any particular class of capital should not fall (rise) relative to national income over time. Producer goods—structures, equipment, and inventories—are such a class.

The clarification of the concept of human capital and its identification have set the stage for a more complete specification and measurement of the accumulation of modern capital. It has also made us aware of changes in the quality of material capital. Thus treating education as human capital is but a step toward a more complete accounting of all capital. Once we embark on this road, it may soon be possible to transform most, if not all, of so-called *technical change* into forms of capital heretofore omitted in capital accounting.

But how to do it is another matter. *Technical change* is ever so elusive. What is it? How can it be identified? Acceptable answers are as yet not at hand. Is it a matter of *definition* or of *evidence*? The distinction between solutions of this problem that depend on definitions and those that rely on evidence is relevant. Dale W. Jorgenson has advanced and clarified this distinction in his argument that "one can never distinguish a model of embodied technical change from a model of disembodied technical change on the basis of factual evidence."[3] An alternative approach is to specify the services of different forms of capital (labor too) and of the stock of each form in terms of refutable hypotheses and by confronting the data.[4]

Although there are still many unresolved questions, what really matters is that *we are moving toward an all-inclusive concept of capital,* and, in doing so, we are greatly strengthening the connections between capital and income and between capital accumulation by investment and economic growth.

The advantages of thinking in terms of the rate of re-

3. Dale W. Jorgenson, "The Embodiment Hypothesis," *The Journal of Political Economy,* 74 (February, 1966), pp. 1-17. I am indebted to Jorgenson for this distinction. The distinction is somewhat too strong if one were to say the embodiment approach solves the problem wholly by definition. It too leads to an appeal to data but in a manner and under what seem to be the implausible assumptions that there is a constant relationship between the rate of technical progress and the rate of investment. On the other hand, although the capital approach is a way of identifying and measuring new forms of capital, it is not possible empirically to account for all of it, and the notion of a once-and-for-all refutable hypothesis settling the measurement problem is too strong. As Zvi Griliches points out, his approach to input and capital accounting succeeds in reducing the unaccounted part. His search in appealing to new information has been highly rewarding; see his "Research Expenditures, Education and the Aggregate Agricultural Production Function," *The American Economic Review,* 54 (December, 1964), pp. 961-974. In terms of capital accounting, see Griliches and Jorgenson, "Sources of Measured Productivity Change: Capital Input," *The American Economic Review,* 56 (May, 1966), pp. 50-61.

4. Despite my strong inclination to rely on "refutable hypotheses," I realize that Robert M. Solow can point out that not all of the observable total factor productivity may be of this sort. A part of it may still prove to be a "residual," whether it is labeled a "return to scale" or something else. Thus it is possible that a part of it may not be imputable to any resource cost, or that whoever makes such a residual technical change is unable to collect the return.

turn are presented cogently by Robert M. Solow.[5] In searching for "the relation between capital accumulation and economic growth in industrial countries,"[6] he finds capital theory unsettled and beset with many analytical difficulties. Solow is convinced, however, that from a planning point of view in dealing with saving and investment, "the central concept in capital theory should be *the rate of return on investment*."[7] I, too, am convinced that the rate-of-return approach has many advantages; and yet it does not tell enough of the story of capital accumulation and economic growth. My plan is to show that the investigations of the economic value of education reveal important supplementary parts of the process of capital accumulation and growth.

Although thinking in terms of the rate of return is fundamental, it will remain an inefficient approach in planning economic development until at least the more important forms of capital, which are the sources of income and economic growth, have been identified. But on this score the omissions of particular forms of capital continue to plague economic growth theory. Human capital is one of the major omissions. Improvement in the quality of non-human capital is another. I do not want to imply that such omissions are endemic to all growth thinking. Yet it comes close to that when "techniques" are treated as exogenous and not as new forms of capital, for this capital must also be identified in allocating investment resources in accordance with priorities set by relative rates of return to alternative investment opportunities.

It may be helpful to comment once again on the attempts

5. Robert M. Solow, *Capital Theory and the Rate of Return* (Amsterdam: North Holland Publishing Company, 1963).
6. *Ibid.*, p. 8.
7. *Ibid.*, p. 16. The italics are Solow's.

to explain the large, unexplained part of modern growth. The challenge, of course, has been the *residual*. I am sure economists will long be indebted to Edward F. Denison[8] for his pioneering endeavor at identifying and measuring the sources of growth despite all the criticism that has been heaped upon it. Although Denison underestimates, in my view, by a large margin the increases in the contributions of nonhuman capital because so much of the improvement in the quality of such capital is concealed in his "increases in output per unit of input"—a large part of which he attributes to "advance in knowledge"—his *labor input* nevertheless represents a marked advance, because it takes account of changes in the quality of labor, including education.[9]

Although the challenge of the residual made "technical change" fashionable, it also gave us Denison's contributions. Furthermore, it led to a realization that there is an accumulation of human capital; and, to cope with it and with conventional capital forms, an all-inclusive concept

8. Edward F. Denison, *The Sources of Economic Growth in the United States and the Alternatives before Us*, Supplementary Paper No. 13 (New York: Committee for Economic Development, 1962). In his "Sources of Postwar Growth in Nine Western Countries," *The American Economic Review*, 57 (May, 1967), pp. 325-332, Denison indicated that he had somewhat modified some of the estimating techniques that he had used in his early United States study.

9. Edward F. Denison, *The Sources of Economic Growth in the United States and the Alternatives before Us*, p. 266, Table 32. Denison sees this issue differently. In his view, his "incorporation of education into the measurement of labor input has the effect of putting labor input on a par with conventional measures of capital input. . . . When labor input is measured by applying weights to education groups, this is comparable to weighting different types of capital by their value in a base year . . . I don't think you really object to my estimates as such but to my classification" (quoted with his permission from a letter from Denison).

of capital is beginning to emerge as set forth by Harry G. Johnson.[10] It is now becoming clear that the question pertaining to technical change has been badly posed. The question facing policy-makers, planners, and entrepreneurs is as follows: How can they allocate investment resources efficiently to the production (formation) of particular new forms of capital?

The advantage of the rate of return approach is also limited, when it comes to investing in education, by the lack of efficiency or shadow prices and by the way the capital market functions in financing students.

Let me turn, however, to the stages through which the investigations of human capital are proceeding for some clarifying clues with respect to unsolved problems inherent in capital accumulation and economic growth. Consider education: Is it a source of earnings? Is it a significant variable in a production function? Can its resource cost be determined? Is it an important form of capital? Do students and schools respond to changes in rates of return? Is the production function applicable to educational activities? Answers to these questions cannot be found without theory and data; and, as might be expected, the analytical task is beset with difficulties on both scores. But some answers are in; others are still in doubt; and, for some of the questions, the search for answers has hardly begun.

Earnings from and Cost of Education

The first stage was simply a matter of determining whether there is any growth mileage whatsoever in education. That there is some mileage of this sort from some education in some countries is now firmly established.

10. In *The Residual Factor and Economic Growth* (Paris: OECD, 1964), pp. 219-227.

Rough as the estimating procedures were at the outset, they showed that it would undoubtedly be worthwhile to undertake more refined and complete analyses of the attributes of the earnings from education. As indicated earlier, Denison found that education seemed to account for about a fifth of the growth of the United States economy from 1929 to 1957.[11] Is education therefore a good investment? His study obviously was not intended to answer that question. My admittedly very rough estimates, which preceded those of Denison, derived from my factor cost of education and some very preliminary notions of the relevant rates of return, were in general consistent with Denison's results—namely, that education appeared to account for at least a fifth of the increase in United States national income during that period.[12] Complementary evidence of a different sort had come from the work of Herman P. Miller[13] and H. S. Houthakker,[14] from Gary S. Becker's first paper[15] in this area, and from a discovery of the relevance of the 1945 study by Milton Friedman

11. Edward F. Denison, *The Sources of Economic Growth in the United States and the Alternatives before Us*, p. 266, Table 32; see second to last column.

12. T. W. Schultz, "Education and Economic Growth," *Social Forces Influencing American Education*, Sixtieth Yearbook of the National Society for the Study of Education, ed. by Nelson B. Henry (Chicago: University of Chicago Press, 1961), Part II, pp. 78-82. See Table 18 covering the period between 1929 and 1956.

13. Herman P. Miller, "Annual and Lifetime Income in Relation to Education: 1939-1959," *The American Economic Review*, 50 (December, 1960), pp. 962-986. Also see Paul C. Glick and Herman P. Miller, "Educational Level and Potential Income," *American Sociological Review*, 21 (June, 1956), pp. 307-312.

14. H. S. Houthakker, "Education and Income," *The Review of Economics and Statistics*, 41 (February, 1959), pp. 24-28.

15. Gary S. Becker, "Underinvestment in College Education?," *The American Economic Review*, 50 (May, 1960), pp. 346-354.

and Simon Kuznets.[16] Jacob Mincer's study,[17] which had dealt with human capital and the distribution of personal income, provided still another type of supporting evidence. But the availability of data on earnings and schooling differs widely from country to country. There are some usable data covering recent decades for the United States, Israel, and Canada. They are better for India than might have been expected, as is clear from the study by A. M. Nalla Gounden.[18] But they are not available from census sources for European countries.[19] One of the favorable surprises, however, is how much can be learned by taking a sample as Martin Carnoy[20] has done in Mexico, Samuel S. Bowles[21] in Nigeria, and as Mark Blaug[22] has in using a British sample of data on earnings and schooling.

16. Milton Friedman and Simon Kuznets, *Income from Independent Professional Practice* (New York: National Bureau of Economic Research, 1945).

17. Jacob Mincer, "Investment in Human Capital and Personal Income Distribution," *The Journal of Political Economy*, 66 (August, 1958), pp. 281-302.

18. A. M. Nalla Gounden, "Education and Economic Development" (Unpublished doctoral dissertation, Kurukshetra University, India, 1965).

19. Mark Blaug in his paper, "The Private and the Social Returns on Investment in Education; Some Results for Great Britain," *The Journal of Human Resources*, 2 (Summer, 1967), pp. 330-346, notes that Sweden is a possible exception. Edward F. Denison has found useful the earnings data collected by the *Institut national de la statistique et des études economiques* (INSSE) in a special survey in France.

20. Martin Carnoy, "The Cost and Return to Schooling in Mexico," (Unpublished doctoral dissertation in economics, University of Chicago, 1964).

21. Samuel S. Bowles, "The Efficient Allocation of Resources in Education: A Planning Model with Applications to Northern Nigeria" (Unpublished doctoral dissertation in economics, Harvard University, 1965).

22. Mark Blaug, "The Private and the Social Returns on Investments in Education; Some Results for Great Britain," *op. cit.*

Once it had been established, however, that earnings were related positively to some extent to schooling, a number of important advances were soon made in developing theoretical models and in using them in estimating earnings from schooling. Becker's *Human Capital*[23] is a landmark. Giora Hanoch's[24] estimation technique and data for estimating the earnings function, which relates expected earnings to age and education after standardizing for other relevant factors, gives us, in my judgment, the best estimates presently available for the United States. Where self-employment predominates, as in agriculture, one turns to Finis Welch's estimates of the relevant earnings function.[25] Meanwhile, in a theoretical paper, Yoram Ben-Porath relates the shape of the life cycle of earnings of individuals to properties of the production function of human capital and examines the implications of these relations.[26] From his model he derives a number of promising hypotheses, which await testing. In another direction, Bowles has developed a linear programming model for the efficient allocation of resources in education.[27]

Educated labor can be introduced as an input in a production function. The presumption here is that, if the estimates of the earnings function of education are valid,

23. Gary S. Becker, *Human Capital* (New York: National Bureau of Economic Research, 1964).

24. Giora Hanoch, "Personal Earnings and Investment in Schooling" (Unpublished doctoral dissertation in economics, University of Chicago, 1965).

25. Finis Welch, "The Determinants of the Return to Schooling in Rural Farm Areas, 1959" (Unpublished doctoral dissertation in economics, University of Chicago, 1966).

26. Yoram Ben-Porath, "The Production of Human Capital and the Life Cycle of Earnings," *The Journal of Political Economy*, 75 (August, 1967), pp. 352-365.

27. Samuel S. Bowles, "The Efficient Allocation of Resources in Education: A Planning Model with Applications to Northern Nigeria," *op. cit.*

education should be one of the relevant variables in estimating the production function of firms. If this variable were significant and its coefficient were positive and well behaved, there would be additional assurance that education is a real source of part of the observed production. Although there is the supposition that education would be less relevant in agriculture than in most sectors of industry, the lack of suitable data—except for agriculture—has restricted the use of this method of analysis predominantly to agriculture. But the indications are that even in agriculture the education of labor is an important input. Zvi Griliches, in his search for the sources of measured productivity growth of United States agriculture, uses an aggregate production function for that sector. His studies indicate that *education* "is a statistically significant variable with a coefficient that is not very different from the coefficient of the man-years worked variable."[28] Micha Gisser, Welch, and Robert E. Evenson, analyzing other economic attributes of United States agriculture, also have used an implicit production function with education as a variable.[29]

28. Zvi Griliches, "Estimates of Aggregate Agricultural Production Function from Cross-Sectional Data," *Journal of Farm Economics*, 45 (May, 1963), pp. 419-428; and "The Sources of Measured Productivity Growth: United States Agriculture, 1940-60," *The Journal of Political Economy*, 71 (August, 1963), pp. 331-346; and his "Research Expenditures, Education and the Aggregate Agricultural Production Function," *op. cit.* The coefficient of "man-years" of labor is .524 and that of "education" is .431 for 1949, with United States agriculture classified into 68 regions.

29. Micha Gisser, "Schooling and the Agricultural Labor Force" (Unpublished doctoral dissertation in economics, University of Chicago, 1962); Finis Welch, "The Determinants of the Return to Schooling in Rural Farm Areas, 1959," *op. cit.*; and Robert E. Evenson, "The Contribution of Agricultural Research and Extension to Agricultural Production" (Unpublished doctoral dissertation in economics, University of Chicago, 1968).

Another method for determining the value of education in production is a planning approach, a linear programming model, of the type developed by Bowles. In applying his model to Northern Nigeria, using a discount rate of 5 percent, he obtained the present value of the net benefits associated with the four educational activities listed below to be as follows: [30]

	Present Value of Net Benefits in £s
Primary school	990
Secondary school	1,210
Technical training school	840
University studies	10,080

But all these studies omit the consumption value of education, as Solow correctly reminds me. It is a serious omission. In my papers and in *The Economic Value of Education*, I have stressed the importance of this consumption value. The available estimates of earnings from education in this respect all underestimate the real value of education. Except for Becker's study, ability differences are not reckoned.

To calculate the rate of return, we must have estimates not only of the earnings from education but also of its cost. But the estimates of the cost are presently not as good as Hanoch's estimates of earnings. The work to measure these costs has fallen behind, and there are deficiencies that affect the reliability of the cost estimates, and these in turn affect the calculated rates of return.

The deficiencies I refer to are not those asserted by John E. Vaizey, who among other criticisms of past work

30. Samuel S. Bowles, "The Efficient Allocation of Resources in Education: A Planning Model with Applications to Northern Nigeria," *op. cit.*, Table 6.4.1. Bowles informs me that the figure for secondary school should be 1,206 instead of 906, before rounding.

seems to make a main point of the assertion that earnings foregone by students should not be included in the cost of education.[31] The economic logic that makes earnings foregone a part of the opportunity cost of education has been presented with care by Mary Jean Bowman and need not be repeated here.[32] Carnoy, Nalla Gounden, and Bowles, for Mexico, India, and Northern Nigeria, respectively, have done as well as they could with their data; but workers on United States data have ignored many factors that influence the cost of education by region, community, and type.[33] I am not so much troubled by our national (aggregate) cost estimates as I am about the way these national estimates are then allocated to various subgroups by region and race without taking account

31. Commenting on John E. Vaizey's views, Harry G. Johnson notes, in *The Residual Factor and Economic Growth, op. cit.*, pp. 225-227, that they "seem to be partly motivated by concern about the political implications," and thus are scarcely relevant to a scientific search for the underlying real cost of education. If the political motive were that of persuading the body politic to increase the government appropriations for education, it would, of course, be convenient to omit earnings foregone. Omitting them in the case of the United States would fully double the calculated rate of return to high school and college education. But this is not the road that leads to economic knowledge.

32. Mary Jean Bowman, "The Costing of Human Resource Development," *The Economics of Education*, ed. by E. A. G. Robinson and John E. Vaizey (New York: St. Martin's Press, 1966), pp. 421-450. Also see Chapters 6 and 7 of this study, and a previous elaboration in my *The Economic Value of Education*, Chapter 2.

33. There is much merit in attaining some historical perspective of the changing composition of the cost of education and thereby improving our understanding of changes now under way affecting these costs, as revealed by Albert Fishlow, "Levels of Nineteenth Century American Investment in Education," *Journal of Economic History*, 26 (December, 1966), pp. 418-436. See also Lewis Solmon, "Capital Formation by Expenditures on Formal Education, 1880 and 1890" (Unpublished doctoral dissertation in economics, University of Chicago, 1968), concentrating on about the same period.

either of the large differences in cost arising from the differences in the regional mix of low-cost community colleges and high-cost private colleges or of the differences in earnings of students who are attending these schools. I am also sure that there are vast differences in the quality of education at all levels among regions—for example, between the farm and nonfarm sectors and between whites and Negroes—and that these differences are related to variations in the cost of education.[34]

I turn now to a consideration of how real and relevant are rates of return in allocating investment resources efficiently to education.[35] The following questions appear pertinent:

1. Should we be worried whether the allocation of resources to education is efficient or not? Yes, because education absorbs a large share of resources, as I shall show, so that misallocations, *within* that sector and *between* education and alternative expenditures, could be wasteful.

2. Is there evidence that private educational choices are privately efficient; that is, do private rates of return to education tend (a) to be equal as among educational options and (b) to be comparable to private rates of return to other private investments? The evidence implies inefficiencies.

3. Are social rates of return and private rates of return proportional in all activities? Evidence is insufficient.

4. If private choices are privately inefficient, are they

34. The economic importance of differences in the quality of schooling is revealed by Finis Welch in "Labor-Market Discrimination: An Interpretation of Income Differences in the Rural South," *The Journal of Political Economy*, 75 (June, 1967), pp. 225-240, and in my "Underinvestment in the Quality of Schooling in Rural Farm Areas," *Increasing Understanding of Public Problems and Policies* (Chicago: Farm Foundation, 1964), pp. 12-34.

35. In clarifying these issues, I owe much to Harry G. Johnson.

nevertheless socially efficient as a consequence of the allocation of public subsidies to education? There is no evidence on this.

If the amount of resources spent on education were trivial, there would be no point in being worried about rates of return as allocative guides in the area of education. But surely in the United States the amount of resources allocated each year to education is far from negligible. In 1956 the total outlay on formal education was $28.7 billion,[36] of which $12.4 billion was earnings foregone, compared with a total gross material capital formation for that year of $79.5 billion.[37] We learn from Kuznets[38] how much investment in man increases the share of gross national product (GNP) that is allocated to the formation of capital. If we start with the conventional concept of material capital, 30 percent of GNP, net of intermediate products, is accounted for in gross capital formation. The direct costs of formal education along with some other investments in man increase the gross capital formation to 42 percent of GNP. Kuznets then adds earnings foregone to GNP, which increases the conventional estimate of GNP by 10 percent; and, since earnings foregone are all part of human capital formation, the share of GNP allocated to gross capital formation rises to 47 percent.[39] In actual amounts, by 1959-1960 the total outlay on formal education in the United States reached $39.5 billion.[40]

On the second question, the evidence shows very high

36. See Chapter 6 of this book, Tables 6.5, 6.6, and 6.7.
37. Simon Kuznets, *Modern Economic Growth* (New Haven, Conn.: Yale University Press, 1966), p. 228.
38. *Ibid.*, pp. 228-230.
39. *Ibid.*, Table 5.2, p. 231, lines 4, 5, and 7.
40. Lewis C. Solmon's estimate, using the same method I used in Chapter 6 of this study; the earnings foregone component was $17.7 billion.

private rates of return to elementary schooling (for instance, see Carnoy for Mexico, W. Lee Hansen[41] and Hanoch for the United States). They are also high for high school and have risen secularly (see Becker's *Human Capital*).[42] These high private rates of return imply that private educational choices are privately inefficient with respect to elementary and secondary schooling. As I see this evidence, it implies that there is an underinvestment partly in quantity but *predominantly in the quality of such schooling*. The private rates of return to college education are, in general, comparable to private rates of return to other private investment, when no allowance is made for the consumption value of such education. On the third and fourth questions, as already noted, there is too little evidence to support firm answers.

Another unsettled question is the response of students (or of their parents) and of the decision-making bodies that organize and operate schools—that is, the suppliers of educational services—to changes in the rates of return. If these responses were nil, it would be pointless to attribute any behavioral importance to these rates of return as allocative guides in the area of education. Such a lack of response on the part of students and schools would imply that the concept of investment in education is meaningless in terms of such economic behavior or that our measures of the rate of return to education are wrong. But what we observe is not a lack of response. Although the story of these responses to changes in rates of return has not yet been told in the language of a Nerlovian dynamic-response model, there is an abundance of historical evi-

41. W. Lee Hansen, "Total and Private Rates of Return to Investment in Schooling," *The Journal of Political Economy*, 71 (April, 1963), pp. 128-140.
42. Gary S. Becker, *Human Capital, op. cit.*

dence that leaves little room for doubt that such responses are occurring and that, in general, they are in the right directions.[43] The search is for behavior models that would be appropriate in analyzing these investment responses.[44]

What is the relevant educational investment horizon in education? It is useful to distinguish between the *apparent behavioral horizons* of students and the *ex post horizons* underlying the estimates of rates of return. In thinking about the first of these, the investment horizon, which will explain the behavior of students and schools, there are strong reasons for believing that it is, in general, fairly short. It is impossible to predict lifetime earnings; for the

43. But it would be a mistake to conclude from such evidence that these responses are *efficient* and that there is no *malinvestment* in education. There is still a tendency toward one or the other of two opposite biases; that is, as extremes, these responses are close to perfect in equating marginal returns or the acquisition of education is determined wholly by social and cultural factors, which are beyond the economic calculus.

44. The first study of this type known to me was by W. Lee Hansen, "Shortages and Investment in Professional Training" (Unpublished Labor Economics Workshop Paper No. 62: 1, University of Chicago, October 16, 1961). Also see his paper, "The Shortage of Engineers," *The Review of Economics and Statistics*, 43 (August, 1961), pp. 251-256. In "Present Values of Lifetime Earnings for Different Occupations," *The Journal of Political Economy*, 74 (December, 1966), pp. 556-572, Bruce W. Wilkinson compares the behavior of teachers and engineers between 1957-1958 and 1961-1962 in Canada, Table 4, p. 570. Richard B. Freeman in "Labor Market for B.S. Engineers, 1948-1965," a paper presented before the Labor Economics Workshop, University of Chicago, January 23, 1967 (part of his unpublished doctoral dissertation in economics, "The Labor Market for College Manpower," Harvard University, 1967), used a cobweb model. Harry G. Johnson, in "The Social Sciences in the Age of Opulence," presidential address before the Canadian Political Science Association, *Canadian Journal of Economics and Political Science*, 32 (November, 1966), pp. 423-442, sees the relevance of a cobweb model in explaining changes in the demand-supply of teachers.

student to do so he would have to predict the changes in the demand for his type of education and the supply consequences of the decisions of others like himself to enter his particular field on his earnings up to 40 or more years ahead. The relevant information available to the student would seem to be mainly of two parts: 1) starting salaries and 2) the relative earnings position of people in their forties at the time the student's decision is made. (His parents will be comparing themselves with contemporaries in other occupations and with respect to those who have made good.)[45]

Thus I would proceed on the assumption that the investment horizon of students is relatively short, except for such traditional occupations as law and medicine. In the case of engineers, Freeman finds that starting salaries of engineers provide a strong clue to the behavior of students entering or leaving this field.[46] But we do not know the relationship between starting salaries and the earnings profiles we use in calculating the rates of return to education, which take account of earnings that accrue from education through the fourth decade after the education is completed. Nor do we know how sensitive these starting salaries are to changes in the real rates of return.

An approach to get at these relatively short investment horizons is to think 1) in terms of the subjective discount rates of students and 2) in terms of the uncertainty they face. The two could be closely linked. But I would presume that the linkage between them is quite loose. The fog of uncertainty is everywhere concealing the more

45. Harry G. Johnson in *ibid.*; also from his comments on my preliminary draft of this chapter.
46. Richard B. Freeman, *op. cit.* These responses of engineers to starting salaries do not necessarily imply short investment horizons; such starting salaries could be good proxies for lifetime earnings.

distant value of education. The subjective discount rates will differ depending upon differences in preferences and in the supply price of capital for this purpose; and, despite such differences, these subjective discount rates may be, in general, not high but close to the going interest rate. Thus it is possible that the relatively short investment horizon, which I have postulated, is a consequence of the general fog of uncertainty.

I do not want to imply that we should dismiss out of hand the possibility that we might find that some of the relevant subjective rates of discount are high. We should therefore search for ways of ascertaining what these rates appear to be, hard as it is to obtain any data that might reveal them to us. Students from families with low incomes and with little wealth in general cannot, even if they wanted to, borrow funds in the capital market to finance education. Even if they could, many of them may impose on themselves forms of internal capital rationing that would keep them from turning to the market for such funds.

But the fog of uncertainty is there. How low and how dense it is really matters. Yet we are ever so vague when it comes to identifying and measuring the level and density of this fog. It is in the nature of things, as a part of the human predicament we must face. Reason and probabilities and the search for solutions will not dispel all this fog, as G. L. S. Shackle reminds us in his presidential address to the British Economic Association, "Policy, Poetry and Success."[47] The future economic value of education is no exception. Estimates of the profiles of lifetime earnings from education are pictures of the past. They reveal *ex post* supply and demand intercepts of the capabilities acquired from education. But when it comes to projecting these esti-

47. G. L. S. Shackle, "Policy, Poetry and Success," *The Economic Journal*, 76 (December, 1966), pp. 755-767.

mates into the future, reason, economic logic and theory, and appeals to probabilities are quite imperfect in making projections that will prove to be right. This limitation of our knowledge about the future is, of course, not unique to investment in education; for this uncertainty is also ever present in the realm of investment in material capital. What we do know is that the dynamics of our type of economy is continuously changing not only the demands for final products and the intermediate components entering into them, but even more important, is improving the quality of old forms of capital and also developing new and better forms of capital. The obsolescence of capital, including the capital that is formed by education, is *real*, in large part *unpredictable*, and *important*.

In planning for economic development, when investment decisions are made by a governmental agency, the investment horizon with regard to education is likewise, so it seems to me, relatively short and for essentially the same reason. Those who make these public decisions are up against the same fog of uncertainty with respect to the more distant economic value of education. They have one advantage, however: such an agency can pool some types of risks that confront a student and treat them in terms of ascertainable probabilities, such as the probability that a particular student is capable of completing some additional education.

If this view of the relevant investment horizons should prove to be valid, it strongly implies that appropriate steps should be taken to maximize the returns from built-in flexibilities for taking advantage of any lifting of the fog as it occurs over time. Such flexibility is possible *by postponing specialization in education* and thus not only starting with but also staying with general education longer than would be warranted if there were no uncertainty with respect to future earnings from the investment in education. The characteristics of this fog also imply that *more* (not all) *of the specialized skills should be acquired from on-the-job training* than would thus be acquired if there were less or no uncertainty.

My purpose here is not to present a catalogue of particulars but to clarify somewhat the problem at hand. We know that the rapid change in the demand for skills is a function of our type of economic growth. The secular shift, which shows that an increasing part of on-the-job training is being acquired by those with a college education, is consistent with the sort of flexibility that my approach implies. In 1939, only one-third of all on-the-job training of males in the United States (which at that time was as large as all formal education) was acquired by college-level males. In 1958, two-thirds of it was acquired by males who already had attained a college education.[48]

It should also be said that our task as educators is to provide instruction that will best serve students in adjusting their skills to the rapidly changing economy in which they will live. Thus we ought to give a low rating to instruction that is specific. We ought to give a high rating to learning principles and theories. We should give the highest priority to instruction devoted to problem-solving using analytical methods. If you ask how this can best be done, do not expect answers. What is odd, however, is that we do not search for answers so relevant to the efficiency of our own work. As economists, we search for ways that will make producers more efficient. We tell everybody else how they can do their work better. But we fail to bring hard, analytical thinking to bear on our

48. See Jacob Mincer, "On-the-Job Training: Costs, Returns and Some Implications," *The Journal of Political Economy* (Supplement), 70 (October, 1962), pp. 50-79.

task as teachers. Surely the rate of obsolescence of what we teach and what students learn is higher than it need be.[49]

In using the distinction between the investment horizon of students and the horizon underlying our estimates of rates of return, I have concentrated on the first of these. If the estimated lifetime earnings profiles, costs, and rates of returns could be projected with certainty, could students then privately invest efficiently in their education if they were informed with respect to only the first half, or some larger part, of such lifetime earnings profiles? Evidence pertaining to this possibility, using Hanoch's estimates, shows, as one would expect, that it would lead to an inefficient investment in education.

This evidence comes from Hanoch's estimates for U.S. males who are white and who lived in the North in 1959.[50] It is restricted to a comparison of the investment in 16 years of schooling over that of 12 years of schooling. Since the net present value at age 20 and the internal rate of return give the same results, I shall refer only to the internal rates of return. They show, using four years for college, large differences:

Time span after age 20 of	Internal rate of return
10 years	2.5
15 years	7.5
20 years	9.6
Full life	11.5

The inference from this evidence, given the conditions set by the problem under consideration, is that there would be an underinvestment in college education if the informa-

49. In this paragraph I draw upon my "Teaching and Learning in Colleges of Agriculture," in my *Economic Growth and Agriculture* (New York: McGraw-Hill Book Company, 1968), pp. 165-171. Harry G. Johnson considers these issues in "The Social Sciences in the Age of Opulence," *op. cit.*

50. Giora Hanoch, *op. cit.*, Table 4.

tion on earnings covering, for instance, only the first 15 years were to guide such private investment decisions. The results shown imply that an expected rate of return of 7.5 percent would then be the guide, whereas the lifetime rate that would be realized is 11.5 percent, which is half again as high, thus calling for additional investment.

Lastly, there is the distinction between the internal rate and the net present value. Much has been written attributing important theoretical advantages to the present value over the internal-rate approach—with authors citing, as a rule, J. Hirshleifer's paper[51] but not Martin J. Bailey's classic paper,[52] which shows that Hirshleifer's analysis is not sufficient to solve the multiperiod case in full generality. Bailey demonstrates formally that "the general solution of investment decision problems cannot rely solely on either the present value or rate of return reasoning."[53] Thus, as with other techniques of analysis in empirical work, neither technique is wholly satisfactory formally. Aside from these formal limitations, each has its advantage. Given the data in this area, the results in terms of the relative internal rates and the relative net present values tend to be about the same; and, since the internal rate of return is a much easier (less costly) statistic to calculate, it has by this token an advantage. But where the data permit, the net present value has an advantage in identifying the large net return from a large additional investment (an extra year in becoming a surgeon), with a relatively small rate of return above the market rate, compared with

51. J. Hirshleifer, "On the Theory of Optimal Investment Decision," *The Journal of Political Economy*, 66 (August, 1958), pp. 329-352.

52. Martin J. Bailey, "Formal Criteria for Investment Decisions," *The Journal of Political Economy*, 67 (October, 1959), pp. 476-488.

53. *Ibid.*, p. 477.

the small net return from an extra year of elementary schooling (going from the seventh and completing the eighth), although the latter produces a relatively high rate of return.

Conclusions

The advantages of thinking in terms of the rate of return are cogent in searching for solutions to investment, capital accumulation, and growth problems, including the problem of an efficient allocation of investment resources to education. I prefer to think of the reciprocal of the rate of return as the *price of an income stream* and then treat this price of an additional income stream as the price of growth. But (staying with the rate of return), my endeavor here at clarifying particular issues would seem to support the following conclusions:

1. The best of the estimates showing the profiles of earnings from education are in good repair (Hanoch), but they omit the consumption value of education and ability differences.

2. Factor costs of education, however, are still far from satisfactory.[54]

3. Estimates of the private rates of return to the different levels of education, despite the limitations with respect to costs, are becoming useful indicators of particular *ex*

---

54. Bruce W. Wilkinson, *op. cit.*, p. 561, for example, proceeds as follows: "Information is not available on incidental high school costs or summer and part-time earnings of high school students, so it will be assumed that they are equal." Giora Hanoch, *op. cit.*, p. 74, is quite aware of the weakness of his cost data in noting that, "direct costs of schooling constitute a main component of these initial sections of the profiles. But due to the shortage of satisfactory data, we actually used here a crude assumption, that direct costs equal the earnings of students."

post disequilibria in the supplies of educated labor viewed privately.

4. The social rates of return are not in good repair, either theoretically or empirically. There is all too little evidence on the relationship between the social and private rates of return.

5. The alleged advantages of present value estimates over internal rate estimates are questionable in theory and in practice; each has its particular advantage.

6. We know very little about the tendency to equilibrium or about the responses of students and schools to the relative rates of return.

7. When it comes to private investment in education, the private investment horizon of students is not known. Despite the substantial additional earnings from education that accrue to the person during the later part of his life span, my feeling is that the private investment horizon is, in fact, relatively short.

8. The economic linkage between recent *ex post* rates of return and future rates of return to investments, in general—including investment in different levels of education —is tenuous. Growth theory does not as yet provide us with any strong links.

9. An approach that treats investment in education as a means of improving the quality of the human agent is an important step leading to the specification and measurement of the quality of both human and nonhuman capital, and thus accounting for the increases in macro production without any appeal to technical change as Griliches and Jorgenson have shown.[55]

55. Zvi Griliches and Dale W. Jorgenson, "Sources of Measured Productivity Change: Capital Input," *op. cit.* Also, their paper "The Explanation of Productivity Change," *The Review of Economic Studies*, 34 (July, 1967), pp. 249-283.

10. In terms of capital accounting, we are moving toward an all-inclusive concept of capital, and, in terms of growth, we have the beginnings of a "generalized capital accumulation approach to economic development,"[56] in which the reciprocal of the rate of return is in theory and in fact the price of growth.

56. See Harry G. Johnson's comment on this approach in *The Residual Factor and Economic Growth, op. cit.*, pp. 219-227.

10 Resources for Higher Education[1]

Iт would be convenient, in good grace, and not too difficult to make a strong case for more funds for higher education. Such a case could be made convincing by simply projecting the recent high rate of increase in higher education, with student enrollment and the cost per student continuing to rise, and proclaiming that soon virtually every high school graduate will require some higher education. This would set the stage for universal higher education with the implication that it should become more nearly free to students and would stress the necessity of supporting more quantity and more quality everywhere. Thus it would seem that there are reasons aplenty for more federal funds, preferably without public control, and for a public package that would finance everybody.

But the problems here that await solution cannot be treated in so convenient a manner. Even the preliminary

1. C. E. Bishop, Mary Jean Bowman, Milton Friedman, Zvi Griliches, A. C. Harberger, Lewis C. Solmon, and Finis Welch commented critically on my first draft of this chapter, and I am indebted to them.

task of identifying the problems that matter is a major undertaking. I am attracted to Professor G. L. S. Shackle's[2] distinction between poetry as a search for beauty and policy as a search for solutions to problems. Our search is for solutions to the problem of financing higher education.

Although poetry is an art, not all of financing is problem solving; for it seems to be true that it has many of the earmarks of an art, subject to convention and tradition as is the art of the poet in his use of words. It could be said that reason, theory, and analysis are quite impotent in challenging any of the following propositions: it is better to maintain an old college than to move it to a superior location; it is better to add new university functions than to eliminate those that have become obsolete; it is better to accommodate classes that have become virtually empty than to reallocate faculty to gain efficiency; it is better simply to project past upward trends than to explain them with the view of altering their course for the better; and it is better to obtain additional outside funds than to raise tuitions.

My plan is to begin with a comment on some of the limitations of economic analysis, then to present a set of propositions and their implications for higher education, and finally, to sketch the search for solutions to financing higher education.

*From Preferences to an
Agenda of Economic Problems*

Consider first the cultural values that determine the preferences of parents, students, and society for higher education. How they may be changed for the better is

2. G. L. S. Shackle, "Policy, Poetry and Success," *The Economic Journal*, 76 (December, 1966), pp. 755-767, presidential address before the British Economic Association.

beyond the economic calculus; such a reform must rest on cultural and political considerations rather than on economic choices among economic opportunities. Economists start with preferences and build on them, treating them as given. Economists have developed powerful analytical techniques, and they are skillful in using them in specifying and identifying the "revealed preferences" of people. With regard to the technical properties of resources, there are some that are "fixed." They consist of particular "original" resources and their attributes, for example, the physical dimensions and space of the United States and the inherited abilities of students and teachers. Other technical properties are not altogether fixed but nevertheless cannot be altered much in any short period of time; for example, the absolute magnitude of the endowment of human and material capital, including the state of knowledge. At best, this endowment can be enlarged somewhat but it would be in the small, and to this extent economists would have something to say on the worthwhileness of such small changes.

When you ask economists for their agenda of problems pertaining to education, you are asking for additional trouble. Propositions about education that have long been treated as self-evident and settled are placed in doubt. The grand monolithic social value of higher education is seen as many little values, each of which is up against a schedule of marginal costs. There is no free instruction. Thus one must ask: Is the additional cost worth the additional satisfactions and earnings? Is it worth as much as the value from an equal expenditure in some other private or public activity? If the federal government were prepared to appropriate an additional billion dollars, would society gain as much from allocating it to higher education as from using it for the conservation of natural resources, reducing water and air pollution, providing more medical care, slum clearance, or for the reduction of poverty? Would an additional billion dollars reduce the job discrimination against educated Negroes, the rate of economic obsolescence of acquired education, or the inefficiency with which resources are allocated within higher education? Would it improve the career choices of students? Would it reduce the social and economic inequities that presently characterize the personal distribution of resources going into higher education? These are some of the troublesome problems on the economist's agenda.

From Propositions to Implications

While altruism is not at the heart of the relationship between education and economics, both gain from an exchange of products. To broaden the exchange, economists are offering some new propositions that should prove useful in planning and in financing education. I shall present seven. Let me indicate what they are about. Organized education produces an array of different forms of human capital of varying durability. Higher education is engaged in three major types of production activities, which entail discovering talent, instruction, and research. But it is not renowned for its gains in the productivity of teachers and students. Educational planning overlooks most of the real costs of higher education because of its omission of the earnings foregone by students. Long-term projections of the demand for higher education are conjectures that undervalue flexibility and overvalue formulas. The advantages of thinking in terms of the rates of return to investment in education and the requirement of efficiency prices in allocating investment resources in accordance with the standard set by the relative rates of return to alternative investment opportunities are strong and clear. There is, however, much confusion with regard to the welfare consequences of higher education, including the consequences of the way in which it is financed and the resulting personal distribution of costs and benefits. I now turn to the meaning of these propositions.

1   *Education Is a Form of Human Capital*   It is *human* because it becomes a part of man, and it is *capital* because it is a source of future satisfactions, or of future earnings, or both. Thus far, however, the concept of human capital has contributed more to economic thinking than it has to the solution of problems in education. In economics, it has become a seminal concept entering into many parts of economic analysis. In international trade, it points to the solution of the Leontief paradox, showing why capital-rich countries nevertheless export labor-intensive goods —we discover that labor entering into these goods requires much human capital. The differences among countries in their capital endowments, when both physical and human capital are taken into account and under the assumption of factor-price equalization, go a long way toward explaining the differences in income per worker among them.[3] When considering the international movement of human capital and the growing international markets for particular high skills, the so-called brain drain is straightaway a form of maximizing economic behavior. In internal migration, also, human capital is a critical explanatory factor. In solving the long-standing puzzle of the *residual*, where the rate of increase in output exceeds the rate of increase in inputs, it has contributed much. As a part of an all-inclusive concept of capital, advances in specification and

3. See Anne O. Krueger, "Factor Endowments and *per Capita* Income Differences among Countries," *The Economic Journal*, 78 (September, 1968), pp. 641-659.

measurement of the services of capital would appear to explain most of the observable economic growth.[4] Furthermore, it sets the stage for a generalized theory of capital accumulation in which investment resources are allocated in accordance with the priorities set by the relative rates of return to all material and human investment opportunities.[5]

There are the following particular implications of this proposition for planning and financing higher education: 1) The human capital that is formed by higher education is far from homogeneous. Parts of it are for consumption and parts are for production. Moreover, both the consumer and producer components are of many different types. To lump them in allocating resources to higher education is bad economics. 2) The value of each type of human capital depends on the value of the services it renders and not on its original costs; mistakes in the composition and size of the stock of each type, once made, are sunk investments. 3) The formation of most of these types of capital requires a long horizon because the capabilities that the student acquires are part of him during the rest of his life. 4) The value of the benefits of higher education accruing to students privately consists of future earnings and of future nonpecuniary satisfactions. It is difficult to measure the latter, but they are nevertheless real and important. 5) Although human capital, as such, cannot be bought and sold, it is comparatively easy to estimate the value of the producer services of this capital because they are priced in terms of wages and salaries in the labor market. 6) Human capital, like reproducible material capital, is subject to

4. Dale W. Jorgenson and Zvi Griliches, "The Explanation of Productivity Change," *The Review of Economic Studies*, 34 (July, 1967), pp. 249-283.
5. See Chapter 9 of this study.

obsolescence. The traditional tax treatment of depreciation is outmoded inasmuch as it excludes human capital. Although earnings foregone do not enter into taxable income, none of the direct private costs is treated as capital formation. The upper limit of the life of this capital is the remaining life span of individuals after they have completed their formal education. An increase in longevity may decrease the rate of depreciation; earlier retirements may work in the opposite direction. More important is the obsolescence from changes in demand for high skills, changes that are a consequence of the characteristics of our type of economic growth. It should be possible to provide instruction that would be less subject to this type of obsolescence than it is presently. Educational planning should search for ways and means of improving higher education in this respect by substituting long-life for short-life instructional components so that it can serve better the changing demands for high skills. Continuing education after graduation is a form of maintenance. 7) Capital formation by education sets the stage for thinking of education as an investment.

2 *The Three Major Functions of Higher Education Are Discovering Talent, Instruction, and Research* Each of these activities requires analysis to determine how efficiently it is organized and whether too few or too many resources are allocated to it. But it must be admitted in all honesty that hard facts and valid inferences pertaining to these issues are about as scarce as they are in the pork barrel realm of rivers and harbors. What is an efficient organization of each of these three activities in higher education in terms of scale of organization, specialization, location of colleges and universities, and importantly, the *complementarity between the discovery of talent, instruction, and research?*

Taking the system of higher education as it is, with regard to instruction, economists have made substantial progress in specifying and identifying the economic value of higher education as it increases the value productivity of human agents as workers. Less, although some, progress has been made in getting at the economic value of university research. The much-neglected activity is that of discovering talent. It, too, can be approached by treating it as a process that provides students with opportunities to discover whether they have the particular capabilities required for the type and level of education at which they are working.

The value of the research function has received a lot of puffing but little analysis. It has prestige, but what about performance? With regard to organized agricultural research, where it is a part of land grant universities, there are some studies with some hard facts. The payoff on this type of research has been very high.[6] But there are no economic studies to my knowledge of other types of organized university research. Is it organized efficiently in terms of combinations of scientific talent, scale of organization, complementarity with Ph.D. research and with other research centers, and division of labor between basic and applied research? Is it for profit or on public account? Despite the importance of these questions and the wide array of experience from which we can learn, scientists are woefully unscientific in the impressionistic answers they give to this question.[7]

---

6. See T. W. Schultz, "Organized Agricultural Research," *Economic Growth and Agriculture* (New York: McGraw-Hill Book Company, 1968), pp. 81-85. See Chapter 12 that follows.

7. For a thoughtful exception see Harvey Brooks, "Can Science Be Planned?" *Problems of Science Policy: Seminar at Jouy-en-Josas on Science* (Paris: OECD, 1967).

There are many signs that indicate that one of the strongest features of higher education in the United States is in discovering talent. Although we are far ahead of western Europe in this activity, the payoff to additional resources used for this purpose is still in all probability very high. If so, three implications are worthy of note: 1) relatively more resources should be committed to this activity; 2) resources should be allocated specifically to support it; and 3) the organization and budgets of higher education should be planned to perform this activity efficiently.

3 *There Appear to Be Few or No Gains in the Measured Productivity of Labor Entering into Higher Education* It follows that if the price of this labor rises and if its productivity remains constant (other things unchanged), the price of the services it renders must rise; that is, the cost of higher education per student must rise. The crude facts, as we observe them, are consistent with this proposition. But these facts do not measure changes in the quality of the educational product, which has been rising markedly in many fields. The advance in knowledge is probably the main reason, and here we have a strong clue to the complementarity between instruction and research.

Nor do we know the possibilities of economizing on the labor entering into education by substituting other educational inputs for this labor or by reorganizing the educational process and thereby obtaining gains in the productivity of teachers and students in terms of the time they spend teaching and learning. These possibilities are undoubtedly of substantial importance, but it is doubtful that they will be found predominantly in new learning machines, in television instruction, or in the computerization of educational activities; instead, they are mainly to be achieved through many small innovative reorganizations of the instructional interplay between teachers and students that will reduce the time spent by each in attaining a given educational product.

The reasons why it is so difficult to make these gains are fairly obvious. The product of teaching and learning is highly labor-intensive like that of barbers. At best, it would appear that there is little room for nonlabor inputs. Nor are cheaper labor inputs the solution; that is, substituting low quality, less costly teachers and students for high quality persons. Although the difficulties here may seem insurmountable, it should be remembered that in classical economics, manufacturing carried the promise of decreasing cost whereas the outlook for agriculture was increasing cost per unit of product. But economic development in western countries has more than offset the drag of diminishing returns to land in farming, and the gains in labor productivity in agriculture have been exceeding those in manufacturing. Not so long ago the conventional view was that the retail sector could not gain appreciably from labor-saving developments, but it has in fact made much progress on this score. The present conventional view that the educational sector is destined to continue as it is regarding the amount of time required of students and teachers also may prove wrong.

The major real problems awaiting solution in higher education in economizing on the time of students and teachers are, in large part, a consequence of the traditional decision-making process in colleges and universities, the ambiguity that conceals the added value of the product, and the lack of strong incentives to innovate. On theoretical grounds there is room for more progress. Decision-making theory is not empty as a guide in improving the traditional process. A theory of the allocation of time[8] is now at hand for determining how efficiently the time of students is allocated. Requiring college students to spend 20 hours a week in class, as is required of many students, may be anything but efficient. The implication is that we might find 15 or 10 or even fewer hours more efficient. But we really will not know what could be achieved by such innovations until we have undertaken carefully planned experiments to discover what the results would be. The specifications of the value added to the capabilities of students by the educational process are being clarified, for example, in the search for a better mix of instructional components that would have a longer life than the present mix.

4   *Earnings Foregone by Students Are Well over Half of the Real Costs of the Human Capital Formation by Higher Education* Earnings foregone by college and university students in the United States exceeded in 1959-1960 the "direct" expenditures in the same period for higher education (minus auxiliary enterprises and capital outlay plus implicit interest and depreciation of physical property), which came to about $4,350 million. Yet we omit these earnings foregone in our planning and financing approach to higher education. We keep them concealed by not entering them in our college and university plans nor in our national income and capital formation accounts. The omission of these earnings foregone by students seriously distorts our view of the economics of higher education. Let me turn to the major implications of this omission of earnings foregone: 1) higher education (leaving university research aside) is more than twice as costly as is re-

8. Gary S. Becker, "A Theory of the Allocation of Time," *The Economic Journal*, 75 (September, 1965), pp. 493-517.

vealed in our budgets; 2) it is simply impossible to plan efficiently when over half of the real costs are treated as "free" resources; 3) there is no incentive to economize on the time of students in educational planning under existing circumstances; 4) educational planners receive no signals that the value of the time of students is rising relative to material inputs; 5) the rate of return to investment in higher education is grossly overestimated when earnings foregone are omitted; 6) so-called "free" education is far from free to students and their parents, which, in turn, implies that many families with low incomes cannot afford to forego the earnings of their children; and 7) savings, investment, and capital formation are all substantially understated in terms of national accounting.[9]

5 *Long-term Projections of the Demand for Higher Education Are Beset with All Manner of Uncertainty* They are conjectures that can be very misleading. As a consequence, flexibility is undervalued and formulas are overvalued in educational planning. Economic logic tells us that in coping with uncertainty, it is necessary to remain sufficiently flexible so that one can act efficiently when new and better information becomes available. But such flexibility is not costless; thus the prospective additional gains from flexibility must be reckoned against the additional costs. Furthermore, to the extent that these projections can be made more reliable, the need for and cost of acquiring flexibility can be reduced.

The available projections of the demands for higher education can be substantially improved. What we have are numbers, which are not a reliable source of information. The concept of demand for education requires clarifica-

9. See the excellent treatment of these issues by Simon Kuznets, *Modern Economic Growth* (New Haven, Conn.: Yale University Press, 1966), pp. 228-234.

tion; as it is presently used, it is beset with ambiguity. So-called need is not demand because the concept of demand implies prices and quantities. But the relevant prices, whether they are shadow prices or actual prices, are not specified in the numbers being projected. The demand behavior of students for places in colleges and universities is a useful approach. Another approach is to determine the demands for the particular capabilities that come from the teaching and learning in higher education—demands that are derived from the production activity of the economy. But it is unfortunately true that there is as yet no satisfactory theory connecting *ex post* rates of increase in the demands for the satisfactions and earnings that accrue to college and university students with future rates of increase in these demands. Projections abound, but they are in principle as naive as exponential population projections. You can take your choice, and if you happen to be correct, it will not be because of reason but because of luck. Manpower studies do not provide the answer, nor are the sophisticated programming models as yet providing an answer.

The rise in per family income undoubtedly increases the demand for the consumer satisfactions from higher education; the income elasticity of the demand for this consumer component is probably such that it is a superior good with a fairly high elasticity. But the demand for the producer component is very hard to determine because it is derived from the production activity of the economy and because the sources of changes in these derived demands over time are still far from clear. Furthermore, the observable responses of students to the array of different prices that students pay for higher education are confounded by all manner of pricing policies and changes in these policies over time.

The lessons to be drawn from all of this are as follows: 1) The game of numbers as it is now played produces unreliable projections of the demand for higher education. 2) Some improvements can be achieved by clarifying and analyzing the economic demands in terms of the factors that determine changes in these demands. 3) But this approach is also severely limited because as yet there is no economic theory for determining the changes in the demands for higher education that are derived from our type of economic growth. 4) At best, any long-term projections of the demands for higher education are subject to many unknowns and to much uncertainty. 5) To be prepared to cope with these, it is the better part of wisdom to pay the price of developing flexibility in the institutional structure of higher education and also within colleges and universities so that they will be capable of adapting their activities to new information with regard to demands as it becomes available. 6) Fixed formulas, like the parity formula in agriculture, lead to inflexibility and, over time, to serious distortions, and they should therefore be avoided in planning and financing higher education.

6 *Seeing that Education Is an Investment in Human Capital, the Central Economic Concept in Planning and Financing It Should Be the Rate of Return to Investment*[10] The advantages of this concept are that it has a firm foundation in economic theory, that it is applicable to both private and public allocative decisions, that in practical economic affairs it is widely used and understood, and that it leads to efficient allocations when all investments are made in accordance with the priorities set by the relative rates of return to alternative investment opportunities. Although it is difficult to use this concept as an allocative

10. For an extended treatment of this approach see Chapter 9 of this study.

guide in view of the way in which education is organized, it is the economist's key in solving the problem of allocating resources; the solution is in equalizing the rates by always allocating investment resources in favor of the highest rate of return.

The practical difficulties in using this concept in education are predominantly consequences of a type of organization that is not designed to provide most of the necessary information and that lacks strong incentives to use the available information. Consider the cost of college and university instruction: earnings foregone by students, which are well over half of the real cost, are concealed; the depreciation and the rate of interest on the investment in buildings used for classrooms, laboratories, offices, and library are as a rule also concealed; the cost of university research and of discovering talent is rarely identified and separated from the cost of instruction. It is also true that the price that the student pays for educational services is only remotely related to the real cost of producing them, and therefore private choices by students, however efficient they are privately, are not necessarily efficient socially. Nor can the allocation of public funds to higher education be made socially efficient under circumstances where information on cost is so inadequate. Consider also the returns that accrue to students and society from these educational services: the organization of higher education provides little or no economic information on returns, pecuniary and nonpecuniary, to guide students in making their career choices, not even with regard to the starting salaries of college graduates; foundation and public subsidies are accepted and awarded to students to get them to enter particular fields without regard to the depressing effects of the increase in supply that is thereby induced upon the lifetime earnings of those who are and will be in these fields; there is inadequate information on the effects upon returns of differences in innate ability of students, in their motivations, and of the differences in the effectiveness of college teaching; although these returns are subject to uncertainty, it is not a unique, distinguishing mark because other investments are also subject to uncertainty. In general, colleges and universities and public bodies that provide funds are poorly organized to provide the necessary information on cost and returns or to use whatever information is available.

Meanwhile, economists who have taken a hand in estimating the returns to education have made substantial progress.[11] These estimates and those pertaining to cost have reached the stage where they arc becoming useful allocative guides. But so far the returns from the nonpecuniary satisfactions that accrue to students have not been reckoned. Nor are the estimates of social returns in good repair.

Turning back to the rate of return as the central concept, the alternative investment opportunities are of course numerous, not only between human and material capital but within each of these two sets. Is there evidence that private educational choices are privately efficient; that is, do private rates of return to education tend 1) to be equal among educational options and 2) to be comparable to private rates of return to other private investments? The evidence implies inefficiencies. To illustrate, consider the available estimates on alternatives within education. In terms of equalizing the rates of return, elementary and secondary schooling appear to have priority. All of the estimates known to me show the highest private rates of return

11. See especially, Gary S. Becker, *Human Capital* (New York: National Bureau of Economic Research, 1964), and Giora Hanoch, "Personal Earnings and Investment in Schooling" (Unpublished doctoral dissertation in economics, University of Chicago, 1965).

Table 10.1—Estimates of Private Rates of Return, United States

	High School[1] Graduates: White Males after Personal Taxes (percent)	College[2] Graduates: White Males after Personal Taxes (percent)	Corporate[3] Manufacturing Firms: after Profit but before Personal Taxes (percent)	U.S. Private[4] Domestic Economy: Implicit Rate of Return after Profit Taxes but before Personal Taxes (percent)
1939	16	14.5		
1949	20	13.+	7.0 (for period 1947-57)	12.6
1956	25	12.4		14.4 (1955-56)
1958	28	14.8		12.3 (1957-58)
1959	Slightly higher than in 1958			9.7
1961	Slightly higher than in 1958			11.2 (1960-61)
1963-65				13.3

1. Gary S. Becker, *Human Capital* (New York: National Bureau of Economic Research, 1964), Table 14, p. 128.

2. *Ibid.*

3. *Ibid.;* here Becker draws on a study by George J. Stigler, see p. 115 and footnote 2.

4. Dale W. Jorgenson and Zvi Griliches, "The Explanation of Productivity Change," *The Review of Economic Studies,* 34 (July, 1967), Table 6, p. 268.

to elementary schooling,[12] and we need to remind ourselves that there are still some children who are not completing the elementary grades. What is more important is the underinvestment in the quality of elementary schooling, especially in many rural areas.[13] While the private rate of return to investment resources entering into high school education is not as high as that for elementary schooling, it nevertheless appears to be about twice as high as that indicated for private investment in completing college. In Table 10.1, the private rates of return to white males after

12. For a word of caution in terms of relationships of these estimates, see Chapter 7.

13. See my "Underinvestment in the Quality of Schooling: The Rural Farm Areas," *Increasing Understanding of Public Problems and Policies* (Chicago: Farm Foundation, 1964), pp. 12-34; also, Finis Welch, "The Determinants of the Return to Schooling in Rural Farm Areas, 1959" (Unpublished doctoral dissertation in economics, University of Chicago, 1966).

personal taxes, in 1958, are 28 percent for high school graduates and 14.8 percent for college graduates. Thus, in allocating resources within education with a view to equalizing the rates of return, the implication is that elementary and secondary schooling appears to be subject to underinvestment relative to higher education. Nevertheless, comparing columns (2) and (4) in Table 10.1, the private rates of return to white male college graduates after personal taxes, without any allowance for the private satisfactions that accrue to students, are on a par with the private implicit rates of return to material capital *before personal taxes* on the income from this capital.

7 *Education Changes the Personal Distribution of Income* The general extension of education and the additional earnings from these forms of human capital have probably been a major factor during recent decades in changing the distribution of personal income. Not only has the supply of educational opportunities increased markedly over time, but the inequality in the differences in the supply of these opportunities has, without doubt, been reduced in elementary and secondary schooling. The differences in the innate capacity of individuals to benefit from investment in education probably remains unchanged for the population as a whole, but the distribution of this capacity of those attending college changes over time as the proportion of individuals of particular age classes attending college increases. Human capital is in fact treated as the key to a theory of the personal distribution of personal income in a pioneering study by Gary S. Becker.[14]

Higher education is certainly *not neutral* in its personal

14. Gary S. Becker, *Human Capital and the Personal Distribution of Income: An Analytical Approach* (Ann Arbor: University of Michigan, 1967).

income distribution effects; some individuals and families undoubtedly gain future income streams partly at the expense of others. Whether it is in general regressive or progressive depends on the distribution of the personal costs and personal benefits of higher education. There are all too few hard facts on this issue.[15]

In clarifying public policy choices, it is necessary to distinguish between the objective of economic efficiency and that of reducing the inequality in the personal distribution of income. There are circumstances when a particular policy will advance the economy toward both objectives; for example, when there is excessive unemployment, a fiscal-monetary policy that reduces such unemployment would normally contribute to both objectives. Similarly, when there is an underinvestment in elementary schooling—that is, a high rate of return to additional investment in such schooling—a policy to invest more in universal elementary schooling of high quality contributes both to economic efficiency and to reducing the inequality in personal income. But under other circumstances, the attainment of one of these objectives is in part at the expense of the other. At this point, the rating of social values underlying such policy choices enters.

I assume that it is not necessary to belabor the fact that economic efficiency rates high among the social values of

15. For a general approach to the many factors entering here, see Mary Jean Bowman and C. Arnold Anderson, "Distributional Effects of Educational Programs," *Income Distribution Analysis*, Series 23 (Raleigh, N.C.: Agricultural Policy Institute, North Carolina State University, December, 1966), pp. 177-214. For hard facts, see W. Lee Hansen and Burton A. Weisbrod, "The Distribution of Cost and Direct Benefits of Public Higher Education: The Case of California," *Journal of Human Resources*, 4 (Spring, 1969), pp. 176-191; also, by same authors, *Benefits, Costs, and Finance of Public Higher Education*, Markham Pub. Co., Chicago, 1969.

our society.[16] This assumption is implicit in my formulation of the six propositions already considered; the principal implications derived from them all pertain to economic efficiency. But how high a social value does our society place on reducing the inequality in personal income? The rating of this social value is not so clear as that which is socially assigned to economic efficiency. Nevertheless, there are strong indications that it also is an important social value. I shall proceed on the assumption that there is a social preference for less inequality in the personal distribution of income than that which prevails presently. Moreover, I shall assume that this social preference is such that society is prepared, should it be necessary, to forego some economic efficiency to bring about somewhat less inequality in the distribution of personal income. Proceeding on this assumption, it becomes relevant and important to determine what the income distribution effects of higher education are and how they can be altered for the better at the least cost in terms of allocative efficiency.

Although higher education is in all probability far from neutral in its effects on the distribution of personal income, it is surprising how little is actually known about these effects. It could be that the financing of higher education is in general quite regressive. It is plausible that it is regressive because it adds to the value of the human capital of those who attend college relative to those who do not go to college, because it increases the lifetime earnings of college graduates in part at the expense of others, and, closely related, because higher education provides educational services predominantly for students from middle and upper income families, a part of the cost of these educational services being paid for by taxes on poor families, as Hansen

16. See Alec L. Macfie, *Economic Efficiency and Social Welfare* (London: Oxford University Press, 1943).

and Weisbrod show in their study of California. (See note 15.) It appears to be true that a much smaller proportion of the undergraduate students in publicly financed institutions receive financial aid for reasons of their having inadequate income than do undergraduate students in private colleges and universities. In either case, the financing is such that substantial amounts of valuable assets are being transferred by society to a particular intellectually elite set of individuals.

In retrospect, given the type of growth that has characterized our economy and the remarkable increase in the stock of education per worker in the labor force, the gains in elementary and secondary schooling and in higher education taken as a whole have been instrumental, it seems to me, in reducing the inequality in the distribution of personal income. The hypothesis I proposed earlier with regard to this issue[17] continues to be consistent with the evidence thus far available. In terms of the income effects of additional education per worker, this hypothesis is: The rise in the investment in education relative to that invested in nonhuman capital increases total earnings relative to total property income, and property income is distributed much less equally than the earnings of persons from labor. Therefore, investment in schooling reduces the inequality in the distribution of personal income. The hypothesis proposed here is that these patterns of investment are an important part of the explanation of the observed reductions in the distribution of personal income.

Becker and Barry R. Chiswick have been analyzing the effects of schooling on the distribution of personal income. For adult white males and for the states within the United States, they report that "about one-third of the differences in inequality between states is directly explained by school-

17. See Chapter 4 of this study, p. 62.

ing, one-third directly by the residual and the remaining one-third by both together through the positive correlation between them."[18]

In a more recent report, Chiswick gives the following results from his analysis of North-South differences: "The education component . . . can 'explain' half of the North-South differences in income inequality. The proportion is slightly lower for white males and slightly higher for all males."[19] But neither the hypothesis I have advanced nor the evidence on the income effects of schooling from Becker and Chiswick implies that the income effects of higher education per se are progressive rather than regressive.

In developing an analytical approach bringing economic theory to bear on the effects of human capital on the personal distribution of income, Becker's 1967 work is full of promise.[20] His distinction between the "egalitarian" and "elite" views is helpful in clarifying the problem. He identifies the egalitarian view with supply conditions; the objective is to reduce the inequality in the differences in the supply of educational opportunities. The elite view, on the other hand, turns on the demand conditions: the actual investment and earning differences are primarily a consequence of differences in the capacity of individuals to benefit from investment in education and from other forms of human capital. What Becker's analytical approach

18. Gary S. Becker and Barry R. Chiswick, "Education and the Distribution of Earnings," *The American Economic Review*, 56 (May, 1966), p. 368.

19. Barry R. Chiswick, "Human Capital and the Distribution of Personal Income" (Unpublished Ph.D. dissertation in economics, Columbia University), Chapter 3, p. 35. 1967, with assistance from the National Bureau of Economic Research.

20. Gary S. Becker, *Human Capital and the Personal Distribution of Income: An Analytical Approach*," op. cit.

will show when it is applied to higher education is still in the realm of unfinished business. Hansen and Weisbrod, using a cost-benefits approach, show that public higher education in California is highly regressive. (See note 15.)

Searching for Solutions

My list of problems that await solution is indicated by the implications that have been derived from the preceding propositions. Although it is a long list, it consists of two major parts in terms of economic logic. The first part pertains to resources for higher education allocated in accordance with the test of economic efficiency; the second part pertains to allocations that reduce the inequality in the personal distribution of income. Rest assured, I shall not present a national budget for higher education all properly allocated. I shall try, however, to clarify some of the organizational changes that would strengthen the tendency toward a more efficient allocation of resources in the area of higher education.

The purpose of the organizational changes on which I shall concentrate is to improve the possibilities of making optimum allocative decisions pertaining to higher education. The substantive changes relate to *economic incentives* and *information*. The decisions that are dependent on these incentives and the state of information consist of economic decisions by students, college and university administrators, and public (social) bodies. The ideal from an economist's point of view is a form of organization that would assure the necessary incentives coupled with optimum information in allocating investment resources to higher education in accordance with the relative rates of return to alternative investment opportunities, an organization in which the rate of return is functionally the price at the intercept of the supply of educational services and the demand for them.

But in making these organizational changes, it will be important not to lose sight of the advantages of the existing organization of higher education that are consistent with this ideal. Among them are: 1) in terms of career choices, higher education in the United States offers students many options; 2) in discovering talent, it has in all probability no equal; 3) the process of admitting many students who do not graduate is not necessarily wasteful, especially when they can readily enter the labor force; 4) there is substantial economic complementarity between discovering talent and instruction and between research and instruction despite the common view to the contrary; 5) although it is obvious that colleges and universities tend to serve an elite measured in terms of intellectual capacity to benefit, they provide places for a much larger proportion of college-age youth than is traditionally served, for example, in western Europe; 6) no college or university has a monopoly on the supply of these educational services —on the contrary, there are many more institutions than would be necessary to assure competition if it were strictly a business sector; 7) as suppliers of these services, colleges and universities show some tendency to adjust to changes in demand, although this tendency could be substantially strengthened; 8) last, and very important, there is much more economic competition within higher education and between it and other sectors of the economy than meets the eye. Colleges and universities purchase virtually all of their instructional inputs in competitive markets. Most of the budget is for faculty, and the job market for their services in this country is actively competitive among colleges and universities and between them and government. Business, too, bids for many of these skills. The range in salaries is subject to some constraints, partly corrected by adjustments in work arrangements. The earnings foregone by students are also determined in a competitive job market. Surely it would be shortsighted to overlook or impair these advantages in our quest to improve the possibilities of making optimum allocative decisions.

How then can we strengthen the tendency toward a more efficient allocation of resources? The required changes in organization to achieve this objective are fundamentally of two parts; namely, better economic incentives and better information for those who make the allocative decisions.

But who should make these allocative decisions? Who is best qualified? There are those who contend that students and their families are best qualified. To support this contention, they appeal to consumer sovereignty and to private self-interest for privately efficient investment in education. Others contend that there are external economies or social benefits that accrue not to the student but to others in society and that these decisions can best be made by public or other social bodies. Those who know and administer the affairs of our colleges and universities see the importance of academic entrepreneurship in managing this complex set of activities, and it can be argued that they are best qualified.

How much truth is there in each of these contentions? Is it all with one and none in the others?

On Behalf of Student Sovereignty   The key to student sovereignty is the private self-interest of students, which provides the necessary economic rationale. Student self-interest is sufficient to bring about an efficient allocation of investment resources to education under the following conditions: 1) competition in producing educational services along with efficient prices of these services, 2) students acquiring optimal information, 3) an efficient capital market serving students, and 4) no social benefits (losses) from higher education.

A clear view of the gains to be had from hitching higher education to the private self-interest of students is blurred by arguments about the underlying conditions. But surely competitive pricing of educational services is in the realm of possibilities. Student loans from public and private sources can be devised to supply the necessary capital. How to reckon the social benefits (losses) of higher education is much more difficult. But if student sovereignty has an Achilles' heel, it is in the domain of information, a long-standing controversial issue as unsettled today as it was when classical economists divided on this issue.[21]

In enlarging the scope and improving the performance of student sovereignty in allocating resources to higher education, the gaps in information and the distortions in incentives really matter. On earnings foregone students are well informed, but on their capabilities as students they are in doubt. With regard to the benefits that will accrue to them, the state of information is far from optimum. But much worse still is the lack of information on the differences in the quality of the educational services of different colleges and universities. Nowhere are students confronted by prices for these services that are equal to the real cost of producing them, and, therefore, the prices to which they respond are not efficient prices. As a consequence, no matter how efficient students are privately in their decisions, from the point of view of the economy as a whole, the allocation of resources to higher education will not be efficient.

On Reckoning Social Benefits (*Losses*) When this box is opened, we are in trouble, for there is so little agreement

21. E. G. West, "Private versus Public Education," *The Journal of Political Economy*, 72 (October, 1964), pp. 465-475.

on what it contains. It is hard to distinguish between fact and fiction because the task of specifying and measuring these benefits has been grossly neglected. No wonder that claims and counterclaims are the order of the day. Most of us have a vested interest in higher education, which is hard on objectivity. We are prone to lay claim to most of the advance in knowledge from which the social benefits are undoubtedly large. University research and instruction are, as a rule, joint products; at the doctoral level, graduate instruction and research are highly complementary. Are there identifiable social benefits from instruction that do not accrue to the college student from his private investment in education? It is plausible that having neighbors who are educated gives a family with such neighbors some positive satisfactions. It is also plausible that having co-workers who are educated is a source of additional satisfactions. It has been argued that parts of our public administration—namely, individuals coping with our "income tax forms"—give rise to an administrative social benefit. But it is also plausible that the private benefits of education accruing to college students leave some other persons worse off. It is argued that some elementary school teachers *favor* the children from homes with (college) educated parents and that this favoritism leaves other children worse off. It is also alleged that in buying and selling homes some educated families act to exclude uneducated families from acquiring property (homes) in their particular neighborhood.

But it is all too convenient to engage in double counting. Education, no doubt, increases the mobility of a labor force, but the benefits in moving to take advantage of better job opportunities are predominantly, if not wholly, private benefits. Educated labor has access to more of the relevant economic information than uneducated labor;

but here too the benefits from this advantage presumably accrue to the persons who have the education. The cultural component embodied in higher education is the source of another benefit which invites double counting. There is also a tendency to claim that higher education makes for better citizens and for a better political democracy. It could be, but our belief with respect to these benefits is a matter of faith. It is not obvious that the political self-interest of college graduates results either in more responsible citizenship or in a more perfect government than the self-interest, say, of high school graduates.

To the extent that there are benefits that accrue to persons other than to the student acquiring the education, there could be underinvestment in higher education, regardless of how efficient students are privately in their investment in education. But there is an important set here that does not qualify; namely, those benefits accruing to the student that make the private investment at least as good as investment in terms of the rate of return as that to alternative investment opportunities. Under these circumstances, presumably, privately efficient investment by students would suffice to bring forth the required education and assure whatever benefits might accrue to others, as was true in investing in physical capital in the case of Henry Ford and his very profitable Model T.

Suppose, however, that there are some potential college students who would not benefit enough privately to warrant the investment privately and that there were some social benefits that were sufficient when added to the benefits accruing to the student privately to raise the (social) rate of return sufficiently to make it a good investment by the standard set by the priorities of the relative rates of return to alternative investment opportunities—then, under these circumstances, some underinvestment in higher education at the margin would be implied.

It follows, of course, that if there were no such social benefits, this bit of economic logic would be wholly empty. Thus we are back to a question of fact; namely, are there any such benefits that can be identified and that are subject to measurement?

On Academic Entrepreneurship   In terms of managerial decisions, the complexity of the modern university places an extraordinary burden on its administrators. But by what economic test are their decisions to be judged? The market test is severely circumscribed by the constraints placed on student sovereignty. Endowment income, private gifts, and public funds confound any economic test of an efficient allocation of resources. Innovation should be rewarded, but where are the incentives to innovate? Surely under the dynamic conditions that now characterize higher education, academic entrepreneurship should be given a vastly better opportunity than is presently possible to allocate resources efficiently.

These observations with respect to student sovereignty, social benefits, and academic entrepreneurship would appear to lend support to the following organizational changes in higher education:

With Respect to the Private Decision Domain of Students   In providing economic incentives that would be allocatively efficient, the ideal price to students for the educational services they acquire should be neither more nor less than the real cost of producing these services. But much of the argument on the differences between private and public tuitions is beside the point. Equalization of tuitions would merely replace one type of price distortion by another type because of the marked differences in the quality and real cost of the educational services that college and universities supply.

This important organizational change implies, however, several complements: 1) that there be developed a capital market that would provide funds to students so they could invest in themselves, which would call for large increases in funds for public loans to students in view of the limitations of the private capital market, 2) that a program of private and public subsidies would be required to finance those and only those qualified students who for welfare or social efficiency reasons should attend college but who privately would not enroll even if there were student loans, and 3) that although the improvement in information that is implicit in the change in pricing set forth above would be very substantial, much more would have to be spent in moving to an optimum in producing and distributing the other types of information already referred to.

On the Social Benefits of Higher Education   In producing these education services, the required organizational changes pertaining to incentives and information are not easy to determine. Consider the problem that arises in planning and financing these components so that public and social bodies would become efficient in allocating investment resources for these purposes. What are the pertinent educational activities that render social benefits? University research is in substantial part one of them. So is a part of the activity pertaining to the discovery of talent. Let me elaborate briefly on why this may be true. My conception of the cost and returns pertaining to the *discovery of talent* could qualify here. There are many colleges that admit at least two freshmen for every one who will survive to graduation. If these colleges charged full costs, I would assume that this ratio of entering freshmen to graduating seniors would decline sharply. Presently, that half of the

entering freshmen who discover that they lack the capabilities and motivation to complete college drop out and
enter the labor market, benefiting sufficiently from the year
or more they spent in college to have made their private
investment in that amount of college work a good investment privately, although when the subsidy entering into
their instruction is taken into account, it was all told a
poor investment. But suppose now that out of the entering freshmen who would not have sought admission at full
costs, there were a substantial number of students (say,
a tenth of the seniors who complete college) who did not
know they had the necessary capabilities. These discovered students could (should) pay full cost; but they would
not have become college educated had it not been for the
extra cost of the discovery process. It would be a matter
for public policy to decide whether this extra cost was
worthwhile. A part of instruction may also belong here;
but the instruction that accrues wholly to the benefit of
students is excluded. It must be admitted that it is exceedingly difficult to specify the particular types of information
and the nature of the incentives that would prove strong
and clear in attaining these purposes. Here we have one
of the unsolved problems in planning and financing higher
education.

On College and University Administrators Academic
entrepreneurship can be made much less frustrating and
at the same time much more efficient once the private decision-making domain of students is subjected to the constraints of a pricing policy, complemented by adequate
student loans and by subsidies to attain the particular welfare and social efficiency purposes set forth above. But
more than this would be required in terms of information
and incentives. The value of the time of students would
have to enter; it is, however, easy to measure earnings

foregone. The value of the time of the faculty is also readily available information, in view of the open market competition for their services; but the internal organization of colleges and universities is anything but efficient in allocating their services within the institution. The most important informational component that is lacking is the *value added* by the instruction, by research, and by the activity I have called "discovering talent." But if we put our minds to it, I am sure we could do a good deal in determining the amount of value added by each of the different activities and proceed from there to internal organizational changes that would provide incentives to take advantage of such information in our academic entrepreneurial and management endeavors.

11 On Priorities in Analysis

THE mainstream of the analytical work on human capital pertains to the economic properties of education. I shall begin with a comment on the advances in this work coupled with some observations on its apparent shortcomings; I shall then consider briefly aspects of the aggregation problem in the treatment of human capital, whatever its source, in analyzing costs and returns, economic growth, migration, educated labor in a production function, and in explaining the personal distribution of income. Third, I shall direct attention to some major omissions.

As Economic Knowledge

The advances are mainly a joint product of theoretical and empirical analysis. In theory they have come predominantly from Gary S. Becker: his distinction between specific and general human capital forms; his recognition of the importance of earnings foregone in an array of economic activities and the development of a theory for the allocation of time to cope with earnings foregone; and, most recently, his rediscovery of the production activities of the household[1]—for example, in the formation of a substantial part of human capital.

Clearly, in economic thinking and measuring, the concept of human capital is a source of many new analytical insights with respect to particular classes of economic behavior. Seminal economic properties are being attributed to human capital. Mark Blaug, in his *Economics of Education*,[2] reviews the progress in this area[3] and then presents the major papers that have been published. His annotated bibliography lists literally several hundred contributions.[4] In determining the role of human capital in the comparative advantage of nations, we turn to Peter B. Kenen.[5] Human capital has received even more attention in analyzing international migration as is clear from the survey by Anthony Scott.[6] The findings of Anne O. Krueger,[7] in her pioneering paper on factor endowments and per capita income, attribute an important new dimen-

1. See Margaret G. Reid, *Economics of Household Production* (New York: John Wiley & Sons, 1934).

2. Mark Blaug (ed.), *Économics of Education* (Middlesex, Eng., and Baltimore, Md.: Penguin Books, 1968).

3. *Ibid.*, "Introduction," pp. 7-9.

4. Mark Blaug, *Economics of Education: A Selected Annotated Bibliography* (Oxford, Eng., and New York: Pergamon Press, 1966). Also see more recent mimeographed supplements by Blaug bringing this bibliography up to date.

5. Peter B. Kenen, "Skills, Human Capital and Comparative Advantage" (Paper presented at the Universities-NBER Conference on Research in Income and Wealth, Madison, Wis., November 15-16, 1968).

6. Anthony Scott, "The Human Capital Approach to International Migration" (Paper presented at the Universities-NBER Conference on Research in Income and Wealth, Madison, Wis., November 15-16, 1968).

7. Anne O. Krueger, "Factor Endowments and *per Capita* Income Differences among Countries," *The Economic Journal*, 78 (September, 1968), pp. 641-659.

sion to human capital. Her conclusion is "that the difference in human resources between the United States and the less-developed countries accounts for more of the difference in *per capita* income than all of the other factors combined."[8] While we await confirmation of her findings, it behooves us to begin thinking through the radical economic implications of her conclusions for economic development. In explaining the personal distribution of income, first Jacob Mincer,[9] and more recently, Becker[10] and Barry R. Chiswick,[11] as indicated in the previous chapter, have turned to human capital. Advances in economic knowledge pertaining to internal migration keyed to education and to costs of migrating as a form of human capital are also impressive (Larry A. Sjaastad,[12] Mary Jean Bowman and Robert Myers,[13] Aba Schwartz,[14] and others). Needless to

8. *Ibid.*, p. 658.

9. Jacob Mincer, "Investment in Human Capital and Personal Income Distribution," *The Journal of Political Economy*, 66 (August, 1958), pp. 281-302.

10. Gary S. Becker, *Human Capital and the Personal Distribution of Income: An Analytical Approach* (Ann Arbor: University of Michigan, 1967).

11. Barry R. Chiswick, "Human Capital and the Distribution of Personal Income" (Unpublished doctoral dissertation in economics, Columbia University, 1967).

12. Larry A. Sjaastad, "Income and Migration in the United States" (Unpublished doctoral dissertation in economics, University of Chicago, 1961) and "The Costs and Returns of Human Migration," *The Journal of Political Economy* (Supplement), 70 (October, 1962), pp. 80-93.

13. Mary Jean Bowman and Robert Myers, "Schooling Experience and Gain and Losses in Human Capital through Migration," *Journal of the American Statistical Association*, 62 (September, 1967), pp. 875-898.

14. Aba Schwartz, "Migration and Life Time Earnings in the U.S." (Unpublished doctoral dissertation in economics, University of Chicago, 1968).

say, there are also other classes of economic behavior and approaches that stem from human capital.

But when we turn to the other side of the coin of these discoveries, there are growing pains, omissions, and a generation gap between those who espouse human capital and those who guard the establishment. Although the guardians of capital theory and economic growth theory may be defending a weak fort, its walls have not come tumbling down.

The beauty of accounting and discounting is that we can take the cost of education or we can transform the earnings from education and call it human capital. But this acquired beauty only conceals the difference between them where there is economic growth. Then, too, the fine art of capital aggregation hides the key to the economic information that makes for economic growth. The aggregation of human capital from education is no exception. As an input, it is well behaved in a production function and it contributes to the output, thus adding to our confidence that educated labor matters in production. But it does not tell us whether all or only a part of this education is worthwhile. Studies of international migration have not been designed to determine whether a well-behaved international market for particular high skills is emerging. The going prices for high skills are not explicit. Nor has the introduction of human capital in analyzing international trade revealed the effects that trade has upon the prices of high skills. Then, too, we consider only a part of education and find it convenient to neglect other parts, notably the large investment in the education of women. By concentrating on education, we are in danger of losing sight of other sources of human capital and, not seeing their contributions, credit some of them to education.

Aggregation Ambiguities

It will not do to continue to bypass the ambiguities of capital theory or of capital in economic growth models because human capital as a part of it is subject to the same ambiguities. The different faces of capital, both theoretically and empirically, lack analytical integrity. What they tell us about economic growth, which is a dynamic process, are inconsistent stories. As the alternative investment opportunities change over time, it alters the difference between the factor cost of a particular form of capital and the discounted value of the stream of services that it renders. But worse still is the capital homogeneity assumption underlying capital theory, and the aggregation of capital in economic growth models. As John Hicks[15] would have it, capital homogeneity is the disaster of capital theory. This assumption is demonstrably inappropriate in analyzing economic growth in a dynamic world that is afloat on capital inequalities whether the capital aggregation is in terms of factor costs or in terms of the discounted value of the lifetime services of its many parts. Nor would a catalogue of all existing models prove that these inequalities are equals. But why try to square the circle? *If we were unable to observe these inequalities, we would have to invent them because they are the mainspring of economic growth.* They are the mainspring because they are the compelling economic force of growth. Thus, what is interesting and what matters in economic growth is concealed by capital aggregation.

One of the major advances of recent years in economic knowledge is the approximate solution of the problem of

15. John Hicks, *Capital and Growth* (Oxford, Eng.: Oxford University Press, 1965), Chapter 3.

the residual. Dale W. Jorgenson and Zvi Griliches have shown us a way of explaining productivity change.[16] The improvement in the quality of labor is an important part of the explanation, and this part is a consequence of investment in human agents, restricted in their empirical work to education. A decade ago, the then growing awareness of investment in human capital followed the observed rise in the quality of labor, and now we have fortified the quality approach in explaining productivity change. The improvements in the quality of nonhuman capital have also been large, perhaps a good deal larger than the best available estimates indicate. But the investment activities that account for this part of the additional quality have not been adequately clarified. In large measure, these activities pertain to advances in scientific and technological knowledge, advances that are truly, in some ultimate sense, a consequence of investment in the scientific skills of man.

Now that we have disposed of the residual, where do we go from here? Clearly, so it seems to me, the real unfinished business is to reckon the costs of and returns to each of these quality components along with the traditional components. But it cannot be done with the family of growth models that presently dominate the literature in economics. These models, including capital theory, begin with the wrong questions for the purpose at hand. What we want to know are the relative rates of return to investment opportunities and what determines the change in the patterns of these rates over time. To get on with this analytical task we must build models that will reveal the very inequalities that we now conceal and proceed to an ex-

16. Dale W. Jorgenson and Zvi Griliches, "The Explanation of Productivity Change," *The Review of Economic Studies*, 34 (July, 1967), pp. 249-283. The references listed in this paper cover the recent relevant literature.

planation of why they occur and why they persist under particular dynamic conditions. The solution obviously is not in the art of producing ever larger capital aggregates.

The growth problem, in terms of economic decisions, requires an investment approach to determine the allocation of investment resources in accordance with the priorities set by the relative rates of return on alternative investment opportunities. It is applicable not only to private decisions but also to public decisions guided by economic planning. The production and distribution of public goods (services) are a necessary part of the process; for example, the investment in research where the fruits of it do not accrue to the researcher or his financial sponsor but are captured by many producers and consumers. Thus we move toward Harry G. Johnson's "generalized capital accumulation approach."[17]

While this approach may be paved with good economic logic, it is in fact a rough road with many detours. For particular investments, and there are many such in the domain of human capital, the value of the resource added (services rendered) is exceedingly hard to come by. It is all too convenient to leave the hard ones out; yet each and every omission falsifies the true picture of the full range of alternative investment opportunities. In analyzing education, we cling to differential earnings and leave aside differential satisfactions with no more than a pious acknowledgment that they exist. Another rough part of this road is the determination of the investment sources and the price of each. The facile assumption of a well-behaved capital market serving the formation of human capital is, I am sure, far from true. When it comes to private invest-

17. Harry G. Johnson, "Toward a Generalized Capital Accumulation Approach to Economic Development," *The Residual Factor and Economic Growth* (Paris: OECD, 1964), pp. 219-227.

ment in human capital, poor people are subject to a great deal of capital rationing. Bruce L. Gardner's analysis of farm family income inequalities in the United States suggests that neither schooling nor migration has been a solution because of the inability of these poor people to respond to shifts in the structure of demand for skills by migrating or acquiring additional skills.[18] The explanation, so it seems to me, is to be found primarily in capital rationing.

Some Omissions

Let me turn to some major omissions in the work on education, in terms of human capital. If one were to judge from the work that is being done, the conclusion would be that human capital is the unique property of the male population, that the only services rendered by it are earnings, that the instructional activities of the educational enterprise are the only source of the educational capital produced by formal education, that the response to changes in educational investment opportunities is restricted to the private decisions of students or their parents, and that advances in knowledge are not altering the quality and value of instruction. There is enough substance to this image of what is being done to be troubled by the implications.

If it is true that investment in human beings is only for males, we would do well to drop the term "human capital" and replace it with "male capital." It would serve notice that human capital is sex-specific! Despite all of the schooling of females and other expenditures on them, they appear to be of no account in the accounting of human capital.

18. Bruce L. Gardner, "An Analysis of U.S. Farm Family Income Inequality, 1950-1960" (Unpublished doctoral dissertation in economics, University of Chicago, 1968).

If females are capital-free, in view of all that is spent on them, we are in real trouble analytically, unless we can show that it is purely for current consumption. There is no way of hiding the fact that females attend elementary and high school to the same extent as males and probably perform a bit better than males. In college attendance they fall behind somewhat; of the 4.9 million students enrolled, October, 1966, about two-fifths were women. Even so, in terms of median years of school completed, of all persons 25 years of age and older in the United States, females are ahead of males slightly, and the difference in favor of females has been increasing over time.[19] Surely, it cannot be denied that the factor costs of all this schooling of females is real and large. Nor is it plausible that all of these direct and indirect costs are only for current consumption. The investment component must be large. But if there is little to show for it, how do we patch up the economic behavioral assumption underlying the investment in education?

Mincer[20] and Becker[21] have each devoted a couple of pages to women. Mincer found that on-the-job training is not for women. Becker observes that the rate of return to females college graduates may not be lower than for males "because direct costs are somewhat lower and opportunity costs are much lower for women."[22] But differential earnings are a small part of the story. The two main reasons for the failure to get at the returns to schooling of women are, so it seems to me, 1) concealment by aggrega-

19. *Statistical Abstract of the United States, 1965*, U.S. Bureau of Census, Table 147, p. 112.

20. Jacob Mincer, "On-the-Job Training: Costs, Returns and Some Implications," *The Journal of Political Economy* (Supplement), 70 (October, 1962), pp. 66-68.

21. Gary S. Becker, *Human Capital* (New York: National Bureau of Economic Research, 1964), pp. 100-102.

22. *Ibid*.

tion and 2) the lack of any accounting of the differential satisfactions that correspond with the differentials in schooling.

There are many puzzles about the economic behavior of women that can be resolved once their human capital is taken into account. Young females leave the better parts of agriculture more readily than young males; these females have a schooling advantage, and they are not held back by any specific on-the-farm training as are males. The explanation of the preponderance of women in most Negro colleges before school integration is to be found in the differences between the job opportunities open to Negro women and Negro men graduates. At a more general level, there is the slow, yet real, economic emancipation of women. It may be viewed as a consequence of growth and affluence. But it is also true that a part of this growth and increase in family income is some function of the rise in the education of women, much more than is revealed by the increasing participation of women in the labor force. At the micro level of the household, there is the shift from household work to work for pay; while a part of the explanation is undoubtedly the relative decline in the price of the services rendered by consumer durables, an important part is a consequence of the rise in the value of the time of women, which in turn is in large measure the result of the education of women.

Another major component that is omitted in our work is the human capital represented by human agents without any education or by children before they enter upon schooling. The distinction between people with some schooling and those with none, educated labor versus raw labor, is a useful distinction for some analytical purposes as Finis Welch has shown.[23] But children before they are old

23. Finis Welch, "The Determinants of the Return to Schooling

enough to attend school are also a form of human capital. I find it hard to believe that there is no economic rationality in the acquisition of this form of human capital. Surely parents derive satisfactions from their children; in traditional societies children provide old age security for their parents, a substitute for retirement "bonds." But the acquisition of children has its price. An approach that treats the production of children, viewed as human capital, in all probability will tell us a great deal about the economics of family planning.[24] In determining the costs of children, it is already clear that the level of schooling of women and changes in job opportunities for women, or, more generally, the economic emancipation of women, and the required school attendance of children, whether cultural or legal, are among the important cost factors.

My conclusions are two: First, there is a class of research, which I have not discussed, where the very idea of reckoning priorities violates the essence of the process of discovery. It is not possible to reckon priorities for it because the problem to be solved is one of the unknowns awaiting to be discovered. I have already commented on the original theoretical analysis of investment in human capital by Becker,[25] his pursuit of the many implications of

in Rural Farm Areas, 1959" (Unpublished doctoral dissertation in economics, University of Chicago, 1966).

24. T. Paul Schultz, "An Economic Model of Family Planning and Fertility," *Journal of Political Economy*, 77 (March-April, 1969); also *A Family Planning Hypothesis and Some Empirical Evidence from Puerto Rico* (Santa Monica, Calif.: The Rand Corporation, M-5405, November, 1967); "An Economic Perspective on Population Growth," National Academy of Sciences Study on the Consequences of Population Change and Their Policy Implications, October, 1969.

25. Gary S. Becker, "Investment in Human Capital: A Theoretical Analysis," *The Journal of Political Economy* (Supplement), 70 (October, 1962), pp. 9-49.

earnings foregone, and his theory of the allocation of time.[26] I find it intuitively plausible that advances pertaining to this part will come largely from micro-analysis, mainly, in response to puzzles and paradoxes revealed by economic data; for example, Lester G. Telser's modification of specific human capital and its formation by firms in his search for the determinants of the differences in the rates of return in manufacturing.[27] Thinking in terms of the activities of the household, it may prove especially rewarding in coping with human capital formation by the family to approach it as a part of the production activities of the household and, also, in getting at the satisfactions that it renders to the family in consumption.[28] The differences in the motivation of students in their school work associated with the differences in job market discrimination following the approach of Welch is another case in point.[29]

Second, a good deal can be said for a reckoning of priorities. The conclusions from this limited endeavor are as follows: 1) As a device for preliminary exploration, it is not wrong to use national aggregates to determine the costs and returns to higher education or to secondary schooling, or to ascertain the amount of human capital in commodities entering into international trade, or to determine the amount of human capital that highly skilled people who

26. Gary S. Becker, "A Theory of the Allocation of Time," *The Economic Journal*, 75 (September, 1965), pp. 493-517.

27. Lester G. Telser, "Some Determinants of the Rates of Return in Manufacturing" (Unpublished paper, Department of Economics, University of Chicago, September, 1968).

28. My reading of an unpublished paper by Gary S. Becker modifying consumption theory is an approach along these lines.

29. Finis Welch, "Labor-Market Discrimination: An Interpretation of Income Differences in the Rural South," *The Journal of Political Economy*, 75 (June, 1967), pp. 225-240.

migrate possess, or to ascertain the economic values of schooling as a quality input in a national production function, *provided these endeavors are viewed as exploratory*. In fact, it has been a necessary first step in discovering whether or not there is any economic value in education or in other forms of human capital. 2) Now that it is established that human capital is both real and important, the question becomes: Where does it stand within the full range of alternative investment opportunities? In entering upon this analytical task, we are beset by the ambiguities of capital theory and of capital, including human capital aggregates, in economic growth models and in national accounting of change in the quality of labor. Also, it is true that the art of capital aggregation conceals a critical part of the information that we must have to understand and explain the dynamics of economic growth. 3) An investment approach, not only to the many different forms of human capital but also to research activities and to traditional nonhuman forms, is in principle the next analytical step. 4) In the work that has been done, the omission of human capital in females and in children before they enter upon schooling should give us pause. But this troublesome omission, so it seems to me, can be taken on, and the reward in terms of additional knowledge is likely to be large.

12 The Allocation of Resources to Research[1]

Education has had the leading role in the formation of human capital in the preceding scenes. In the next scene research is the principal actor, while education plays a supporting role. Research activities are an integral part of the economy, firmly established and enjoying a growth rate that puts the growth of GNP to shame. There are all manner of research enterprises and many of the newcomers are growing like Topsy. Only a few of them have been around long enough to have become mature and sedate in their behavior, as has organized agricultural research. Despite all of the diversity, it is obvious that research has prestige, is expensive, and is influential in acquiring private and public resources. But what is not obvious is the economic value of all of this research. Moreover, there is much confusion in economics on what it is that research

1. I am indebted to Gregory C. Chow, Robert E. Evenson, Zvi Griliches, Yujiro Hayami, Lowell Hardin, Richard R. Nelson, Vernon Ruttan, Larry A. Sjaastad, George Tolley, and Sterling Wortman for comments and suggestions.

contributes to the economy and on how to treat it in economic analysis.

My plan is first to consider the economic attributes of research; this part is devoted mainly to definitions and concepts. I shall then present the factors that determine the demand and supply that explain the behavior of nonprofit research agents. Lastly, I shall advance a number of propositions pertaining to the demand, supply, price, and efficiency of agricultural research and also consider some of the more important implications of these propositions.

Economic Attributes of Research

The weakest link in the analytical chain that connects research to the economy is in the accounting of the value of the contributions of research to the economy. To start the accounting, I shall define research as a specialized activity that requires special skills and facilities that are employed to discover and develop special forms of *new information*,[2] a part of which acquires the properties of economic information. By this definition, such research is an *economic activity* because it requires scarce resources and because it produces something of value. Although there

2. The choice of a well-defined, meaningful concept for the purpose at hand is beset with difficulties. In view of the literature on research, the choice appears to be between "knowledge" and "information." My attempt to gain clarity and precision by defining the term "entity" appropriately for this purpose and substituting it for the other two terms was criticized cogently by Richard R. Nelson and Zvi Griliches. As between the other two terms, I prefer the concept of information because it is subject to fewer ambiguities; the term "knowledge" has all too many different meanings. I also prefer "information" because of the advances in the treatment of the economics of information. See, for instance, George J. Stigler, "The Economics of Information," *The Journal of Political Economy*, 69 (June, 1961), pp. 213-235.

are several subsets of new information depending on the class of research, I shall consider only one of them, namely the new information represented by the advances in science and associated activities. I shall assume that this subset of new information is of two separate parts dependent upon whether it can be appropriated and whether it is of sufficient value to warrant appropriation. The part that is appropriated has, by my definition, the properties of economic information.

The scarce resources that are allocated to this research are readily observable and not difficult to measure. But the value it renders is exceedingly hard to get at. Research renders satisfactions to research workers in professional recognition for discovering new information and in the value they place on such new information for its own sake.[3] There are also some social satisfactions, even national prestige, in winning Nobel Prizes. But this research also produces information that becomes valuable to households, firms, and agencies of government. In general, then, the value of this research[4] is 1) in the satisfactions that accrue to the research workers and society, and 2) in the information that acquires economic properties for which there is a demand from other parts of the economy.

Thus there is room in this formulation of the contributions of research for the pursuit of wholly self-serving research by anyone who believes he has the special skills and who can afford to devote his time to it; for it may be

3. No doubt many scientists (others too) acquire satisfactions from research work per se regardless of whether they are successful in discovering and developing some new information. There are, of course, other classes of work that also render satisfactions to those who do the work.

4. Other classes of "research" not considered here, for instance that pertaining to the fine arts including literature, also may render a "product" that has a value.

worth all of his opportunity cost in terms of the satisfaction it gives him. Then, too, the realized reward of the salaried research worker is his salary plus the satisfactions that accrue to him. Under the assumption of an economic equilibrium and with higher paying alternative work opportunities open to research workers, and even though they would accept less pay employed doing research by an amount equal to the value they place on these satisfactions, they need not accept less pay if they are sufficiently scarce.

There is confusion when it comes to specifying and measuring the economic properties of the new information from research and the value of these properties beyond the satisfactions that accrue directly to researchers and society. Most of the confusion arises out of misconceptions of what it is that this research contributes and what determines the economic value of the part that can be and is appropriated. The process of transforming this part into components that acquire economic value from the demand for them by households, firms, and government agencies, is usually considered as development, and the two are then joined in "research and development." The literature in economics abounds with proxies for the contribution from this research—inventions, patents, know-how, techniques and technology. The dominant proxy in economic growth models is "technological change," and it is presumed to be neither capital nor labor but it is something that may substitute for either of them, or for both. A variant of this proxy is a capital embodiment process.

While inventions and patents have proven useful in empirical analysis,[5] they are only a small part of the story.

5. Jacob Schmookler, *Invention and Economic Growth* (Cambridge, Mass.: Harvard University Press, 1966); Richard R. Nelson (ed.), *The Rate and Direction of Inventive Activity* (Princeton, N.J.: Princeton University Press, 1962), a 635-page conference

In terms of common-sense perceptions, the phrase "technological change" is also useful as a form of shorthand in discussing the dynamics of modern economic growth. But in terms of economic analysis, what is "technological change" at a macro level empirically? As a proxy that is used to explain a part of modern economic growth, it is an economic omnibus with passengers who are not well behaved. It is akin to that old puzzle, the residual. It also is related to the "unexplained" gains in productivity. The view taken here is that, in short, it is subject to serious analytical limitations because of the unequal, dissimilar, and distinct components that account for "technological change." Furthermore, these disparate components imply economic incongruity and incompatibility. The differences in the attributes of the passengers in this omnibus really matter. They are not exclusively techniques or know-how, or even some combination of these two. Consider the new information from research. When it is in a form that it can be appropriated and then acquired and used by households, firms, and government agencies, it is not capital free. On the contrary, at that stage it is always a form of either human or nonhuman capital.

Returning to the subset of new information that is discovered and developed by the class of research under consideration, we must elaborate further.[6] The first step is to distinguish once again between the new information from

---

report of the Universities-National Bureau Committee for Economic Research and the Committee for Economic Growth of the Social Science Research Council; Richard R. Nelson, Merton J. Peck, and Edward D. Kalachek, *Technology, Economic Growth and Public Policy* (Washington, D.C.: The Brookings Institution, 1967), Part 3, "The Invention Industry," pp. 44-65.

6. I have benefited especially from discussions with Zvi Griliches in my endeavor to clarify the critical attributes of this subset of new information for purposes of economic analysis.

this source that is transformable into components which are appropriable and the new information that is not appropriable. The latter consists of new ideas, new scientific and technical concepts, models, and theories. They are assumed to be in a form that is not appropriable, and for this reason it is not possible to "control" their utilization. It follows also that they are, in general, not sufficiently specific to be patented. New information of this type is usually published in scientific and technical journals, and when this has occurred it is in the public domain and thus accessible to anyone.

The new information from this research that is appropriable and of some economic value is of two fundamental parts, namely, 1) that which is transformed into *new skills*,[7]

7. These skills are *new* if and only if they originate from a new advance in science. Whenever such an advance in science is the source of particular new "know-how," the acquisition of it is here defined as a new skill. But it also encompasses new "know-how" and in "knowing where." Thus this concept of new skills includes, for instance, new diagnostic skills on the part of doctors made possible by new information from research, new computer skills from an advance in computer programing, new farming skills in the use of new information with regard to nutrition in feeding farm animals, and new skills entering into household activities when housewives acquire and use new information pertaining to human nutrition. These new skills may be acquired in sundry ways—in school, on the job, or in the home. Farmers may acquire them by learning from reports in farm journals, from talks by extension agents, or from radio and television programs.

I quote with permission a perceptive comment by Robert E. Evenson: ". . . in the use of the term 'new skills' . . . I am reminded of Finis Welch's distinction between 'allocative' ability (and its crucial relationship with information and decoding of information) and the 'worker effects.'" [See my citation of the paper by Richard R. Nelson and E. S. Phelps and the paper by Finis Welch in footnote 20.] "The research that is transformed into human capital is in part information about marginal products of new and old material inputs (and about optimal input combinations such as rules for optimal herbicide application). It is human capabilities of economic value, and when such skills have been acquired, they represent new forms of human capital; and 2) that which is transformed into *new materials*,[8] and when this transformation has been achieved, such materials represent new forms of nonhuman capital.

But why not simply aggregate all of these new skills and new materials in analyzing economic growth? Presumably, such an aggregate could be in terms of the value of the services that they render or in terms of their value as a stock of capital. The answer is that there are some in-

---

dominated by information about new inputs, and I am impressed by the magnitude of the effort devoted to this information and its development and transmittal in agriculture. The rate of generation of new materials largely determines the return to such effort, since diminishing returns set in fast as far as 'old' materials are concerned. This aspect of information seems best captured by Welch's allocative effect. The 'worker effect,' based on manual dexterity and the knowledge of more or less complex rules of machinery operation, building construction, or engine repair is affected in different ways by research. It would seem to depend crucially on the new materials. These may require an increase in the degree of complexity with which production takes place. On the other hand, a reduction in complexity could occur. It may be worthwhile to distinguish between the information associated with new materials (adoption) and old or established material inputs. An important allocative ability is associated with the elements of agricultural production which are non-routine (for routine process only the worker effect is important). Here I am referring to the decisions that must be made when weather disturbances, price changes, machine breakdowns, etc., require knowledge of prices and marginal products for decisions. I would suggest a three-way delineation of your 'skill' term, the worker effect, the allocative effect associated with research that is transformed into new material inputs, and the allocative effect associated with the non-routineness of production."

8. The concept of new materials includes all manner of materials of economic value; for example, new inputs (hybrid seeds), new processes (complex capital goods), and new final commodities (from cake mixes to television sets). They are all forms of nonhuman resources that are appropriable, and there is an economic incentive to appropriate them.

surmountable difficulties in constructing such an aggregate, given the present state of economic analysis. There is, for example, the difficulty of distinguishing between the new skills from the new information under consideration and all other classes of skills, old and new, that are being augmented by investment in human capital. Similarly, there is the distinction between new materials from the new information from this research and all other materials that are increased by capital formation. Even if it were possible to identify the particular skills associated with advances in science, the analytical task of aggregating them is presently not in the realm of what is possible. It is no less true for the new materials under consideration.

With respect to the new information that becomes skills, consider engineers; those who graduate from engineering colleges presently acquire some valuable skills that engineers who graduated two decades ago did not have at the time they completed college.[9] The reason for this difference is primarily a consequence of the advances in engineering information discovered by means of research. Then, too, specialization in engineering has led to an array of different specialties, and the advances in engineering have added additional specialties as well as new skills on the part of old specialties but not necessarily in the same proportions. Moreover, each specialty represents some unique properties in terms of skills that determine the limits of substitution among them. The process of change in skills from the discoveries of research is, obviously, not restricted to engineers. The growing array of technicians in the labor force is proof of the proposition that the advances in science are a source of new skills. It is also evident in the change in skills associated with the advances in the agri-

9. It is of course true, as Richard R. Nelson has noted, that old engineers can also learn new engineering tricks.

cultural sciences and with the agricultural technicians who acquire new skills. The specialized skill that is required to take the new biological materials from biological research and transform them into inputs that have an economic value is an example of this process. In economics, as in engineering, the advances in economics are a source of new, valuable skills. There is room also for new skills from research entering into households, as, for instance, the skills of housewives to use new information pertaining to nutrition. Each of these new skills is a new form of human capital. The interesting economic questions are in the different forms of this capital. Suppose they were aggregated; *it would conceal the demand and supply inequalities of the different skills and thus it would hide precisely the economic information that is required to determine the alternative investment opportunities in skills.*

Consider next the new information that is discovered and developed by this research and then transformed into valuable new materials, either as producer or consumer materials. These materials have only one thing in common: they are new in the sense that they were unknown prior to the research that discovered the new information. But they are far from homogeneous in their economic properties. As consumer goods or as producer goods, they differ with respect to durability, divisibility, and rate of obsolescence. They differ as complements or substitutes in combination with each other and with other items and goods in the economy. Then, too, they differ with respect to the economic information required by households, firms, and government agencies to determine their value. As forms of capital, they are a paradigm of heterogeneity. As economic opportunities, either for consumption or production, it is not sufficient to date them according to vintage.

Some examples may be helpful. New consumer items

may be highly divisible and their utility may be exhausted the day they are purchased, as in the instance of a new cake mix or a new variety of carrots high in vitamin A, whereas consumer durables, such as refrigerators and air conditioners for homes, have a relatively long life. The special properties that determine the productivity of hybrid seeds may be exhausted the first time they are sown,[10] while a mechanical cotton picker may last for a decade. A new producer good may be highly divisible like seeds by the peck, or it may be a large, indivisible plant, such as the new compressors used in producing nitrogen (fertilizer), a single-stream plant that costs several million dollars. It may call for few, if any, additional skills to use it in production, or it may require a corps of engineers with new special skills to use the new process efficiently. The difference in the rates at which these producer goods become obsolete has obvious economic implications. The discovery of decades ago that potassium is a valuable plant nutrient has not been superseded by a new input that would substitute for potassium. But in corn hybrids, additional information from research has led to the improvement and replacement of the earlier varieties by newer ones, an impressive parade of new and better varieties superseding the old. Another attribute pertaining to obsolescence is that there is a class of new biological inputs that are subject to "sudden" obsolescence in their struggle for survival in nature. A new high yielding variety of wheat may be destroyed quite suddenly by an outbreak of a new rust that it is unable to resist. Thus, unless biological research is successful in developing a new strain of wheat that is resistant to this particular race of rust, the yield of wheat cannot be main-

10. The theory of hybridization as scientific information is, of course, not diminished; nor is there any loss of information about the inbred lines that are required to produce hybrid seeds.

tained at its former level. There is, accordingly, a branch of biological research that should be treated as *maintenance research*.[11] The cost of it is the price that must be paid to keep the yield from falling.[12]

Up to this point, I have dealt mainly with definitions and concepts. What is readily visible are research workers who are paid salaries and who require facilities, and there is the obvious fact that research is an expensive activity. Also, increasingly visible, is that research is an organized economic activity, that it is an *endogenous sector* of the economy, and that it is of increasing importance in the dynamics of modern economic growth. Conceptually, organized research is that sector of the economy that discovers and

11. Robert E. Evenson, in "The Contribution of Agricultural Research and Extension to Agricultural Production" (Unpublished doctoral dissertation in economics, University of Chicago, 1968), introduces this concept of maintenance research.

12. To see this attribute of biological research in biological terms, I draw upon an unpublished paper by Dr. A. H. Moseman, "Agricultural Research Institutes in the Developing Countries," Agricultural Development Council, New York, presented at Chicago, November 28, 1968:

The serious outbreak of Race 15-B of stem rust of wheat destroyed 65-75 percent of the durum wheat crop in the United States in 1953 and 1954; it was then brought under control.

The oat diseases from 1943 to 1953, caused by *Helminthosporeum septoria* and the new races of crown and stem rust, brought down the yield of oats.

The new virulent form of bunt in the Pacific Northwest resulted in a sharp increase in "smutty" wheat in the early fifties.

In tobacco in the Carolinas and Kentucky there were the losses from black shank disease.

In the western range lands, the spread of the poisonous weed "Halogeton" took its toll.

Dr. Moseman adds to this list of one-time serious threats to output that were brought under control by biological research the outbreaks of green bugs or aphids on small grains, corn root worms, cereal leaf beetles, Mexican fruit fly, and the eradication of the screwworm, which had caused heavy losses in livestock production in parts of the United States.

develops primarily new forms of information that are then transformed into new skills and new materials, a transformation that sets the stage for the formation of particular new classes of human and nonhuman capital.

As an economic sector, all research activities in terms of costs and returns, private and social, can be classified as follows: 1) research that is undertaken by firms *for profit*, and 2) research that is financed and administered by public and private agencies *not for profit*. The distinction in terms of economic incentives and behavior between these two classes of research enterprises is essential for the purpose of economic analysis. The fundamental economic logic for this distinction is firmly established.[13] It depends on who captures the benefits from research.[14] If all of the benefits accrue to those who pay the cost of the research, profit-oriented firms (persons) under competition presumably would arrive at a general optimum (private and social) by equating marginal costs and marginal returns. If, however, not all of these benefits accrue to these firms (persons), they would equate marginal cost only to the point where the marginal returns that they can capture are equalized. Since there is a class of research whose benefits, in whole or in part, are widely diffused and end up ultimately as a *consumer surplus*, it is necessary to "socialize"[15] this part of research in order to arrive at a general economic optimum.

Both of these classes of research enterprises have become important subsectors of the research sector. In the United

13. See Richard R. Nelson, "The Simple Economics of Basic Scientific Research," *The Journal of Political Economy*, 67 (June, 1959), pp. 297-306.

14. Although clear in theory, it is very difficult to specify and identify these benefits for this purpose in empirical analysis.

15. Either by organizing nonprofit research enterprises or by subsidizing such research when it is undertaken by firms (persons) for profit.

States, in terms of factor costs, they appear to account, when combined, for more than $20 billion annually. The size and the division of agricultural research between these two classes is instructive. In fiscal 1965, the total expenditures on agricultural research in the United States came to $854 million, of which about 55 percent was accounted for by industry. In terms of research workers, the agricultural experiment stations and the United States Department of Agriculture accounted for about 10,900 scientists man-years, and the number employed in industry on research related to agriculture was about the same.[16]

The theory of the firm presumably explains the allocation of resources to research within firms that are operating for profit. In principle, therefore, this class of research presents no new theoretical problems. But it must be said that all too few empirical analyses have been undertaken to determine the efficiency of firms in allocating resources to research.[17]

In terms of the profit incentive, they should perform efficiently. But in terms of demand and supply information pertaining to such research, it is not clear that entrepreneurs, who are responsible for the decisions within firms, are better or even as well informed as are the agents in the domain of nonprofit research. The puffing of research and development that is presently so popular in corporate an-

16. *A National Program of Research for Agriculture* (Washington, D.C.: Association of State Universities and Land Grant Colleges and the U.S. Dept. of Agriculture, October, 1966), Table F-1 and pp. 6-7.

17. Jora Minasian, "The Economics of Research and Development" (Unpublished Ph.D. dissertation in economics, University of Chicago, 1960).

Edwin Mansfield has done pioneer work in this area. In addition to his technical papers and an earlier book see his *Industrial Research and Technological Innovation* (New York: W. W. Norton, 1968).

nual reports, designed to impress stockholders, leaves room for serious doubts that entrepreneurs are, as a rule, well informed with regard to the profit potentials of research.

Besides the question of the state of information, there are a number of unsettled issues about the research activities of firms operating for profit. The economic efficiency of patents is still unsettled despite many studies of the economic function of patents. Are government contracts, that provide funds to corporations mostly "gravy"? The favorable tax treatment of expenditures for "research and development" granted to business firms is a closely related issue, the effects of which have not been ascertained. How much of so-called "development" is disguised sales promotion? Then, too, what are the possibilities of developing new institutional arrangements by means of which business firms could finance jointly research activities in proportion to their respective shares of the prospective profits? Private profit-oriented firms that engage in research presumably benefit from the (basic) research information discovered by nonprofit research agencies. Would it be efficient in economic terms to tax these firms in accordance with the benefits they obtain from the work of nonprofit agencies, as Larry A. Sjaastad has proposed?[18]

18. Larry A. Sjaastad, "On the Economics of Research and Development (Unpublished paper on program evaluation prepared for the U.S. Bureau of Budget, Department of Economics, University of Chicago, December, 1967). The difficulties that I see in this proposal are: 1) it would be well nigh impossible to identify the particular basic research component that a particular firm utilizes in its applied research; 2) corporate firms now pay federal corporation taxes far in excess of the costs of nonprofit research and surely a part of it may be viewed (treated) as public revenue used to support nonprofit research; and 3) the social-economic optimum is not necessarily attained by an endeavor on the part of nonprofit research enterprises selling the new information they discover and develop to the highest bidder.

From this point on, I shall restrict my analysis to non-profit research, except where it overlaps with that of profit-making firms. There is an unsettled problem with regard to the division of labor between firms for profit and non-profit agencies; the specialization between them is, in practice, subject to substantial inefficiency.[19]

Nonprofit Research Subject to Demand and Supply

Although it is obvious that human agents decide the allocation of resources both to and within these research programs, it is not obvious that they respond to changes in demand and supply conditions pertaining to this subsector of research. I plan to show that when the demand and supply conditions are specified, there is evidence that they tend to respond. Moreover, there are many allocative puzzles that can then be solved. The tendency to respond may not be as strong or clear as it is in producing traditional products, but it is, nevertheless, a significant tendency. Economic research can, I am sure, strengthen this tendency by providing information that would reduce the lags in these responses; but it is a serious mistake not to take the existing tendency into account in an endeavor to improve the resource allocation process of this subsector. This tendency is also an important source of economic information that, among other things, reveals some of the shadow prices that are determining the allocation of resources to and within these research programs. The purpose of this section is to clarify the nature and substance of these "prices" and the response of these agents to them.

It will be necessary to distinguish between two sets of

19. T. W. Schultz, "Efficient Allocation of Scientists in Modernizing World Agriculture," *Economic Growth and Agriculture* (New York: McGraw-Hill Book Company, 1968), pp. 94-107.

agents in this domain; namely, 1) agents who determine the allocation of private and public funds to nonprofit research, and 2) agents who act as *research entrepreneurs* in obtaining these funds and in using them. The first set of agents consists of members of legislative committees, members of the executive branches of government (for instance, the staff of the Bureau of Budget) and the members of private foundations, and of other groups and persons who support research. The second set represents all persons who enter into the decision-making process within experiment stations, research laboratories, research bureaus, and centers, including persons in charge of research projects. All of them are in some manner for the purpose at hand research entrepreneurs. I shall consider mainly the second of these two sets.

There are several assumptions underlying this approach. It is assumed that the new information from the research of this subsector, whether it is transformed into new skills or into new materials, is, in general, not patented either because it is not patentable or because no economic purpose is served by patents. Where there are exceptions to this generalization, patents are used only to protect the public interest in its utilization. It is also assumed that the demand and supply conditions pertaining to this research change over time; and it is further assumed that both sets of agents, in different ways, depending upon the economic and technical environment in which they operate, obtain and take account of a wide array of information, both economic and technical, in making their decisions. Lastly, it is assumed that both sets of agents have a high level of education, which gives them, in general, a comparative advantage over persons with less education in evaluating new information with regard to changes in demand and supply conditions and in responding and adjusting to these conditions (a decision-making advantage in terms of allocative ability akin to that of entrepreneurs with a high level of education in other economic activities).[20]

Some Allocative Puzzles

In presenting these puzzles, I shall restrict my comments to organized agricultural research because it is more observable than other sectors, because it has been under way for decades, and because I have some knowledge about it.

Organized agricultural research was established in India before independence, but until very recently few resources were devoted to the development of high yielding varieties of rice and wheat. The puzzle is, why this long neglect of the advances in biological information in developing new and better varieties? There are competent agricultural scientists in India who were specializing on rice and wheat. It is my contention that they saw the demand of farmers as a demand for varieties that would perform best given the depleted soils, the weather uncertainties, the limited control of water, and the poor farm equipment that characterize so much of India. Their assessment was undoubtedly correct. It was also clear to them that the new high yielding varieties of wheat and rice are strongly dependent upon fertilizer. They, however, were serving a country with virtually no commercial fertilizer. To argue *ex post* that Indian agricultural scientists should have anticipated the recent remarkable increases in the supply of fertilizer available to farmers in India, is pointless. It should also be

20. See Richard R. Nelson and E. S. Phelps, "Investment in Humans, Technological Diffusion, and Economic Growth," *The American Economic Review*, 56 (May, 1966), pp. 69-75; and Finis Welch, "Education in Production" (Unpublished paper, Department of Economics, Southern Methodist University, Dallas, Tex., December, 1968).

noted that until recently neither the government nor farmers were aware of the modern possibilities of research and they, therefore, did not bring their influence to bear in favor of such possibilities. Instead, they concurred, at least tacitly, particularly with the most talented scientists, that they engage in the type of scientific and academic pursuits that was their wont. Now that there is an awareness of new possibilities, government and farmers are using their influence in bringing about a change. Now too, scientists are responding. They are now actively at work improving the quality of the new wheat and rice varieties as food, determining the proper application of fertilizer that the new high yielding varieties require, and searching for effective means for controlling diseases and pests, for better seeding techniques, and for improvements in land management that the new varieties and the fertilizers call for.[21]

The puzzle with regard to the use of resources in agricultural research in Japan is not akin to the apparent puzzle throughout South Asia referred to above. Investment in irrigation was undertaken several decades ago, even earlier than in Taiwan.[22] As a purchased input, starting with

21. Sterling Wortman's comments, and a paper by W. David Hopper and Wayne H. Freeman, "India's Rice Development Moves from Unsteady Infancy to Vigorous Adolescence," have been most helpful in clarifying this issue.

22. I quote, with permission, a comment on Taiwan that I have received from Professor Yujiro Hayami:

Prior to the 1918 Rice Riot in Japan, the Government had concentrated its agricultural development efforts in Taiwan on sugar cane, because sugar had been one of the major foreign exchange losers in the Japanese Empire and it did not compete with Japanese agriculture. After the 1918 Rice Riot, the Japanese Government decided to assign to Taiwan (and Korea) the role of rice supplier of the Empire and funds were allocated to the development of rice production in Taiwan. The research sector responded to this request of the government to produce and propagate fertilizer-responsive varieties by adapting Japanese varieties to the local ecology of Taiwan. In fact, although the fertilizer price had declined

fish meals and oil seed meals, even before commercial chemical fertilizer became available in substantial amounts, there was some fertilizer for agricultural production, and instead the supply price of fertilizer declined. It is clear that research entrepreneurs in Japan responded to the demand of farmers for high-yielding varieties of rice under these conditions. The puzzle in Japan is the decentralization of organized agricultural research. In solving this puzzle, I would propose the following hypothesis: To keep these research enterprises close to farmers and their specific demands, it was decided in allocating public funds to support such research so that, ideally, each prefecture would have its own *small* research enterprise. The reasoning back of this decision by the public bodies that provide the funds for this research would require a good deal of historical research. But what is clear, *ex post*, is that, as a result of this decision, Japan benefited in making sure that the local requirements of farmers were served by the research.[23] It is noteworthy in this connection that the question of the optimum extent of decentralization in agricultural research is still far from settled.

---

in Taiwan as in Japan before 1918, the development of fertilizer-responsive varieties of rice had not been signficant in Taiwan until after the change in government policy.

Also see Yhi-Min Ho, *The Agricultural Development of Taiwan, 1903-60* (Nashville, Tenn.: Vanderbilt University Press, 1966).

23. Here, too, I am indebted to Sterling Wortman of the Rockefeller Foundation. With permission I quote from a comment from Professor Yujiro Hayami:

The National Experiment Stations set up in 1893 had six major regional branches (the number of branches changed over time) under its direction. Although all prefectures have acquired their own stations after the passage of the State Subsidy Act for Prefectural Agricultural Experiment Stations in 1899, they have been coordinated by the Central Government through subsidies. In 1926-27 the so-called "Assigned Experiment System" (System of Experiment Assigned by the Ministry of Agriculture and Forestry) was established. For rice, the National Ex-

There is general agreement that organized agricultural research in Mexico has achieved an outstanding record during the last 25 years, in large part as a consequence of the successful cooperative work of the Government of Mexico and the Rockefeller Foundation. But, it is fair to say that it has been more successful in its work on wheat than on corn, although corn is grown more generally throughout Mexico and is, in terms of economic value, a more important crop. The puzzle here is why this should have occurred. Is it not an example of a malallocation of research resources? It is, no doubt, in part, a result of some wrong allocations. But is it more so than might be expected given the particular uncertainties that usually characterize dynamic economic processes? Here I advance the following hypothesis, which is of two parts: 1) the wheat-growing areas are increasingly concentrated under irrigation where additional water has become available and the use of commercial fertilizer has become profitable as the price of it has declined, and 2) the production of corn is not concentrated in particular areas, and the availability of water and fertilizer is very uneven throughout Mexico—accordingly corn is grown almost everywhere, mainly on small plots that are not irrigated, and many new corn varieties are required because of the heterogeneity of the soil and climate.[24] If this hypothesis is valid, it follows that it is less

periment Stations (especially the one at Konosu) were assigned to conduct the hybridization up to the selection of F_2. Eight local experiment stations were assigned, one for each of eight ecological regions, to make further selection (all expense paid by the central government up to this point). Other local stations were assigned to test the adaptability of the varieties thus selected for their specific local ecologies. This system was successful in generating the Norin varieties of rice and wheat (Mexican dwarf wheat which has been revolutionizing Mexican and Indo-Pakistan agriculture was based on the Norin variety of wheat produced by this Assigned Experiment System).

24. My formulation of this hypothesis owes much to the Ph.D. research at the University of Chicago by Nicolas Ardito-Barletta

costly to respond to the demand for better varieties of wheat than to that for corn. The malallocation from the vantage point of hindsight is in the early commitment to corn hybrids instead of concentrating on improved open-pollinated varieties and synthetics.[25]

Regarding the United States, try to explain the growth of the state experiment stations. Start with the year just prior to the Hatch Act (1887) when the aggregate expenditure came to about $100,000[26] and account for the $247 million in fiscal 1967. But the difference in the rates of growth of the different experiment stations is even more fascinating. Among the states that had an equal start ($5,000) prior to the Hatch Act, the largest station is now over 25 times as large as the smallest station. The passage of the Hatch Act is not the source of the subsequent inequality among the state experiment stations. The 1887 Hatch Act was a model of equal financial treatment of the several states; it gave each the beneficent sum of $15,000, and it accounted for most of the income of the state experiment stations. As of 1900, two-thirds of the total income of the state experiment stations was still from Hatch appropriations. Then came the Adams Act in 1906, and,

---

and Reed Hertford on the recent growth in agricultural production in Mexico.

25. It is also true that until recently it had not been realized that it was as important in breeding corn, as in wheat, to reduce its sensitivity to day length and temperature.

26. Alfred Charles True, in *A History of Agricultural Experimentation and Research in the United States 1607-1925* (Washington, D.C.: U.S. Dept. of Agriculture, July, 1937), gives an account of 14 state agricultural experiment stations, 1875-1888 (pp. 82-106), and a reckoning of his accounts indicates that they had about $60,000 of income for the year. He then describes the agricultural experimentation under way in 13 additional states having no experiment stations (pp. 106-118); from his account, it is my guess that upwards of $40,000 was spent for this latter purpose.

again, there is equal financial treatment with its additional $15,000 of federal funds for each state. It was not until 1910 that the total nonfederal funds of the state experiment stations were equal to the federal funds they received. The marked disparity in the growth of these stations since then is predominantly a consequence of the differences in the increase in state appropriations to these stations.[27]

There is also a geographical picture of the uneven growth of the state experiment stations. Appalachia lost out; the South, with nearly half of the farms of the United States, fared badly, except for Florida, a newcomer, North Carolina, Louisiana, and also Texas, if it is considered South. The intermountain states have relatively small experiment stations. The Corn Belt has not lost out, but the puzzle is why its northern fringe came off so well. Then, there is New York, mainly Cornell, which is not in the mainstream of United States agriculture, and yet it has developed at Cornell University one of the largest experiment stations. The Pacific states have done well indeed; they, of course, include California with its gigantic enterprise of organized agricultural research.

27. Compare the California and Vermont stations, two of the oldest, both having been established before the passage of the Hatch Act and with about the same resources at the outset. For fiscal 1967 we have:

	Vermont	California	Ratio
Federal Funds	$498,000	$ 1,680,000	1:3.4
State Appropriations	$372,000	$20,028,000	1:53.8

The source of these figures is *Funds for Research* at State Agricultural Experiment Stations and other State Institutions, 1967, CSRS 15-12, U.S. Dept. of Agriculture, January, 1968.

In a 1956 paper, I examined the changes in financial support of agricultural experiment stations by regions from 1929-1930 to 1954-1955 and also in terms of the difference in such funds per farm person among regions. The research implications were considered. See T. W. Schultz, "Agriculture and the Application of Knowledge," in *A Look to the Future* (Battle Creek, Mich.: W. K. Kellogg Foundation, 1956), pp. 54-78.

The uneven growth of the state experiment stations is explainable, so it seems to me, along the following lines: 1) the differences in the size and changes in the relative size over time of the agricultural sector in the several states; 2) the differences in the applicability of advances in science in terms of research possibilities that could contribute to the agricultural production of the several states; 3) the differences in financial ability of several states to appropriate funds to support these research enterprises. No one would contend that differences in scientific entrepreneurship, legislative leadership, and organization have not played a part in accounting for the differences in these rates of growth. A comment on this point by Sterling Wortman is pertinent: ". . . one of the major factors contributing to the high pay-off from investment in agricultural research in the United States has been the high degree of focus on solution of problems of high priority in the economic development of the regions (states) served. There have been good reasons for this. Certainly, the nature of much of the agricultural research undertaken by university experiment stations has been dictated by state legislatures as they appropriated funds for specific lines of work. However, this does not mean necessarily that the ideas or the demand for such specific research originated in the farm sector. Rather, the scientists at the experiment stations (at least the more effective ones) were the ones who could see the possible impact of certain research efforts, demonstrated some of these to farm producers, and thereby created a desire on the part of the farm sector that such research be done. The scientists played a very useful function is explaining to farm leaders what it was reasonable to want from research. This interaction between scientists and farm leaders caused activities at experiment stations to be oriented toward service to the farm sector and toward economic development. Essentially, the scientific establishment said, 'here is what we can do for you' and leadership of the farm sector replied, 'yes, we want some of these things done. Here are the funds.' "

Specifying the Demand for What Research Does

The satisfactions that research workers derive from what they discover are a part of the demand. The difference between academic and industrial salaries for comparable scientists is a clue to the difference in these satisfactions. The satisfactions that accrue to workers directly from new skills created by research are exceedingly hard to identify. I shall leave both of these demands aside, however, and concentrate on the demand for the new skills and new materials from other parts of the economy.

It should be said that demand analysis is still a weak reed for this task. Consumer demand analysis is cogent and useful, for instance, in determining the demand for food. But when it comes to analyzing the demand for new skills and new materials, we are in trouble. The treatment of demand in economic growth theory is, as yet, of little use for this purpose. Consider, by way of an example, the lack of a theory of demand capable of explaining the apparent marked increase in the demand for persons with the skills associated with the completion of high school that occurred during recent decades in the United States. Not only has the relative supply increased markedly, but the price (rates of return to this schooling) also has risen sharply. Specifically, for the male civilian labor force, 18 to 64 years old, those who had completed high school rose from 16.6 to 28.1 percent of all males in the labor force between 1940 and 1959.[28] Meanwhile, private rates of return to males (white) who had completed high school rose from a rate of 16 to 28 percent between 1940 and 1958.[29] From whence this extraordinary increase in demand for this particular level of skills?

Given the present state of economic knowledge, we are unable to explain all of the dynamics of the demand for skills and materials. What we can do is very limited, but important nevertheless. The economic attributes of the agricultural sector are such that some analysis of the dynamics of the demand for new skills and materials is possible. Farmers produce highly standardized products; the price and income elasticities of the demand for these products are fairly well established; the utilization of old and new skills and materials by farmers gives some useful signals with respect to change in their demand for them. But are these signals sufficiently explicit so that the agents who make the allocation decisions in the nonprofit subsector of organized research can interpret them, at least in part, as firm economic information? I believe that the answer is in the affirmative. But I do not wish to imply that this type of economic information cannot be improved, or that the incentives to respond to it cannot be strengthened. On the contrary, one of my purposes is to show how these objectives can be attained.

The setting of the stage in general terms, and much oversimplified, can be done very briefly. Research produces new information, as already defined, that is then transformed into new skills or new materials. If these skills or materials are of some economic value in farming, farm-

28. *Educational Attainment of Workers,* Special Labor Force Report No. 65, U.S. Dept. of Labor, March, 1965, Table A-1, page A-6. By 1965 this percentage had risen to 32.8.

29. Gary S. Becker, *Human Capital* (New York: National Bureau of Economic Research, 1964), Table 14.

ers will reveal a demand for them and the alacrity with which they act to satisfy that demand will depend on the *absolute profitability* to them of the new skills or new materials.[30] But this is a demand that is derived from production, which is dependent not only upon the farm product price, which may fall as a consequence of the new skills and new materials, but importantly, upon the cost of information and the production possibilities as they are determined by substitution and complementarity, along with the uncertainty that is inherent in anything new.

The different sources of the demand for the contributions of agricultural research are as follows:

1. Industries that are suppliers of producer and consumer goods for farm people are, undoubtedly, aggressive in their demand for the new information from such research.

2. The demand of farmers for the contributions of this research is much maligned in the sense that there is a widely held belief that an inordinate amount of "persuasion" is required to induce farmers to adopt them. I shall show that it is a mistaken belief.

3. The demand of housewives for the new information from research that is of value in the "production activities" within households appears to be mixed; for new information regarding nutrition, it has been weak, but for the birth control pills, it has been anything but weak.

4. With respect to the demand of government agencies for these new research entities, there is no evidence that is known to me.

I shall concentrate on the demand of farmers because it is still misconceived so generally, and because a useful

---

30. Let me assume at this point that these research entrepreneurs, because of past experience, are capable of anticipating the classes of new materials and new skills that would have some economic value in agricultural production.

economic approach for analyzing this demand has been developed. The pioneering work of Zvi Griliches in his Ph.D. research (University of Chicago, 1957) laid the foundation for this approach. It is also applicable to firms that produce the new materials, as in the case of hybrid corn. The thrust of Griliches' paper in *Science* is that "geographic differences in the use of hybrid corn are explained by differences in the profitability of that use."[31] He found that "seed producers first entered those areas where the expected profits from commercial production of hybrid corn seed were largest." The market density for corn hybrids turned out to be closely correlated with the cost of entry. The evidence of the rate of acceptance of hybrid corn by farmers supported his hypothesis; namely, that "the rate at which farmers accept a new technique depends, among other things, on the magnitude of the profit to be realized from the change-over."[32] In their objection to the hypothesis advanced by Griliches, L. Brander and M. A. Strauss[33] argued that the acceptance of hybrid sorghum in Kansas proves that "congruence to the existing pattern" rather than "profitability" is the explanation of the dif-

31. Zvi Griliches, "Hybrid Corn and the Economics of Innovation," *Science*, 132 (July 29, 1960), pp. 275-280. Prior to this Griliches had published, "Hybrid Corn: An Exploration in the Economics of Technological Change," *Econometrica*, 25 (October, 1957), pp. 501-522, and "Research Costs and Social Returns: Hybrid Corn and Related Innovations," *The Journal of Political Economy*, 66 (October, 1958), pp. 419-431, reprinted with corrections in Carl Eicher and Lawrence Witt (eds.), *Agriculture in Economic Development* (New York: McGraw-Hill Book Company, 1964), pp. 369-386.

32. Griliches, "Hybrid Corn and the Economics of Innovation," p. 276.

33. L. Brander and M. A. Strauss, "Congruence versus Profitability in the Diffusion of Hybrid Sorghum," *Rural Sociology*, 24 (1959), pp. 381-383.

fusion process. A. E. Havens and E. M. Rogers[34] also objected, arguing for "interaction" and against profitability. In replying to these objections, Griliches gives both the analytical reasons and additional evidence why "congruence versus profitability" is a false dichotomy[35] and why "profitability versus interaction" is also a false dichotomy.[36] Commercial fertilizer is another new input for most United States farmers, although the technical properties of the major classes of fertilizer as plant nutrients, in general terms, have long been known. But the demand of farmers within this country for fertilizer, except for use on cotton and some specialty crops, was small prior to World War II. Then, as the *real* price of fertilizer fell by 50 percent between 1940 and 1950, farmers responded with alacrity, trebling their use of it between 1940 and 1952. In support of the profitability hypothesis, Griliches concluded his "Demand for Fertilizer"[37] study by noting that ". . . it is possible to explain almost all of the variations in fertilizer consumption on the basis of changing relative prices, without invoking or even mentioning 'technological change.'"

There is, however, the question of divisibility. Hybrid seeds come in small bags, but cotton pickers are large, expensive machines. Frank Maier's findings show, however, that the rate of acceptance of mechanical cotton pickers by farmers is very similar to that for hybrid corn and for the

34. A. E. Havens and E. M. Rogers, "Adoption of Hybrid Corn: Profitability and Interaction Effects," *Rural Sociology*, 26 (1961), pp. 409-414.

35. Zvi Griliches, "Congruence versus Profitability: A False Dichotomy," *Rural Sociology*, 25 (1960), pp. 354-356.

36. Zvi Griliches, "Profitability versus Interaction: Another False Dichotomy," *Rural Sociology*, 27 (1962), pp. 327-330.

37. Zvi Griliches, "The Demand for Fertilizer: An Economic Interpretation of Technical Change," *Journal of Farm Economics*, 40 (August, 1958), p. 604.

same reasons.[38] The rapid mechanization of United States agriculture after 1920, measured in terms of farm tractors and the factors determining the demand for this durable input, also supports strongly the absolute profitability hypothesis.[39]

The payoff on new skills, or on a higher level of skills than formerly in farming, as a consequence of advances in agricultural research, is much harder to determine than for new material inputs. In traditional agriculture, where the state of the agricultural arts has long been stationary and where farmers have arrived close to an optimum in terms of economic efficiency in the use of the agricultural resources available to them, the allocative process remains unchanged from one generation to the next and in this sense becomes routine.[40] But the dynamics of modern agriculture is a wholly different process; an array of new materials is becoming available; they must be evaluated by farmers to determine when and how to use them; and new allocative decisions are constantly required. It is this dynamic process of modern farming that holds the key to the payoff on high-level skills in farming. Welch has advanced the following proposition: "If educated persons are more adept at critically evaluating new or reportedly improved input varieties, if they can distinguish more quickly between the systematic and random elements of productivity

38. Frank Maier, "An Economic Analysis of Adoption of the Mechanical Cotton Picker" (Unpublished Ph.D. dissertation, Dept. of Economics, University of Chicago, 1969).

39. See Zvi Griliches, "The Demand for a Durable Input: Farm Tractors in the United States, 1921-57," in *The Demand for Durable Goods*, ed. by A. C. Harberger (Chicago: University of Chicago Press, 1960), pp. 181-207.

40. This is the economic conception of traditional agriculture advanced in my *Transforming Traditional Agriculture* (New Haven, Conn.: Yale University Press, 1964).

responses, then in a dynamical context educated persons will be more productive. Furthermore, the *extent* of the productivity differentials between skill levels will be directly related to the *rate* of flow of new inputs into agriculture."[41] His empirical analysis of high school and college education in farming provides appreciable support for the proposition.

The conclusion to be drawn from the preceding comments on the demand for new skills and new materials from research is as follows: the demand depends on profitability; although research workers often overrate the profitability of the new information they discover and develop, they are aware that profitability matters; the lags in adoption puzzle them, but economists have as yet done all too little to resolve this puzzle for them.

Thus, in specifying the demand, the absolute profitability of new skills and new materials is fundamental. But, from the point of view of the contributions of an experiment station, a farm is a mere postage stamp attached to the economic landscape. There are 11 states with less than 10,000 farms. Alaska in 1966 had only 340 farms, and the value of all farm sales came to less than $13,000 per farm from a long list of crops and livestock products.[42] The agricul-

41. Welch, "Education in Production," quoted here with his permission. Welch's findings support the reasoning on innovative ability being positively related to education as advanced by Richard R. Nelson and E. S. Phelps in "Investment in Humans, Technological Diffusion, and Economic Growth," *op. cit.*

42. *Alaska Agricultural Stations*, U.S. Dept. of Agriculture Statistical Reporting Service, Alaska Experiment Station, 1966, p. 3. The total value of farm sales was $4.3 million and the total value of farm production came to $5.5 million in 1966. By comparison, the value of farm sales to California (1964) was $3.5 billion, and the farm value of one crop (corn) in Iowa (1964) was $1,127 million.

tural production of Appalachia does not add up to much in terms of the demand for any new skills or new materials, whereas the opposite is true in the Corn Belt and in California. It is, of course, obvious that state experiment stations tend to specialize with a view to serving the agriculture of the state (region) in which they are located. Clearly, the aggregate demand for any new skills or materials from research depends on the density and specialization of agriculture and the size of the market served by each experiment station. It is my hypothesis that the nonprofit research agents are informed about these matters and that they tend to respond, given the research possibilities. I shall postpone, however, any further examination of this tendency; for we must also take account of the research possibilities in explaining this tendency.

There is, however, a critical omission in this approach. Workers and firms (farms) that take advantage of these new skills and new materials under competitive conditions are compelled to transfer any benefits above normal profits into lower product prices and thus ultimately to consumers. What is, therefore, omitted is the *consumer surplus*. Given the state of economic information with regard to consumer surpluses, it is not possible for research agents to evaluate them and to take them into account in their role as research entrepreneurs. The analytical task of providing this information should be high on the agenda of economists. Economic theory is not lacking. But the empirical analysis is wanting. It is undoubtedly very difficult to identify and measure the benefits that are transferred to consumers through competition and become consumer surpluses. Until this is done, however, it is not possible to allocate efficiently investment resources to research in accordance with the priorities established by the relative rates of return to alternative investment opportunities.

Specifying the Supply

Given the funds for research, the research output depends on the prices of scientists and of facilities and on the state of the research art. The prices of the research inputs are determined in competitive markets, and they are for all practical purposes readily available. Substitution and complementary considerations in combining different scientists and facilities and the optimum scale of the research enterprise also depend on the research art. The state of the research art is the heart of the problem in specifying the research possibilities, hence the supply of new information from research.

In terms of economic analysis, we are far from determining the right questions to ask. Is it a matter of rating the research possibilities of alternative projects (research opportunities)? Is the conventional production function approach appropriate for this task? Or is it necessary to incorporate the probabilistic characteristics of research projects into the production function in analyzing the relationships between research inputs and outputs? Is the concept of diminishing returns applicable? Are changes in relative prices in the economy of some significance in allocating resources efficiently to research?[43] My views with respect to these and related questions are as follows: Changes in relative prices matter. The increase in the amount and the decline in the price of commercial fertilizer relative to food grains in India, is firm evidence on this issue. The probabilistic characteristics of research must be reckoned with, and therefore an "engineering" type production function will not suffice. The question of diminishing returns is of two general parts; in terms of economic theory, any narrowly well-specified research project by

43. I am indebted here to Robert E. Evenson for his comment.

assumption is under the constraints that imply diminishing returns; but research, in general, as we observe it empirically (historically) appears not to have reached the stage of general diminishing returns. The rating of research projects depends in large part on information with respect to the preceding issues; and to get at the scientific possibilities for purposes of economic analysis, economists are very much dependent on what scientists know.

My reading of the early history of the agricultural experiment stations, before and also for a time after the passage of the Hatch Act, is that the research art consisted mainly of some advances in chemistry applied to fertilizer. What could, therefore, be achieved did not account for much in agricultural production because fertilizer was not profitable at that time in most of United States agriculture. For a later period, an examination of the records of each of the stations, say between 1890 and 1920, would probably reveal some small improvements in the scientific research possibilities; I doubt, however, that in the aggregate they contributed much. In other words, when the art of agricultural research is virtually stationary, it is only a matter of time when the worthwhile output from it will be exhausted. This stationary period is, undoubtedly, the reason why many land-grant workers turned during that period to the practices of the more successful farmers in the community for new knowledge about production. But this is not a rich source of new high-payoff skills and materials.[44] Advances in science are the source that matters; as these advances are realized, the frontier of the research possibilities is extended.

44. The early corn yield tests, which were based on searching for superior seed corn on Iowa farms for 12 years from 1904 to 1915 and testing these seeds on 75,000 field plots, as summarized by Martin L. Mosher, indicate how slow and difficult it was to improve corn yields by this approach—even with exceptionally competent and inspired workers and leadership. Corn yields in Iowa

There is little room for doubt that agricultural research in the United States entered upon a very dynamic period soon after World War I. Moreover, new advances in science are maintaining this dynamic process, and there are many signs that these new research possibilities are far from having been exhausted. According to my rating of the

---

which had averaged 32.4 bushels an acre from 1896 to 1905 averaged only 33 bushels during 1913, 1914, and 1915. See, Martin L. Mosher, *Early Iowa Corn Yield Tests and Related Later Programs* (Ames, Iowa: Iowa State University Press, 1962).

The farmers of Japan contributed substantially to the discoveries of better rice varieties and associated practices, according to Professor Yujiro Hayami. I quote from his comment with permission:

Some improved rice varieties prior to 1920 were selected by farmers. The experiment stations, before the establishment of Assigned Experiment System, propagated these varieties by conducting comparative yield tests and adaptive research. New techniques requiring high skills were also developed by farmers. A good example is the technique of selecting rice seeds in salt water discovered by Jikei Yokoi in 1882. Yokoi ...later became the foremost leader of agriculture and agricultural science in Japan. As a young instructor at a vocational agricultural school at Fukuoka Prefecture (Fukuoka was one of the most advanced rice producing prefectures in early Meiji period), he found this technique practiced by farmers in the prefecture. Yokoi recognized that this technique was a high pay-off on skills. It is interesting that Yokoi who had strongly criticized the *ad hoc* nature of such farmer techniques and advocated the superiority of modern science throughout his life, played an important role in propagating this technique. The examples are not limited to Meiji Era. The technique of vinyl covered rice nursery bed preparation, which is considered an important agricultural innovation in the post-World War II period, was developed by a farmer in Nagano prefecture. The high pay-off of this practice was recognized by an agronomist of the Prefectural Experiment Station, who improved it in cooperation with scientists at Tokyo College of Agriculture and Mechanic Arts. The very high pay-off of this technique was demonstrated by the fact that in ten years almost all Japanese farmers had adopted this technique. It seems to me that in Japan the relation between farmers and agricultural scientists in the creation of new high pay-off information has been a kind of dialectic process. Not only did the scientific establishment say "here is what we can do for you," and the leader of the farm sector replied, "yes, we want some of these things done, here are the funds." Farmers, also, said "here is what we found through our practices," and the research establishment replied "O.K., we will test them and determine their scientific possibilities."

advances in science that determine the research possibilities of the experiment stations, taken in their entirety, the dominant source is biological in making it possible to produce new biological materials; chemistry is next, and of least importance in terms of the work of experiment stations is engineering that leads to more mechanization[45] and better control of water. This rating would differ somewhat by regions; for example, the Corn Belt compared to the Pacific Coast states.

In specifying the factors determining the supply, it is clear from Evenson's[46] study that the size of the experiment station is important; the largest stations appear to have a marked comparative advantage over the rest of them. I shall return to this issue of scale a bit later.

Let me now return to the role of the research agents who act as research entrepreneurs in the classification presented above. They presumably know the state of the research possibilities in their respective areas of competence. But these possibilities, as a rule, are not of the type that can be transformed into a well-behaved production function of the "engineering" type. The research game of problem solving is not that simple. It requires a probabilistic approach; another requirement is that we build on the scientific (technical) and economic information of the research scientist. The information that he has about the choices open to him pertaining to their relative prospects and their costs are the primary source of the shadow prices that are essential in allocating resources efficiently to research.[47] My approach is close to that described by Richard R. Nelson in his study of the transistor.[48]

45. Industries that produce inputs for agriculture account for most of the advances in farm tractors and machinery and also for many of the new chemical materials.
46. Evenson, "The Contribution of Agricultural Research and Extension to Agricultural Production."
47. I assume that there is an *incentive* for the research worker

Propositions and Implications

The propositions that I shall advance pertain to non-profit agricultural research. My purpose in presenting them is, first, to suggest that they are sufficiently important to warrant careful investigation and, second, to use them in an attempt to clarify related unsettled questions.

(agriculture) in the state experiment station to contribute to the agriculture of that state (region). In large part, the sources of the experiment station funds and the organization of the station have kept the interest of agriculture in the foreground and have provided the incentive. But post-World War II developments have provided several new sources of funds and the incentives to serve agriculture have become weaker and diffused. Director Glenn S. Pound, College of Agriculture, University of Wisconsin, in "U.S. Agriculture and World Food Needs," presented to the Centennial Symposium of the Land Grant University, University of Illinois, October 18, 1967 (unpublished) on this point said as follows:

> Our problem is accentuated by the source and distribution of research funds. The relatively high level of support during the past decade from the federal foundations for basic research and the decreasing support in many states for applied research pose a delicate question of balance between the two. In table 5 are shown data from the University of Wisconsin to illustrate this point. It can be seen that during the last two decades, Wisconsin has surrendered a significant portion of its equity in agricultural research to the federal foundations. The foundation grants are, for the most part, obtained by direct communication between the individual scientists and the foundations. In terms of directing scientific effort to high priority needs of the state, college administrators have little left to them but persuasion. The kind of research done, therefore, is largely dictated by the scientist and the foundation, and indirectly by the foundation by granting or not granting the funds. The foundations have been interested totally in basic research. Individual departments and individual scientists who are oriented heavily to applied research suffer in lack of support. We will experience a steady retreat from the applied research field because scientists are going to adjust their programs to provide security for their professional advancement.

(I owe this reference to Sterling Wortman.)

48. Richard R. Nelson, "The Link between Science and Invention: The Case of the Transistor," *The Rate and Direction of Inventive Activity*.

1   *As the Modernization of Agriculture Proceeds, the Demand for the Contributions of Agricultural Research Becomes Stronger and More Effective*   The following developments support the validity of this proposition. 1) Agriculture becomes increasingly commercial as modernization proceeds. Commercialization of agriculture implies production for markets; thus production for home (on-farm) consumption declines in both relative and absolute terms. 2) Market-oriented farmers obtain information about new inputs more readily and at less cost than self-sufficient farmers. It is for this reason that the response of nonprofit research agents to cash crops is stronger than to crops for on-farm consumption. It is also the reason why plantations producing farm products for export have historically turned to agricultural research more readily than traditional farmers producing largely for home consumption and local markets. 3) Commercialization of agriculture also implies that farmers become increasingly dependent upon purchased inputs. It is well known that industries that produce these inputs are aggressive in taking advantage of any new information from research applicable to their production. 4) There is also a better supply of agricultural inputs that are complementary to new varieties or to other new inputs from research where agriculture has become commercial in contrast to where it is still largely self-sufficient. 5) Last, but surely not least in importance, is that farmers become better educated.

Several implications of this proposition are worth noting. 1) Although the number of farmers in a country may decline as the modernization of agriculture proceeds in the United States down from 6 to 3 million, the demand of farmers for new materials and skills from research, nevertheless, becomes stronger and more effective. 2) Interregional shifts in agricultural production, however, may reduce the agricultural sector in some regions (states) to the point that the market for the new entities from the research of a state experiment station becomes all too small to warrant the continuation of the station. An increasing number of state agricultural experiment stations are becoming obsolete as a consequence of regional shifts in agricultural production. 3) The higher rate at which new agricultural inputs are adopted by farmers as modernization proceeds implies that the ultimate benefits from the research leading to the development of new inputs are transferred more rapidly than formerly to consumers in the form of lower consumer prices. 4) There is, probably, a tendency on the part of industries serving agriculture to have the nonprofit research agents carry as much of the development costs as possible, thus shifting these costs to the "public" sector. 5) The economic logic of agricultural modernization also implies that increasingly more of the costs of providing information about new agricultural inputs can be borne by the industries serving agriculture; there appears to be a substantial lag in adjusting the agricultural extension services that are supported by public funds to this fact. 6) The payoff to education in agriculture tends to rise.

2 *As the Advances in Science Proceed, the Agricultural Research Possibilities Are Enhanced, Thus Setting the Stage for a Supply of Additional New Information from Agricultural Research* It is obviously true that there have been during the recent past remarkable advances in science. In view of the growth and magnitude of the scientific establishment and its continuing success in new discoveries, it is hard to believe that it will not continue to achieve additional advances during the time span that matters in

making decisions to invest in agricultural research. It is also true that the agricultural research possibilities are dependent upon the advances in science.

When we turn to the implications of this proposition, the following are important: 1) The agricultural research possibilities have not been exhausted; on the contrary, they afford more research opportunities presently than at any time in the past. 2) As science has become vast in scope and increasingly more specialized, it has become ever more difficult for agricultural research workers to stay abreast of the advances in science. In order to cope successfully with this difficulty, agricultural research workers must also specialize as have other scientists, so as to make use of the advances in science. 3) The benefits of a close association of agricultural research workers with other scientists increases over time; thus the comparative advantage of an agricultural experiment station associated with a *major research-oriented university* is strong and clear.[49] 4) There are only a few states that have the resources to provide enough public funds to support a major research-oriented university.[50]

49. See Robert E. Evenson, "The Contribution of Agricultural Research and Extension to Agricultural Production."
50. The nine state experiment stations reeciving the largest state appropriations and the five receiving the smallest amounts in 1966-1967 along with expenditures on all organized research in each university and all income from its state appropriations in 1962-1963 were as follows:

	State Appropriations to Experiment Stations 1966-1967[1] (Millions)	University Expenditures on All Organized Research 1962-1963[2] (Millions)	Income from State Appropriations to Universities 1962-1963[2] (Millions)
Univ. of California (Berkeley, Davis, Riverside, etc.)	$20.0	$319.0	$143.5
Univ. of Florida	6.9	13.0	25.6
Louisiana State Univ.	5.4	7.1	21.5
Cornell Univ. (New York)	5.2	32.6	18.0
Univ. of Minnesota	4.8	19.8	35.1
North Carolina State Univ.	4.4	8.1	11.6

3 *The Social Rate of Return to Investment (Expenditures) in Nonprofit Agricultural Research Is, in General, High Relative to That on Most Alternative Investment Opportunities* The high rate of return is predominantly a consequence of the low supply price of new research information; and this price is low mainly because the research possibilities are highly favorable as a result of the advances in science. (The price here is the reciprocal of the rate of return; a 50 percent rate of return, for example, implies that the price of a $1.00 per year income stream is only $2.00). While it is true that the salaries of researchers are high, their overall productivity is such that the supply price of new information from research is nevertheless low.

The studies at hand support the validity of this proposition. As a benchmark against which to compare the estimated rates of return to agricultural research, I turn to alternative investment opportunities, including schooling. The Jorgenson and Griliches[51] estimates of the implicit rates of return for the private domestic economy of the United States, after profit taxes and before personal income taxes, for selected years between 1949 and 1963-65, range from about 10 to 15 percent. For education, the estimates of Becker[52] of the private rates of return to college gradu-

Univ. of Wisconsin	4.3	26.1	31.2
Univ. of Illinois	4.0	27.1	69.2
Michigan State Univ.	4.0	8.5	31.3
Univ. of New Hampshire	.32	1.3	3.8
Univ. of Rhode Island	.34	2.2	5.4
Alaska (Palmer Exp. Station)	.36		
Univ. of Delaware	.36	1.6	4.7
Univ. of Vermont	.37	1.9	3.3

1. *Funds for Research,* 1967, Cooperative State Research Service, U.S. Dept. of Agriculture, CSRS 15-3, Table 4.
2. *Statistics of Land Grant Colleges and Universities,* Office of Education, U.S. Dept. of Health, Education and Welfare, OE-50002-63, 1965, Tables 13 and 15.

51. Dale W. Jorgenson and Zvi Griliches, "The Explanation of Productivity Change," *The Review of Economic Studies,* 34 (July, 1967), pp. 249-283.
52. Becker, *Human Capital.*

ates (white males) after personal income taxes, range from 12 to 15 percent for selected years between 1939 and 1958; for high school graduates, his estimates show an increase in the private rates of return after personal income taxes from 16 percent in 1939 to 28 percent in 1958. The estimates of the social rates of return to agricultural research are, in general, higher than the benchmark rates cited above for the particular alternative investment opportunities cited. The estimates from the recent competent econometric studies pertaining to all agricultural research are of the same order of magnitude as were the implied estimates from my simple arithmetic of 17 years ago.[53] My treatment of the value of the agricultural inputs *saved* by the advances in the agricultural arts from 1940 to 1950, along with my estimates of the cost of all nonprofit (public) agricultural research implied a 35 percent rate of return as the lower limit and a 170 percent rate of return as the upper limit per dollar spent on all agricultural research.[54]

Table 12.1 summarizes the econometric studies to which I have referred above. The implications of these findings is that investment in agricultural research should be given a high priority in terms of the standard established by most alternative investment opportunities.

In view of the above propositions and their implications, what determines the economic efficiency of nonprofit research in terms of resource allocation? Here, too, I shall restrict my analysis to the performance of organized nonprofit agricultural research.

53. T. W. Schultz, *The Economic Organization of Agriculture* (New York: McGraw-Hill Book Company, 1953), pp. 112-122.

54. These estimates were made by Zvi Griliches, using my inputs saved and research costs. In adjusting the research cost for the private research component, Griliches doubled my estimate of the nonprofit agricultural research cost. See Griliches, "Research Costs and Social Returns: Hybrid Corn and Related Innovations," pp. 427-428.

Table 12.1—Estimates of the Social Rates of Return to Investment in Agricultural Research

STUDY	SOCIAL RATES OF RETURN	
	A	B
	Returns at end year above a 10 percent discount rate[1]	Returns distributed internally[2]
1. Particular U.S. farm products		
a. Hybrid corn research, public and private, as of 1955[3] and internalized over 1910-1955	700	35-40
b. Hybrid sorghum research, public and private, as of 1967[3]	360	
c. Poultry research, public, 1960 and internalized over 1915-1960[4]		
Feed efficiency	178	25
Total productivity	137	21
2. U.S. agriculture, 1949, 1954, and 1959 Public and private agricultural research and extension adjusted for excess capacity[5]	300	
3. U.S. agriculture, 1938-1963		
a. Public agricultural research and extension[6]		54-57
b. Adjusted for private research[6]		46-48
4. Agricultural research in Mexico		
a. Wheat research, 1943 to 1963[7]	750	
b. Corn research, 1943 to 1963[7]	300	
c. Total agricultural research in Mexico, 1943 to 1963[7]	290	
5. Japanese agriculture, 1880-1938 Predominantly investment in education; for example, in 1880, education 23.6 million yen, and agriculture research and extension, 0.3 million yen; and in 1938, 185 and 21.5 million yen, respectively, lower bounds[8]	(35)	

1. Estimate A is obtained by applying a 10 percent discount rate to the flow of cost incurred over time accumulated and also to the flow of benefits obtained over time accumulated. The 10 percent discount rate is assumed to be a reasonable proxy for the rate of return to alternative social and private investment.

The use of estimate B, the internal rate of return, may attribute an inordinately high value to a dollar spent in the more distant past. For example, in the case of hybrid corn, the internalized rate of return attributes a value $2,300 to a dollar spent in 1910 in developing hybrid corn. (See p. 425 of Griliches' paper cited in note 3 on why this is an objectionable procedure.)

    2. Estimate B is that rate of return that equates the flow of costs and flow of returns over time; it thus distributes the net benefits equally over the entire period measured in terms of the internal rate of return. Estimates A and B are different ways of interpreting the same set of cost and benefit facts.

    3. Zvi Griliches, "Research Costs and Social Returns: Hybrid Corn and Related Innovations," *The Journal of Political Economy,* 66 (October, 1958), pp. 419-431.

    4. Willis Peterson, "Returns to Poultry Research in the United States" (Unpublished Ph.D. dissertation in economics, University of Chicago, 1966).

    5. Zvi Griliches, "Research Expenditures, Education and the Aggregate Agricultural Production Function," *The American Economic Review, 54* (December, 1964), pp. 967-968.

    6. Robert E. Evenson, "The Contribution of Agricultural Research and Extension to Agricultural Production" (Unpublished doctoral dissertation in economics, University of Chicago, 1968).

    7. Nicolas Ardito-Barletta, "Costs and Social Returns of Agricultural Research in Mexico" (Unpublished Ph.D. dissertation in economics, University of Chicago, pending).

    8. Anthony M. Tang, "Research and Education in Japanese Agricultural Development, 1880-1938," *The Economic Studies Quarterly,* 13 (February and May, 1963), pp. 27-42 and 91-100.

In solving the problem that is implied by this question, it would be a serious mistake not to take account of the response of nonprofit research agents to the economic and scientific environment in which they are located. The agents who act as research entrepreneurs, given the constraints of the scientific community in which they are situated, are better informed with regard to the scientific research possibilities than anyone else. I find it hard to believe that they do not make use of this information in formulating their research projects. Moreover, this scientific information is essential in arriving at, or close to, an optimum in allocating resources. They also have substantial information pertaining to the cost of undertaking the research along with an awareness of the demand for the potential contributions of the research to the economy (to farmers, agricultural industries, and even to farm households). But what they do not know is the prospective value of the consumer surplus. It is a serious omission in allocation of resources to research.

In this approach, an experiment station has the economic attributes of a firm, a merger of many subenterprises—as many as there are projects. There are cost considerations and shadow prices. To analyze and explain the behavior of the director and of those who are in charge of projects, what is required is a family of economic models designed to test the effects of specific economic and scientific factors on the responses of these research entrepreneurs. I find it highly plausible that such models, accompanied by empirical analysis, would reveal 1) the research contributions that are expected, given the scientific research possibilities, 2) the expected economic value of the contributions to the agriculture served by the station, and 3) little or no information on the expected consumer surplus that would result from the research contributions.

This approach, however, will not suffice because it will not get at the predominant sources of the malallocation of resources pertaining to this subsector. These malallocations are, primarily, a consequence of the dynamics of modern economic growth. In principle, the sources of these malallocations are the same as the sources that account for the disequilibria of other economic sectors under rapidly changing dynamic conditions. I shall do no more than to mention some of them:

1. Overall, there is an underinvestment in nonprofit agricultural research in view of the relatively high social rates of return to this activity.

2. This underinvestment is in substantial part a result of the obsolete organization of public finance. The reason why this is true is fairly obvious. These social rates of return are high mainly because of benefits from nonprofit

research that result in consumer surpluses; they are, however, widely diffused. Accordingly, they are not specific to the state, or even to the nation, that appropriates funds for the research.

3. The advances in science that account for the strong advantage of agricultural research in close association with a major research-oriented university, are another cause of the obsolescence of existing organization of public finance.

4. A national agricultural research center (U.S. Department of Agriculture plus the National Research Center at Beltsville, Maryland) that is not an integral part of a major research-oriented university is, under present conditions, inefficiently located for such research. Here, too, the advances in science have made what was formerly a fairly efficient place into an obsolete location. Even the prestigious Rockefeller research enterprise (New York City) has found it necessary to transform itself into a university.

13 Institutions and the Rising Economic Value of Man[1]

THERE is a strong connection between the investment in human capital and the secular rise in the economic value of man. The institutional implications of this development are, however, far from clear. My purpose is to show that the rise in the economic value of human agents makes new demands on institutions, that some political and legal institutions are especially subject to these demands, that these institutions lag in adjusting to the new demands and these lags are the key to important public problems, and that economic theory is a necessary analytical tool in clarifying and solving these problems.

It might be said that human capital is protesting the status quo of institutions as it seeks participation rights for itself. Be that as it may, there is enough historical perspective to see that the ownership of land is declining as a

1. I am indebted to Earl J. Hamilton and Albert Rees for their incisive comments on an earlier draft of this chapter. I also have benefited from a discussion with Dale Hathaway.

source of economic leverage, and so is the ownership of physical capital relative to that of human capital. We have long known that Ricardian rent is not the fulcrum of economic values; nor is physical capital the critical historical factor as Marx believed. The institutions governing private rights in land and in other forms of physical capital when Ricardo and Marx made their contributions would be far from adequate in contemporary society with its large investment in human capital. Would that economics could have been blessed by the marriage of Irving Fisher's all-inclusive concept of capital and John R. Commons' legal foundations of that capital.[2]

It is currently a mark of sophistication in presenting economic models not to mention institutions. But for all that, it is a significant trait of contemporary economics that despite this omission, it manages somehow to find support for institutional changes. It is a neat trick, but it cannot hide the fact that in thinking about institutions, the analytical cupboard is bare. There are a few old boxes on the back shelf labeled "institutional economics," which have been pushed aside and which have long been thought to be empty. When we look more closely, we find that there are virtually no terms of reference, no concepts with specifications that can be identified, and no economic theory to guide the analysis. Yet, it is obvious that particular institutions really matter, that they are subject to change and are, in fact, changing, and that people are trying to clarify social choices with regard to alternative institutional changes to improve the economic efficiency and the welfare performance of the economy.[3]

2. Irving Fisher, *The Nature of Capital and Income* (New York: The Macmillan Company, 1906), and John R. Commons, *Legal Foundations of Capitalism* (New York: The Macmillan Company, 1924).

3. A part of the literature pertaining to the welfare of economics

My plan is, first, to define and comment on the attributes of the institutions that render services to the economy, then to present and evaluate three approaches for the analytical task at hand, and lastly, to use the third of these approaches to explain particular institutional lags in adjusting to the rise in the value of human agents.

Defining Institutions

I shall define an institution as a behavioral rule. These rules pertain to social, political, and economic behavior. They consist, for example, of rules that govern marriage and divorce, rules embodied in constitutions that govern the allocation and use of political power, and rules that establish market capitalism or governmental allocation of resources and of income. Since I shall deal only with those institutions that perform economic functions, I shall leave aside all institutions that perform purely social functions. It is my aim to consider particular political, including legal, institutions that in one way or another influence, or

---

is relevant here. *The Journal of Law & Economics* is a rich source of papers on the economic implications of property rights; see, for instance, Scott Gordon, "Economics and the Conservation Question," 1 (1958), pp. 110-121; S. R. Dennison, "The British Restrictive Trade Practices Act of 1956," 2 (1959), pp. 64-83; R. H. Coase, "The Problem of Social Cost," and Jacob Viner, "The Intellectual History of Laissez Faire," both in 3 (1960), pp. 1-44 and pp. 45-69, respectively; Edgar S. Bagley, "Water Rights Law and Public Policies Relating to Ground Water 'Mining' in the Southwestern States," 4 (1961), pp. 144-174; Robert W. Gerwig, "Natural Gas Production: A Study of Costs of Regulation," 5 (1962), pp. 69-92; Harold Demsetz, "The Exchange and Enforcement of Property Rights," 7 (1964), pp. 11-26; and Kenneth W. Dam, "Oil and Gas Licensing and the North Sea," 8 (1965), pp. 51-75. Another relevant source in bringing economic theory to bear on political decisions is the work by Anthony Downs, *An Economic Theory of Democracy* (New York: Harper, 1957).

are, in turn, influenced by, the dynamics of economic growth. It is a concept of institutions which takes me into the domain of political economy. A partial list includes the following institutions: 1) those that contribute to the extension of the market (such as money, credit, debts, future markets), 2) those that influence the allocation of risk among the owners of the factors of production (among them, contracts, share tenancy, cooperatives, corporations, insurance, public social security programs), 3) those that provide the linkage between functional and personal income streams (for instance, property, including inheritance laws, seniority and other rights of labor, and forms of human capital), and 4) those that establish the framework for the production and distribution of public goods (services)— among them, highways, airports, schools, agricultural experiment stations.

Some elaboration of the economic role of these institutions may be in order. There are those that belong to an older vintage. Money, clearly, is one of them. As the quantity of international transactions increases, the supply of international money may be subject to serious stresses. Consider the steps taken to internationalize "paper gold" thus presumably freeing the supply of high-powered money from the constraints that determine the production of gold. Closely related are credit instruments including debts. I recall with pleasure the first assignment at the University of Wisconsin by John R. Commons asking those of us in his class to search for the historical circumstances that gave rise to negotiability of a debt. The legal assignment of private rights in property is still, obviously, an important institution, the economic implications of which remain high on the agenda at Wisconsin, especially so in agricultural economics. Contracts, of course, are a viable institution, and they, also, are undergoing change—for example, in obtaining access to the capital market to invest in one-self, the formation of human capital.

A recent vintage includes the legal rights of labor; they now loom large. But they, too, are in a state of flux with many unsettled issues. The rights to organize and to use all of the bargaining power that organized labor can muster can impair economic efficiency sufficiently to induce the political process to alter some of these rights. Meanwhile, the rising economic value of man is compelling society to establish additional rights favoring the human agent. Organized economic planning by government is another recent institution with respect to which advances in economic theory have contributed much in clarifying the function of prices, whether they are market prices or shadow prices, in allocating resources by organized planning. Lastly, there is the institutionalization of public transfers of income. But here, too, the guiding principles and the appropriate arrangements are still far from settled.

It is hard to believe that institutions such as these are protected by nature in ways which may make them immune to economic analysis. The analytical job is to specify their functions, measure their influence, and determine when they are efficient. To get on with this task requires a theoretical approach from which testable hypotheses can be derived; hopefully, these hypotheses will lead to empirically supported propositions pertaining to the economic performance of these institutions.

The Economic Functions of Institutions

In analyzing the economic functions of institutions and the value of these functions, it is helpful to think in terms of three approaches.

First, there is the approach that omits or impounds in-

stitutions by abstracting from them. As noted at the outset, this is the approach of modern economics. We have a large family of growth models that treat institutions as a part of the "state of nature"; thus institutions are impounded and they are not subject to change either exogenously or as a variable adjusting to the dynamics of growth. It is, of course, true that there are some short-run growth problems that can be solved by using this approach. But most growth problems cannot be solved in this manner. Modern economics with all of its analytical tools is presently not up to the job of analyzing the connections between institutional changes and growth dynamics.

Second, there is the approach that treats institutions as subject to change exogenously. In this approach institutional changes may matter, but the critical simplifying assumption is that these changes are independent of growth. Accordingly, institutions are treated as an exogenous variable in the sense that they are altered by political acts, including legal decisions independent of the process of economic growth. There are, undoubtedly, some institutional changes that are of this type and in considering their economic effects, it is an appropriate approach. But most institutions that perform economic functions undergo change in response to the requirements of the dynamics of economic growth, and the nature and strength of these responses are not within the province of this scheme of analysis.

I would be remiss if I did not give credit to those few hardy economists who remain committed to "institutional economics." They are concerned predominantly with the allocation of property rights in natural resources, and they are best known for their analyses of and arguments for land reform. The essence of their work is to begin with an *ad hoc* institutional change. It is, therefore, not an approach that treats an institution as an endogenous variable in an economic growth model. It is primarily concerned with the effects of a particular reform upon the distribution of personal income and welfare. It is not guided by economic theory, no doubt in part because theory has so far not integrated the functional distribution of income and the distribution of personal income. Likewise, institutions that produce human capital (such as education and on-the-job training), institutions that are the source of new entities of knowledge entering the economy (research and development among them), and laissez faire competition are also usually treated in this fashion.

Third, I propose an approach that treats these institutions as variables within the economic domain, variables that respond to the dynamics of economic growth. Although not all institutional changes can be treated thus, there is an important set that can be taken on analytically in this manner.

Instead of omitting or impounding these institutions in the "state of nature," or introducing them on an *ad hoc* basis, the analytical task is to bring them into the theoretical core of economics. To get on with this task, two key concepts are required: the economic value of the function performed by an institution and the concept of an economic equilibrium. First, how are we to get at their economic value and the factors that determine their value? We begin with the assumption that these institutions are suppliers of particular services. They may supply a convenience, which is one of the attributes of money; they may supply a contract, which reduces transaction costs as in the case of leases, mortgages, or commodity futures; they may supply information, as do markets and economic planning; they may pool particular risks, which is an attribute of insurance, corporations, cooperatives, and public social security arrangements; and they may supply public goods (services), as in the case of schools, highways, health facilities, and experiment stations. For each of these services there is a demand. It is, therefore, within the province of economic theory to approach the determination of the economic value of each of these services by subjecting them to a supply and demand analysis. The next analytical step is to place this supply and demand approach in an equilibrium framework.

Consider now several variants of the process of economic growth. Suppose that it were conceivable that an economy could produce additional income streams over time in such a manner that everything would increase in exactly the same proportion. If this were to occur, presumably there would be no disequilibria, and thus the economy would not be confronted by the problem of returning to an equilibrium. But in explaining actual economic growth as we observe it, growth models built on this assumption are, so it seems to me, toys rather than analytical tools.

The process of modern economic growth is beset by all manner of disequilibria, which are consequences of the growth process. Institutions that perform economic functions are not spared. Some of these disequilibria persist and even become chronic, as anyone who is informed about economic problems confronting United States agriculture knows. It is obvious that we are involved in a long-standing disequilibrium, which has burdened human agents in agriculture greatly and which still persists despite the extraordinary migration out of agriculture. C. E. Bishop, in his perceptive and challenging paper, clearly identified the lags in adjusting community institutions.[4] With respect

4. C. E. Bishop, "The Urbanization of Rural America: Implications for Agricultural Economics," *Journal of Farm Economics*, 49 (December, 1967), pp. 999-1,008.

to this and other disequilibria, the question to ask is: How strong is the tendency towards equilibrium? Can it be strengthened? Can the lags in the adjustment be facilitated at a cost where the benefits will exceed or at least equal the costs?

By way of summary, then, our theory is designed to explain those changes in institutions that occur in response to the dynamics of economic growth. The institution is treated as a supplier of a service that has an economic value. It is assumed that the process of growth alters the demand for the service and that this alteration in the demand brings about a disequilibrium between the demand and the supply measure in terms of longer run costs and returns. Although it is possible for the supply of the service of an institution to be altered independently of economic growth considerations, our theory cannot explain such a change in an institution; it can be used, however, to determine the resulting economic effects of such a change.

I shall digress at this point and consider briefly several testable propositions pertaining to institutions and agricultural production in countries that have long been in equilibrium of the type that characterizes traditional agriculture.[5] Suppose the policy objective is to attain a sustained rate of increase in agricultural production and the rate of increase is both efficient in economic terms and higher than the rate associated with population growth (farm labor) in the case of traditional agriculture. In negative terms, I would propose the following propositions: 1) a planned increase in the supply of money at a rate that would be higher than formerly will not suffice to bring about the desired increases in agricultural production; 2) nor will an institutional reform that would increase the supply of credit available to farmers achieve the objective;

5. As defined in my *Transforming Traditional Agriculture* (New Haven, Conn.: Yale University Press, 1964), Chap. 2.

3) nor will a change in tenancy laws that would reduce the share rents of tenants bring about the desired sustained rate of increase in agricultural production.

Let me now reformulate these and closely related propositions in positive and more readily testable terms. When agriculture acquires a growth momentum, as it recently has in parts of Asia (China aside for lack of information and Japan aside for reasons of her prior successful modernization of agriculture), a growth momentum that is a consequence of favorable farm product prices, of the available new varieties of food grains that are fertilizer-responsive, and of a cheaper and larger supply of fertilizer will induce farmers in these parts of Asia to *demand institutional adjustments*. They will demand a larger supply of credit with stress on its timeliness and terms, and they will organize cooperatives should these be necessary for this purpose. They will demand more flexibility in tenancy contracts. They will join with neighbors to acquire tube wells and to undertake minor investments to improve the supply of water. Both tenants and landowners will also use whatever political influence they have to induce the government to provide more and better large-scale irrigation and drainage facilities. These are all testable propositions. There is, so it seems to me, a growing body of evidence in support of each of these propositions.[6] So much by way of digression. I now return to the mainstream of the analysis.

In terms of the economic incentives for institutional responses, incentives that are a consequence of economic growth, there are several more general propositions: 1) In

6. I am indebted here to W. David Hopper and his formulation as it appears in "Regional Economic Report on Agriculture," Sect. III, 1, of the *Asian Agricultural Survey*, Asian Development Bank, Manila, March, 1968.

a market economy achieving growth, the demand for the convenience of money shifts to the right. (This proposition is supported by competent empirical studies.) 2) In an economy in which the income per family is rising, the demand for contracts and property arrangements serving the economic activities of the nonfarm sectors increases relative to that associated with the farm sector. (This is an obvious proposition.) 3) As economic growth becomes increasingly dependent upon the advance in useful knowledge, the demand for institutions that produce and distribute such knowledge shifts to the right. Here we have a modern development with respect to which the less developed countries are in general substantially more in disequilibrium than are the technically advanced countries.[7] 4) When economic development reaches the stage during which the economy needs increasingly sophisticated skills, the demand for high skills that require schooling including higher education increases relative to the demand for low skills and for reproducible forms of nonhuman capital. (There is a strong evidence that the United States economy has been in this stage since World War II.) 5) The proposition on which I shall concentrate during the remainder of this chapter is as follows: In an economy where growth increases the economic value of human agents, the demands for services of a number of different institutions are altered by this type of growth. As human lives become less cheap, the demand per worker for additional safeguards protecting workers from accidents shifts to the right; so does the demand per person for health services and for life insurance. The demand for additional legal protection of personal rights, for instance protection

7. T. W. Schultz, "Efficient Allocation of Scientists in Modernizing World Agriculture," *Economic Growth and Agriculture* (New York: McGraw-Hill Book Company, 1968), pp. 94-107.

from invasion by police that impairs the privacy of persons, also shifts to the right, as does the demand more generally for civil rights. As a factor in production, human agents demand greater equality in obtaining jobs especially so with respect to jobs that require high skills. Closely related is the increase in the demand for less discrimination in having access to schooling and higher education to acquire the higher skills. As consumers, human agents demand greater equality in having access to consumer goods and services, notably so in the case of housing and family planning information. Then, too, as the value of a person's time rises, there is a reallocation toward goods-intensive and away from time-intensive consumption activities.[8]

Lagging Institutional Adjustments

It is my thesis that the remarkable secular rise in the economic value of human agents that has been and is occurring in the United States is the source of major disequilibria in the economic functions performed by institutions. Let me be explicit in noting that it is not my contention that all of this rise in the economic value of human agents is wholly a consequence of the type of economic growth that characterizes our economy. A part of it, but surely it is a small part, is a result of the curtailment of the immigration of persons who are allowed to enter from abroad to become members of the United States labor force. The extension of civil rights, the additional public provisions for legal services for the poor, the programs to alleviate poverty,[9] and the Supreme Court's

8. Gary S. Becker, "A Theory of the Allocation of Time," *The Economic Journal*, 75 (September, 1965), pp. 493-517.

9. Walter Gellborn, "Poverty and Legality: The Law's Slow Awakening," *Proceedings of the American Philosophical Society*, 112 (April, 1968), pp. 107-116.

decisions with regard to schooling are developments that have enlarged the choices open to individuals. While it might be argued that these developments, including urbanization as an intermediate influence, were not dependent upon the growth of the economy enhancing the economic value of human agents, it is a superficial view if it is true, as I contend, that these developments are predominantly a consequence of the type of economic growth that has been and is occurring in the United States. These legislative acts and legal decisions, in large part, were made possible and necessary because of the process of economic growth. In brief, these legislative and legal developments are lagged accommodations to the profound institutional stresses and strains brought about by the marked, secular rise in the economic value of human agents.[10]

It is hard to imagine any secular economic movement that would have more profound influence in altering institutions than would the movement of wages relative to that of rents (the price of the services of property). I am sure that economic historians would find the secular movement of wages relative to rents a rich vein. The symmetry of the institutional changes that follow in the wake of such movements, regardless of the type of government, is one of the findings of B. H. Slicher Van Bath.[11] We are presently in a long secular movement that is running in favor of the economic value of the human agent.

Clearly, then, the institutional changes that occur in response to the rising economic value of the human agent call for a family of new economic models. I shall consider

10. Albert Rees has called my attention to the fact that courts are more and more explicitly considering earning power in determining the size of the judgments in cases of accidental injury or death.

11. B. H. Slicher Van Bath, *The Agrarian History of Western Europe A.D. 500-1850* (New York: St. Martin's Press, 1963).

briefly three that belong to this family; namely, 1) institutional responses to increases in the market price of work, 2) institutional responses to increases in the rate of return to investment in human capital, and 3) institutional responses to increases in consumer disposable income.

First, assume that growth increases the value productivity of workers per unit of time (and thus the wage per hour) relative to the rate of return to investment in property, and also that the value productivity of workers with high skills increases in absolute terms compared to that of workers with low skills. What are the institutional implications? What is implied in terms of substitution possibilities? At the level of allocative decisions made by firms operating for profit, we are not burdened with serious institutional rigidities in our type of competitive market economy. Contracts, including leases entered into by tenants in agriculture, are a case in point; there is, of course, a lag, but it is not a long lag in adjusting such contracts to changes in the better earning opportunities of human agents. What is true, however, in a national context is that workers with low skills have access to less job information than workers with high skills, and, in the case of higher skills, there is job market discrimination against nonwhite workers.

The institutional lags pertaining to wages that arise out of the dynamics of economic growth are predominantly in the realm of internal migration, occupational shifts, and discrimination against nonwhites. These lags are revealed in terms of less than optimum job information, less on-the-job training than is consistent with an equalization of the benefits and costs of such training, and of living accommodations in job-expanding areas that are in part rationed by discrimination. In the report, *The People Left Behind*,[12] we have a landmark in analysis and recommendations for lines of public action to reduce the institutional lags in this general area.

Second, in approaching the problem of investing in man, the key assumption is that economic growth is of a type in which the production activities require relatively more high skills than formerly and that the derived demand from these activities increases the rate of return to investment in human agents. Again we ask: What are the institutional implications?[13] It would appear that our system of education has been flexible in expanding the supply of educational services sufficiently to accommodate the private demands of middle and upper income families. The rub is, however, that it has lagged seriously in supplying educational services, both quantitatively and qualitatively, for many children of farm families, for poor whites generally, and most patently, for Negroes. In terms of social rates of return to investment in poor people, there is a growing body of evidence that supports the inference of a continuing disequilibrium, especially so with respect to elementary and secondary schooling. Higher education is an institution that raises complex and difficult organizational issues. The tendency toward an efficient allocation of resources is weak; economic incentives and information are poor. The self-interest of students is not mobilized adequately, the accounting of social benefits (losses) is haphazard, and academic entrepreneurs have all too little opportunity for allocating resources efficiently. (See Chapter 10.)

Third, in thinking about institutional lags that impair

12. Washington, D.C.: President's National Advisory Commission on Rural Poverty, September, 1967.

13. Professor Earl J. Hamilton has reminded me of the insights Alfred Marshall gave on some aspects of this issue in *Principles of Economics* (8th ed. London: The Macmillan Company, 1930), Book VI, Chaps. 12 and 13.

consumer sovereignty, the central problem is that of accessibility where rationing occurs as a consequence of discrimination. Here, too, let us assume that disposable consumer incomes rise as a result of economic growth. Although it is true that, in general, market forces have a strong tendency to adjust to the changing demands of consumers, it is not true in the case where particular consumer goods and services are subject to market discrimination between people by color. There is little room for doubt that many Negro families with rising incomes are subject to such markets in traveling, at least until very recently, in acquiring health services and family planning information and techniques, and above all, in renting or purchasing housing.

With the economic value of human agents rising, we are in the realm of new and better opportunities. The range of private and social choice is enlarged. It is, indeed, an optimistic set of circumstances that all too few people of the world enjoy. But even so, this favorable type of economic growth is not without its institutional stresses and strains. Since we can specify and identify these institutional lags, we can also analyze the benefits in terms of efficiency and welfare that could result from reducing these lags. Meanwhile, it is not simply a matter of catching up because there are strong reasons for believing that the economic value of man will continue to rise.

Index